Bookstore

ACC Library
840 Bay Road
Queensbury, NY 12804

Annual Editions: Child Growth
and Development, 22/e

Chris J. Boyatzis
Ellen N. Junn

D1613709

http://create.mheducation.com

Copyright 2016 by McGraw-Hill Education. All rights
reserved. Printed in the United States of America. Except as
permitted under the United States Copyright Act of 1976, no part
of this publication may be reproduced or distributed in any form
or by any means, or stored in a database or retrieval system,
without prior written permission of the publisher.

This McGraw-Hill Create text may include materials submitted to
McGraw-Hill for publication by the instructor of this course.
The instructor is solely responsible for the editorial content of such
materials. Instructors retain copyright of these additional materials.

ISBN-10: 1259406199   ISBN-13: 9781259406195

Contents

Preface

We are delighted to welcome you to this edition of *Annual Editions: Child Growth and Development*. The amazing sequence of events of prenatal development that lead to the birth of a baby is an awe-inspiring process. Perhaps, more intriguing is the question of what the future may hold for this newly arrived baby. For instance, will this child become a doctor, a lawyer, an artist, a beggar, or a thief? Although philosophers and prominent thinkers such as Charles Darwin and Sigmund Freud have long speculated about the importance of infancy on subsequent development, not until the 1960s did the scientific study of infants and young children flourish.

Since then, research and theory in infancy and childhood have exploded, resulting in a wealth of new knowledge about child development. Past accounts of infants and young children as passive, homogeneous organisms have been replaced with investigations aimed at studying infants and young children at a "microlevel"—as active individuals with many inborn competencies who are capable of shaping their own environment—as well as at a "macrolevel"—by considering the larger context surrounding the child. In short, children are not "blank slates," and development does not take place in a vacuum; children arrive with many skills and grow up in a complex web of social, historical, political, economic, and cultural spheres.

As was the case for previous editions, we hope to achieve at least four major goals with this volume. First, we hope to present you with the latest research and thinking to help you better appreciate the complex interactions that characterize human development in infancy and childhood. Second, in light of the feedback we received on previous editions, we have placed greater emphasis on important contemporary issues and challenges, exploring topics such as understanding development in the context of current societal and cultural influences. Third, attention is given to articles that also discuss effective, practical applications. Finally, we hope that this anthology will serve as a catalyst to help students become more effective future professionals and parents.

To achieve these objectives, we carefully selected articles from a variety of sources, including scholarly research journals and texts as well as semiprofessional journals and popular publications. Every selection was scrutinized for readability, interest level, relevance, and currency. In addition, we listened to the valuable input and advice from members of our board, consisting of faculty from a range of institutions of higher education, including community and liberal arts colleges as well as research and teaching universities. We are most grateful to the advisory board as well as to the excellent editorial staff of McGraw-Hill Create™/Contemporary Learning Series.

Annual Editions: Child Growth and Development is organized into four major units: Prenatal Development and Child Cognition, Language and Learning; Social and Emotional Development; Parenting and Family Issues; and Cultural and Societal Issues.

In addition, we provide student learning outcomes, critical thinking questions, and relevant web links for each article so that instructors will have a variety of important resources and options available for students.

Instructors for large lecture courses may wish to adopt this anthology as a supplement to a basic text, while instructors for smaller sections might also find the readings effective for promoting student presentations or for stimulating discussions and applications. Whatever format is utilized, it is our hope that the instructor and the students will find the readings interesting, illuminating, and provocative.

As the title indicates, *Annual Editions: Child Growth and Development* is by definition a volume that undergoes continual review and revision. Thus, we welcome and encourage your comments and suggestions for future editions of this volume.

Editors

Chris J. Boyatzis
Bucknell University

Chris J. Boyatzis is professor of psychology at Bucknell University, where he received the Lindback Award for Distinguished Teaching, and serves as director of the Bucknell in Denmark summer program. He received his BA with Distinction in psychology from Boston University and his MA and PhD in developmental psychology from Brandeis University. His primary research interests are religious and spiritual development from childhood into early adulthood and cultural differences in parenting. He was formerly president of Div. 36 (Society for the Psychology of Religion and Spirituality) of the American

Psychological Association, is associate editor of *Psychology of Religion and Spirituality,* and serves on the editorial board of several other journals.

Ellen N. Junn
California State University, Dominguez Hills

Ellen Junn is provost and vice president for academic affairs and professor of psychology at California State University, Dominguez Hills. She received her BS with distinction in psychology and with high honors from the University of Michigan and her MA and PhD in cognitive and developmental psychology from Princeton University. Dr. Junn's areas of research include student success, educational equity, college teaching effectiveness, faculty development, and public policy as it affects children and families. She served as a Past President for the California Association for the Education of Young Children and as a Governing Board member of the National Association for the Education of Young Children.

Editors/Academic Advisory Board

Members of the Academic Advisory Board are instrumental in the final selection of articles for each edition of ANNUAL EDITIONS. Their review of articles for content, level, and appropriateness provides critical direction to the editors and staff. We think that you will find their careful consideration well reflected in this volume.

Kathleen E. Fite
Texas State University - San Marcos

Mary Helen Spear
Prince George's Community College

Kelly Cartwright
Christopher Newport University

Nicole Martin
Kennesaw State University

Paula Tripp
Oklahoma State University, Stillwater

Linda A. Sidoti
The College of Saint Rose

Mary Eva Repass
University of Virginia

Carlene Henderson
Sam Houston State University

Leilani M. Brown
University of Hawaii - Manoa

Kathleen Sheridan
National Louis University

John W. McNeeley
Daytona State College

Claire N. Rubman
Suffolk County Community College

Jean Kubeck
New York City College of Technology, CUNY

Sandra M. Todaro
Bossier Parish Community College

Frankie Rabon
Grambling State University

Stephen T. Schroth
Knox College

Robert Stennett
University of North Georgia, Gainesville

Angela Sullivan
Concordia College

William A. Mosier
Wright State University

Ronald Hixson
Southwest Texas Junior College

Carol LaLiberte
Westfield State University

Nancy McCarley
Armstrong Atlantic State University

Deborah Harris-Sims
University of Phoenix

Terri Pardee
Spring Arbor University

Unit 1

UNIT

Prepared by: Chris J. Boyatzis, *Bucknell University*
Ellen N. Junn, *California State University, Dominguez Hills*

Prenatal Development and Child Cognition, Language, and Learning

Former carefree and more conventional sentiments of starting a family were exemplified by the old nursery rhyme, *"First comes love. Then comes marriage. Then comes baby in a baby carriage."*

However, this old adage belies the much more complex family realities facing pregnant couples and women today. Moreover, the new and exciting science regarding the critically important role that a healthy prenatal environment may play in ensuring optimal development after birth and into childhood and beyond continues to expand and fascinate the public. For example, new prenatal and infant research shows the powerful influence of both genes and the environment depending on specific domains—such as brain development, temperament, or personality development—in shaping and supporting the genetic foundations for a given infant, and underscore the critical importance of optimal prenatal and infant development.

We have come a long way from the days when the characterization of the minds of infants and young children included phrases like "tabula rasa" and "booming, buzzing confusion." Today, infants and young children are no longer viewed by researchers as blank slates, passively waiting to be filled up with knowledge. Current experts in child development and cognitive science are calling for a reformulation of assumptions about children's cognitive abilities, as well as calling for reforms in the ways we teach children in our schools.

Researchers today continue to discover the complex interplay between brain maturational development and external or environmental experience in scaffolding and supporting the emergence of abilities such as language acquisition, perceptual and cognitive advances, and early learning.

Hence, the articles in this subsection highlight some of the new knowledge of the impressive and foundational cognitive abilities of infants and young children in the areas of language, cognitive and conceptual learning, reading, creative activity, and problem solving and how these abilities may be influenced by parents, teachers, and schooling.

Indeed, today perhaps more than ever in the last few decades, public and parents' thirst for not only knowing about these foundational cognitive skills, but more importantly, how they can, as parents, teachers, and educators, further promote and nurture these cognitive skills has increased dramatically.

We hope that readers will enjoy the variety of articles, research, approaches, and real-life applications in thinking about how to optimize the development of young children presented in this unit.

Article

Prepared by: Chris J. Boyatzis, *Bucknell University*
Ellen N. Junn, *California State University, Dominguez Hills*

Should You Bring Your Unborn Baby to Work?

Research shows that babies are far more sensitive to the prenatal environment than we once believed. How should today's stretched-to-the-brink parents respond?

MOISES VELASQUEZ-MANOFF

Learning Outcomes

After reading this article, you will be able to:

- Describe how the prenatal environment can affect the development of embryos and fetuses.

- Understand the new field of "fetal-origins" science.

- Evaluate the potential impact of nations' maternity leave policies on mothers and early development.

Last year, as my wife and I prepared for the arrival of our second child, I began to worry. My wife is a mid-level manager at an advertising agency with offices around the world. She heads a team, and she's ferociously dedicated to her work—which translated, late in her pregnancy, to a couple of 80-hour weeks and chronic sleep deprivation. When she came home from work at 2 A.M. for the second time in as many weeks, I started to fear that her grueling schedule might affect her health, and that of our unborn son.

As a science journalist, I've become familiar with a burgeoning area of research called the fetal origins of disease. It examines how what happens to your mother during pregnancy can affect your vulnerability to any number of lifelong disorders, including asthma, heart disease, obesity, diabetes, and schizophrenia and other psychiatric problems. We've internalized some of this science already—we know, for example, that excessive drinking while pregnant isn't good. Less well known are the consequences of things like infection and severe stress. They, too, may leave a legacy.

My wife's salary keeps the lights on and a roof over our heads, and funds our 3-year-old daughter's adventures in preschool. What I earn as a freelance journalist, by contrast, more resembles an allowance, so I do the bulk of the child care.

I knew that my wife wouldn't take well to a conversation about her working too much. Any suggestion that she scale back would probably add to the stress I was arguing she should avoid. Not only might it sound like recrimination, but she was in the final stretch of a major project and probably couldn't (or wouldn't) change her work situation just then anyway.

So what did I do when she came home at two in the morning? I bit my tongue.

Today, some 70 percent of mothers work outside the home. For many of them, that means one of two scenarios: the uncertainty and low pay of variable or part-time work, or in the white-collar world, full-throttle commitment and near-constant availability. According to the American Psychological Association, women report more stress than men, from worry over money, work, and the economy, in that order. And each new generation reports more stress than the previous one did.

Given the growing body of research on the importance of Mom's health during pregnancy, I wondered how it was that women seemed to have so little recourse during this period—to work less, to change duties, to merely acknowledge that gestation might be the least bit taxing.

Partly subsidized by my wife, I set out to better understand why this was the case, and what the fetal-origins research really indicated about potential conflicts between pregnancy and the workplace. What solutions had been devised elsewhere, and how well had they worked?

One remarkable aspect of this new field of research is how it has upended medical convention. For decades, many scientists viewed the fetus as a "perfect parasite." Whatever happened to Mom short of death, the thinking went, the fetus would continue developing unperturbed. (As Annie Murphy Paul points out in *Origins: How the Nine Months Before Birth Shape the Rest of Our Lives,* not long ago women about to give birth were liquored up by their doctors, because the fetus was considered invulnerable to the mother's drinking. Maternity wards smelled like bars.)

Then, in the late 1980s, a British epidemiologist named David Barker found that he could predict which populations would be most vulnerable to heart disease in middle age by looking at rates of infant mortality and low birth weight. Both measures, Barker believed, were partly determined by mothers' nutrition during pregnancy. At that time, the medical consensus was that your lifestyle—what *you* ate, whether *you* smoked, the exercise *you* did or didn't do—determined your risk of heart failure. Disease resulted solely from an interaction between genes and personal choice, in essence. Barker's findings suggested a more complicated reality: conditions in the womb could increase your chances of falling dead from heart failure decades later.

Your mom might shake off flu symptoms after a couple of weeks. But if those weeks of misery occur during gestation, they could forever alter the course of your life.

When Barker began publishing his findings, skeptics charged that birth weight was a poor indicator of maternal nutrition. Also, they noted, those regions with the highest prevalence of heart disease were the poorest, and bad habits were known to accompany poverty. Maybe those habits, not the prenatal environment, elevated the risk of cardiovascular problems.

So Barker turned to a data set whose variables were easier to control. In 1944, toward the end of World War II, Allied forces liberated half of the Netherlands but were stopped at the Rhine River. The Nazis blockaded the remaining Dutch territory, preventing shipments of food and fuel. Then a bitterly cold winter set in, and the Dutch began to starve.

The Dutch Hunger Winter, as it's sometimes called, provided an ideal laboratory: a previously well-nourished population starved for roughly four months and then, after liberation in May 1945, returned to a life of relative plenty.

Barker collaborated with Dutch scientists who were researching this population, and what they found helped change how we think about chronic disease. Children born to mothers who

were pregnant during the famine had double the risk of heart disease later in life compared with children whose mothers didn't starve. They were more prone to asthma and other lung diseases, as well as to obesity.

The early months of gestation are an especially sensitive time, and how far along the mothers were in their pregnancy when the starvation began also seemed to matter. Ezra Susser, a Columbia University epidemiologist and psychiatrist who studied the Dutch famine around the same time as Barker, found that children whose mothers went hungry early in pregnancy had double the risk of schizophrenia compared with those whose mothers starved later in pregnancy or didn't starve at all.

Scientists have since sought to explain how prenatal conditions can incur long-lasting consequences. In the nine months before birth, a fertilized egg multiplies from one cell to trillions. If that process is like building a house, then a sudden scarcity of brick and mortar—a famine—might change the kind of house that gets built. These alterations don't determine our destiny; they're one factor among many that affect our vulnerability to disease. And they don't necessarily qualify as damage; they may in fact represent an attempt by the fetus to adapt to a world of scarcity. (Take height, which tends to increase as nutrition improves and infections decline. A smaller body is, in theory, better suited to a world with less food, where constant battle with pathogens and parasites drains energy.) But adaptations that aid survival in certain circumstances may increase the risk of disease in others. Some of these changes are "epigenetic," meaning that they affect how our genes get translated into flesh and blood.

The early fetal-origins research hinted at the possibility that simple interventions during pregnancy might yield huge payoffs later in life. "The next generation does not have to suffer from heart disease or osteoporosis. These diseases are not mandated by the human genome," Barker, who died in 2013, once said. "We could prevent them, had we the will to do so."

To some degree, that prophecy has proved true. The observation of spina bifida and certain other problems in children whose mothers survived the Dutch famine contributed to the discovery that folic acid is necessary for proper development of the fetal brain. Pregnant women now take it routinely—a cheap pill prevents devastating conditions. But not all fetal-origins research yields such easy solutions.

Scientists who study prenatal development are increasingly interested in the maternal immune system. In a 2004 study, a group of researchers including Susser and Alan Brown, another Columbia University epidemiologist, analyzed blood samples collected from pregnant women between 1959 and 1966 for evidence of infection. They matched the results to the mental-health outcomes of the women's now-adult children.

The presence of antibodies to the flu virus during the first half of pregnancy, they found, correlated with triple the risk of schizophrenia. (Animal studies, including on monkeys, have since shown that activating the mother's immune system as if it were fighting off an infection can alter the fetal development of the brain and other organs.) While many scientists argue that schizophrenia, thought to afflict about 1 percent of people in the United States, must be genetic, this research suggests that with enough planning and foresight, we might be able to reduce its incidence by preventing infections during pregnancy.

In the late aughts, Douglas Almond, an economist at Columbia, and a skeptic of fetal-origins research, published a study testing the possibility that infections during pregnancy could have ramifications decades later. In 1918, the Spanish Flu raged around the world. An estimated one-third of American women of childbearing age contracted the virus. When Almond followed up with people whose mothers were pregnant around the time of the pandemic, he found a generation that had been permanently hobbled. They were less educated, earned less, and were poorer overall than trends had predicted.

If gestation is like building a house, then a sudden scarcity of brick and mortar–a famine—might change the kind of house that gets built.

The asymmetry of what Almond observed was stunning: Your mom might shake off flu symptoms after a couple of weeks. But if those weeks of misery occur during gestation, they could forever alter the course of your life.

In retrospect, perhaps it's not surprising that famine and major infections can affect fetal development. But scientists think it may be the immune-system response—not the infection itself—that causes harm. And the immune system has other triggers besides infection, Susser told me. One of them is stress.

A kind of subspecialty has emerged examining the long-term consequences of acute prenatal stressors—sudden and extreme conditions that hit an entire population but then disappear, allowing for during-and-after comparisons. The associations unearthed in these circumstances should be treated as "clues," Susser said, "so you can look for the factors that operate in more-ordinary situations."

In June of 1967, Israel and its Arab neighbors fought a war that lasted just six days. In 2008, scientists in New York and Israel released a study of adults whose mothers had been pregnant during the conflict, and reported a more than fourfold increased risk of schizophrenia among women in that group. (Why not men? One possibility is that male fetuses, often observed to be more sensitive than female ones, may have been miscarried.)

In California, women with Arabic names saw a reduction in their babies' birth weight following the September 11 attacks, possibly due to hostility directed their way, or anxiety over reprisal attacks. Research on Arab women in Michigan didn't confirm this finding, but another study indicated that across the United States that September, there was a greater occurrence of male fetal death among pregnant women generally. Another study has observed a heightened risk of birth complications among children born to mothers who were pregnant during hurricanes along the Gulf Coast. Still others have looked at bereavement—women who lose a close family member during pregnancy. The children from these pregnancies may have a higher rate of mental illness.

Some of the studies are small, and not all of them find that the stressors affect the babies' health. But that doesn't disprove causation, Susser notes. How people respond physiologically to war or grief depends on hard-to-measure variables such as upbringing, culture, and social support that may lead to seemingly contradictory findings.

Health writers suffer from a version of medical-student syndrome. We read about what can go wrong and then become sure we're developing those very symptoms. Only in my case, I projected these worries onto my wife. I could see from the slight bags under her eyes that she wasn't sleeping enough. And I could sense, from her preoccupied demeanor, that even when she was home, she never stopped thinking about work. But I reminded myself that my wife had a well-paying job that, whatever its demands, provided fulfillment. Her situation was very different from living through a war, losing a loved one, or contracting the flu.

The research that looks more directly at work stress and pregnancy is inconsistent, and much of it suffers from methodological problems. Still, the findings troubled me. In 2012, a study of female orthopedic surgeons found that those who worked more than 60 hours a week while pregnant had nearly five times the risk of preterm birth—meaning delivery before 37 weeks of gestation, which can indicate unfavorable conditions in the womb and predict ill health throughout a child's life—compared with those who worked less. But one glaring problem with this study was that it surveyed women after they gave birth, asking them to remember how much they had worked during pregnancy.

A 2009 study from Ireland that followed 676 pregnant women was better designed. Experiencing two or more work-related stressors—including shift work, temporary work, or working 40 hours or more a week—was associated with a more than fivefold increased risk of preterm birth. A much larger subsequent study from Denmark, however, found no such relationship between "job strain" and preterm birth.

What was I to think? I called up Sylvia Guendelman, a professor of maternal and child health at the University of California at Berkeley. The research could be inconsistent, she said. "But the bulk of evidence seems to suggest that something is there."

It's when support is lacking and the stressors begin piling on that obvious problems begin to emerge.

One possible explanation for the differing outcomes is this: contrasting social realities may affect how citizens of different countries respond to stressors. Denmark and other Nordic countries have legendary social safety nets, including laws that require employers to accommodate pregnant women by changing their duties or, if they can't, allowing the women to go on leave. The absence of a relationship between maternal stress and preterm birth in Denmark, Danish scientists note, may really show that preventive measures are working, not that job strain never causes problems.

Research from France suggests as much. By the 1970s, French scientists had established that job strain and physically demanding work were clearly correlated with an elevated risk of preterm birth. But in later studies, the relationship seemed to have disappeared. What happened?

National policies first implemented in 1972 permitted women to reduce their hours, change duties, or take time off while pregnant. (These days, France also requires women to get prenatal medical care and take prenatal leave—a government-in-your-business approach that can seem jarring to Americans.)

Preterm birth is a leading driver of infant mortality in the United States and predicts an increased risk of numerous chronic diseases later in life. So one notable facet of France's experience is that, as provisions protecting pregnant women in the workplace expanded in the late 20th century, the incidence of preterm birth fell. By 1988, it had declined to 3.8 percent—a 45 percent decrease from the early 1970s, and less than half the U.S. rate today. (It has since inched back up, possibly because of an increasing number of elective C-sections.)

Numerous studies, meanwhile, have linked maternal stress and anxiety during pregnancy to preterm birth. One problem with this research, however, is that much of it relies on mothers' subjective descriptions of stress. Scientists try to circumvent this issue by measuring biological factors, including the stress hormone cortisol and markers of immune function. These studies are somewhat more compelling, although they're also relatively small and don't necessarily show causation. One such study, from 2012, led by scientists at the University of Colorado at Denver, linked pregnancy-related stress and inflammation to preterm birth.

Considering the world we evolved in, populated by lions—and other humans—we should be able to handle stress. But even among wild primates that still fend off lions, unremitting social stress quickly erodes health. In baboon troops, the dominant male greatly determines the culture of the group, and observers have noted that when highly aggressive males take over, pregnant females can become so distressed that they spontaneously miscarry.

Controlled experiments on primates are even more compelling. In studies at the University of Wisconsin at Madison, scientists exposed pregnant monkeys to intermittent horn blasts once daily for 10 minutes toward the end of their terms—in the grand scheme of things (think lions), a relatively mild stressor. The monkeys born to these mothers grew up more anxious, and had a slightly depressed immune response in youth.

Only once when my wife was on maternity leave did I ask about her work experience during pregnancy. Had she worried? No, she said. Apparently only I, the nonpregnant one, had fretted. "I know my limits," she said. How? Years earlier, after weeks of work-related sleep deprivation, she'd been talking with someone when she woke up mid-sentence and realized she'd been speaking gibberish. She vowed never to end up there again.

How close had she come this time? If 10 was delirium and talking nonsense, she said, she'd reached a five. And if the dial had turned much further, she would have bowed out.

I found this somewhat reassuring, especially when she explained the techniques she'd developed for managing a job so rife with chaos and uncertainty that whenever she related the day's insanity over dinner, I became tense. She always created contingency plans, she said. She informed clients of problems when they arose, not at the 11th hour—a way of managing fallout from unmet expectations. And maybe most important, she'd learned to remind herself that, whatever catastrophe seemed to be looming, it wasn't the end of the world. "I'm not saving lives," she said.

All of this echoed what scientists had told me: how you respond to stress isn't written in stone; managing it is a skill that can be learned.

In California, women with Arabic names saw a reduction in their babies' birth weight following the September 11 attacks.

I still had one lingering anxiety: her sleep deprivation. Experiments on human volunteers suggest that a lack of sleep can induce a derangement of the immune system similar to what's seen under chronic stress. Michele Okun, a researcher at the University of Colorado at Colorado Springs, has linked sleep deficiency to an increased risk of preterm birth.

The fact is, though, success in upper-echelon positions sometimes requires 80-hour weeks, pregnancy be damned.

Marissa Mayer, the CEO of Yahoo, launched an ambitious effort to turn around the company while six months pregnant. Sheryl Sandberg, the COO of Facebook, worked through what sounds like severe morning sickness. I'm not suggesting that these women, who have become symbols of female ascendancy, did something wrong.

Here's why: the science indicates that how we respond to stress depends in large part on how much control we think we have over it. If you're excited by your job, invigorated by its challenges, made to feel alive by it, it's probably not going to wear you down. And Mayer and Sandberg have more control than most. Sandberg's book, *Lean In,* begins with her "lumbering" while pregnant across the parking lot at Google, where she worked at the time, wondering why no designated spaces existed for expectant mothers, and then promptly fixing that problem. Mayer had a nursery built in her office, and stafed it with a nanny.

Indeed, both women had plenty of help—from husbands, assistants, and so on. And my wife has me—providing the child care, cooking dinner, and trying to make sure she eats her vegetables. All of this, which scientists describe as "social support," can shape our response to stress.

It's when support is lacking and the stressors begin piling on—a lack of job security, anxiety-provoking relationships, falling behind on the rent—that obvious problems begin to emerge. "You put everything in a bucket," Okun told me, "and eventually the bucket is going to overflow."

One damp evening last November, I squeezed into a small conference room at the University of California at San Francisco, accompanied by perhaps 40 others, many of them medical professionals. We'd come for a discussion titled "The Placenta and the Neighborhood," in which Paula Braveman, the head of the university's Center on Social Disparities in Health, would explore new thinking on the persistent discrepancies in health tied to class and race in the United States, and how those discrepancies likely begin before birth.

Though I'd set out to investigate how the pressures on my wife might affect her health, and our child's, I knew I couldn't write about stress and pregnancy without looking at the consequences for women near the bottom of the socioeconomic ladder, where a qualitatively different kind of stress prevails. If famine and infection are the first two pillars of the fetal-origins field, poverty is quickly becoming the third.

Braveman laid out the argument: Experiences that tend to correlate with class and race—neighborhood violence, social isolation, financial insecurity—induce a state of chronic stress. This response, meant to protect us from acute threats like man-eating bears, ends up wreaking havoc on our bodies over time, altering immune and circulatory function. In pregnancy, these changes may affect the placenta, birth outcomes, and the long-term health of the child.

At least, that's the theory. There's little doubt that poverty is bad for you. The prevalence of nearly every factor known to erode health—lousy diet, lack of exercise, smoking, and so on—increases as one descends the socioeconomic ladder. But when scientists try to control for these factors—comparing rich smokers with poor smokers, say, or affluent couch potatoes with poor ones—they still find a disparity. The growing suspicion, says Braveman, is that stress is "a missing piece of the puzzle."

This is not the stress of working late to finish a presentation. This is better understood as rage, humiliation, and shame capped with a sense of powerlessness. This type of stress begins shaping vulnerability to disease, Braveman and others think, during pregnancy. Variations in preterm birthrates by class and race provide evidence. Poor whites have an elevated risk of preterm birth compared with more-affluent whites, suggesting that poverty drives the disparity. But there also seems to be something about the experience of being African American that, poverty aside, can affect pregnancy. Middle-class and affluent black women have much higher preterm birthrates than similarly well-to-do white women, and blacks in general are one and a half times as likely as whites to have a child prematurely. Is genetics responsible? It seems not. Black women who immigrate to the United States don't have the same risk of preterm birth as those who are born here do.

What these findings suggest, Braveman told the mostly non-minority-female audience, is that "there's something toxic about being a woman of color in the U.S."

One ongoing study of 560 inner-city children whose parents have asthma or allergies highlights the idea that social conditions can influence the health of unborn babies. Scientists began following the children's mothers, most of whom are black or Latina, during pregnancy, and they've found that prenatal stress, from sources including money and neighborhood problems, seemed to predict altered immune function at birth. Asthma, which is prevalent among certain urban minorities, doesn't usually show up until later in childhood. In this cohort, however, the children whose mothers were most stressed during pregnancy were more likely to wheeze as 1-year-olds.

Even this research doesn't show direct causation: the same genetic traits could, in theory, underlie both the mother's physiological response to stress and the child's susceptibility to asthma. But then again, the findings parallel those from the monkeys whose mothers were stressed with horn blasts—their immune function was similarly altered.

In a recent *Nature* essay titled "Don't Blame the Mothers," Sarah Richardson, a historian of science and philosophy at Harvard, and others, including leaders in the fetal-origins field, warned that the science too often gets translated into mother-blaming. As the research has gained momentum and edged toward scientific fashionability, accusatory-sounding headlines have begun to appear. "The Nutritional Sins of the Mother," read a recent one in *Science*. Another, in the United Kingdom's *Daily Mail*, proclaimed, "Babies Can 'Contract' Depression in the Womb."

At its worst, the reporting on fetal-origins science gives mothers a new source of anxiety (or even guilt, if they're looking back in time). Tommy not only requires plenty of extracurricular activities for his college application; to succeed, he needs to have had an optimal prenatal experience, whatever that is.

We should be cautious about prescriptive advice. Research shows that in the right amount, stress may be good for pregnant mothers and their unborn children. Janet DiPietro, a professor at Johns Hopkins University, has found, for example, that moderate stress during pregnancy seems to beneficially accelerate development of the fetal nervous system. Completely eliminating such stimuli may pose its own risks.

At its worst, the reporting on fetal-origins science gives mothers a new source of anxiety (or even guilt, if they're looking back in time).

The other problem is that the narrow focus on mother and fetus ignores other interfaces—between Mom and the multiple spheres in which she dwells. "We assume complete agency of the individual in our society," Janet Rich-Edwards, a Harvard scientist who studies maternal health and who co-authored the *Nature* essay, told me. "That ignores a lot of the truth about women's situations." That's a primary takeaway of the research on poverty: part of what makes poverty toxic may be the lack of control over what's happening to you.

Fetal-origins science may not yet yield many useful guidelines for individual pregnant women (and their husbands) wondering whether their jobs are too stressful. But research by economists does suggest that public policies can improve infants' health by helping mothers manage work/family conflicts.

In the late 20th century, many European nations expanded maternal-leave policies incrementally, with a rather striking result: even in relatively wealthy populations, the rates of infant mortality declined.

The numbers aren't huge. On average, providing 10 weeks of leave corresponds with a 1 to 2 percent reduction in infant mortality. But the improvements keep growing as the leave increases. Twenty weeks yields a reduction of 2 to 4 percent. Thirty weeks gives you between 7 and 9 percent. Infant health also improves.

No one is certain how a few months away from work can have this effect. Public-health experts have assumed it is due solely to time off after the baby's birth—women who take maternity leave may breast-feed more, and be more diligent about doctor visits and vaccinations. But the economist Sakiko Tanaka notes that birth weights increased after paid-leave mandates took effect, suggesting that the policies somehow improved prenatal conditions. How? One explanation is that many European women start maternity leave before delivery—in Norway, women begin their paid leave at least three weeks before their due date.

Not everyone buys that maternity leave improves infant health. Critics charge that the studies don't show causality, and economists in Canada have not found the same benefits there as in Europe. Even if the associations hold, the lesson isn't that all women need to take time off before birth, or that they necessarily should. There's still a lot we don't know, including when in pregnancy time off might be most beneficial, or under what circumstances.

Evidence from the U.S. also suggests that simply providing leave—whether or not women use it before their babies are born—could improve birth outcomes, in part by reducing pregnant women's stress.

The 1993 Family and Medical Leave Act allows women up to 12 weeks of unpaid maternity leave without fear of losing their jobs. Only about 60 percent of American workers qualify (the company has to have more than 50 employees in a 75-mile radius, and the employee needs to have worked for at least a year and logged 1,250 hours), and few poor women can afford to go without a paycheck for three months (only 12 percent of women in the private sector get paid leave from their employers).

Even so, when Maya Rossin-Slater, an economist at UC Santa Barbara, compared birth outcomes from before and after the law went into effect, she found that the preterm birthrate declined slightly and birth weights went up. As in Europe, fewer children were dying.

Since American women tend not to take prenatal maternity leave, Rossin-Slater thinks the improvements at birth were largely because women weren't stressed out during pregnancy about rushing back to work after delivery—or worried that there might not be a job for them to come back to. They may also have found it easier to take time off for prenatal care, which the law allows.

One policy that seems to improve birth outcomes is allowing pregnant women to scale back or temporarily change their duties at work.

The changes are very slight, and Rossin-Slater observed them only among college-educated and married women, the group most able to take time off. One in seven American women lives in poverty. If this cohort could have a similar reprieve, Rossin-Slater suspects, the U.S. would see greater improvements in infant health.

A version of that experiment has occurred. After the 1978 Pregnancy Discrimination Act was passed, five states— California, Hawaii, New Jersey, New York, and Rhode Island— began offering temporary-disability pay to pregnant women. In a working paper, Jenna Stearns, a doctoral candidate at UC Santa Barbara, looked at how birth outcomes changed as a result. Stearns found that the incidence of low birth weight declined by 3.2 percent, and early births (between 37 and 39 weeks of gestation) fell by 7.2 percent. The effect was greatest among single mothers and African American mothers.

Parental-leave policies can be too generous. Studies in Europe have found that at some point after six months, parental leave stops producing measurable benefits, says Rossin-Slater, and overly long leaves may begin to hold women back, or make them more likely to drop out of the workforce altogether. But the U.S. lags so far behind—out of the 185 countries that report to the United Nations' International Labor Organization, we're one of only two without a national paid-maternity-leave policy—that we are in a sense ideally situated to make dramatic gains.

The other policy that seems to improve birth outcomes is allowing pregnant women to scale back or temporarily change their duties at work. In 1979, Quebec followed the French example and passed a law giving women the right to request a change in job responsibilities. A 2007 study on female workers there found that cumulative job strains and stress correlated with double the risk of preterm birth. But the risk dissipated when women invoked the law and switched to less strenuous positions.

When I asked about doing something similar here, I got strong reactions. "Good God, no!," one researcher said. "What a setback for the equality of women in the workplace." Harvard's Sarah Richardson said that she had concerns about policies focused on the health of the fetus: "Well-intended support can move into coercion."

She pointed to the 1908 Supreme Court case *Muller v. Oregon*. Curt Muller, who owned a laundry business, was found guilty in a state court of making a female employee work more than 10 hours a day, then Oregon's workday limit for women. He appealed, but the Supreme Court upheld the conviction (and the $10 fine). As one justice put it, because "healthy mothers are essential to vigorous offspring, the physical wellbeing of woman becomes an object of public interest and care in order to preserve the strength and vigor of the race."

Looking back, many scholars see *Muller v. Oregon* as establishing the precedent for half a century of laws that limited women's participation in the workplace, all ostensibly to protect unborn children. With court approval, legislation prevented women from working in restaurants at night, and from working in factories in Ohio. Numerous states limited women's workdays to 10 hours.

Even after the 1964 Civil Rights Act made gender-based discrimination illegal, many companies refused to hire women for certain positions, out of concern for their yet-to-be-conceived children. By 1980, an estimated 100,000 jobs were off-limits. No one seemed to consider that women could make these decisions themselves, or that a mother's inability to secure her livelihood might be the most toxic exposure of all for the fetus. Because of these restrictions, some women sterilized themselves to stay employed.

These issues continue to arise even today. In December, the Supreme Court heard the case of *Young v. United Parcel Service*. Peggy Young, a delivery person, was pregnant with her third child in 2006 when her doctor and her midwife both recommended that she should not lift more than 20 pounds. When she relayed this medical advice to her superiors, UPS forced her to take unpaid leave. Young sued, charging that UPS had violated the Pregnancy Discrimination Act. The government's Equal Employment Opportunity Commission recently clarified that, under the law, employers must make "reasonable" accommodations for pregnant women.

One legacy of the *Muller* decision may be a fear of inadvertently opening the door to further discrimination through legislation aimed at helping women. Joan Williams, the head of the Center for WorkLife Law at UC Hastings's College of the Law, told me that a prominent feminist once confided to her that because she didn't want anything resembling special treatment written into law, she'd fought against maternity leave. "Inside-the-Beltway feminists killed it," Williams said. She suspects that as a result, unpaid leave came to American mothers a decade later than it might have, folded into the Family and Medical Leave Act—which applies to everyone, not just to women.

The U.S. is one of only two countries without a paid-maternity-leave policy.

Williams argues that it's time to reframe the debate as one about families and the workplace, not just women and work. Research suggests that after a woman has a baby, she's seen as less reliable and dedicated, and her superiors are more likely to pass her over for promotions. She'll likely earn less in the course of her career. Over time, though, a fatherhood penalty has also become apparent, albeit only for dads who take paternity leave. For most men, becoming a father increases their earnings. But those who take time off are more likely to be demoted. Their colleagues see them as weak, and they, too, may earn less during their careers.

The Center for WorkLife Law runs a hotline for reporting discrimination involving parental leave. Complaints by men have ballooned, from less than 2 percent of all calls in 2000 to a quarter today. This is good news, Williams said—a sign that men are pushing back against old, rusted-in-place expectations: you put in 40 years, never get sick, take very little vacation, then retire. That 1950s ideal doesn't work well for today's mothers or fathers—or for anyone, really. The solution, says Williams, isn't to fit women into an untenable norm, but to change the norm.

In the end, our son arrived a week late, large and healthy. He's grown into a solid, bright-eyed baby who laughs and babbles plenty. Between company maternity leave, disability insurance, and a month and a half at partial pay from the State of California (which implemented the country's first paid-parental-leave program in 2004), my wife cobbled together roughly three and a half months of semi-paid leave. Her employer granted an additional three months unpaid.

All of my fretting over her work was perhaps misplaced. My wife was respected; she had control. She was compensated well enough to fund her own European-length leave. If anything, my wife stood as evidence that more women should be in higher positions, and paid better—to no small degree, having power and money equals health, because it gives you more control over your time.

But if there's one clear takeaway from the research on fetal health and workplace strains, it's that such control shouldn't be a luxury afforded only to affluent women. In January, President Obama announced that he would direct federal agencies to allow employees to take six weeks of paid sick leave for the arrival of a child. He also proposed creating a $2.2 billion fund to help states develop their own paid-leave programs for all workers. That proposal seems unlikely to get much traction—which is a shame, because the research suggests that paid leave could not only help parents manage the demands of work and family but also decrease infant mortality and improve infant health, particularly for those at lower socioeconomic levels. Maybe Americans could finally start living as long as Swedes, who have three years on us, or at least Canadians, who outlive us by two and a half.

Critical Thinking

1. What does evidence from fetal-origins research tell us about the roles of nature and nurture in early development? What are some studies in the article that capture how nature and nurture influence each other?

2. Based on the fetal-origin research in the article, how does early development appear to be much more complex than straight forward, with multiple influences on the developing baby?

3. What are some reasons why the United States does not have a good maternity leave policy? What could be some possible benefits on babies, mothers, and the nation of adopting better leave policies in the United States?

Internet References

Aboutkidshealth.com
http://www.aboutkidshealth.ca/en/resourcecentres/pregnancybabies/pregnancy/healthcareinpregnancy/pages/things-to-avoid-during-pregnancy-teratogens.aspx

Babycenter.com
http://www.babycenter.com/pregnancy-week-by-week

Healthychild.org
http://www.healthychild.org/saferpregnancyebook/?gclid=Cj0KEQjwyoCrBRCl-aa97pKX_t8BEiQAbrs_9Btb_rJK1gj8kuXR4b0WvYcTlFFxMFz8e3kjJ5RL_r4aAkRY8P8HAQ

National Institute of Health (NIH)
http://www.nlm.nih.gov/medlineplus/ency/article/002398.htm

Women'sHealth.gov, USDHHS
http://www.womenshealth.gov/publications/our-publications/fact-sheet/prenatal-care.html

Velasquez-Manoff, Moises. "Should You Bring Your Unborn Baby to Work?," *The Atlantic*, March 2015. Copyright © 2015 The Atlantic Media Co., as first published in The Atlantic Magazine. All rights reserved. Distributed by Tribune Content Agency, LLC. Reprinted by permission.

Prepared by: Chris J. Boyatzis, *Bucknell University*
Ellen N. Junn, *California State University, Dominguez Hills*

Article

"Possibly the Worst Approach"

In an effort to protect kids from food allergies, American parents have been doing the opposite.

MELINDA WENNER MOYER

Learning Outcomes

After reading this article, you will be able to:

- Describe evidence of the benefits of exposing babies to different foods, including some that may cause allergic reactions.

- Explain when babies should be exposed to solid foods, including foods that might cause allergies.

- Use evidence from allergies in different countries to evaluate the basic hypothesis that exposure to foods can lower babies' sensitivity to them.

The news last month of a clinical trial showing that infants at a high risk for peanut allergies were much less likely to actually develop these allergies if they were fed regular peanut snacks made me want to reach for a spoonful of peanut butter to shove down my 7-month-old's throat. But then visions of hives and red puffy welts danced in my head and I reconsidered. Like many parents, I have long been under the impression that the best way to prevent food allergies in kids is to *delay* giving them allergenic foods such as peanuts and eggs until they're older. So before presenting my daughter with a bowl full of Jif based on a single finding, I decided to dig into the research.

If your kid seems a little sensitive to a particular food, the worst thing to do may be to stop giving her that food.

The simplest way to sum up my conclusion is to say that my daughter tried her first bite of peanut butter last week. She made a stink face but was otherwise fine. As it turns out, the outcome of the recent trial, which was covered by many news organizations as if it shattered current established dogma, was actually not terribly surprising if you've been following current advice and research on food allergies. It's been clear for a while that waiting a year or longer to feed your child peanut butter and eggs is useless at best. Some research even suggests that the earlier you introduce these foods the better—4 months, in other words, may be better than 6 months, even though the American Academy of Pediatrics' official recommendation is to wait until 6 months to give babies any solid food. Even crazier: If your kid seems a little sensitive to a particular food—perhaps dairy gives her a minor rash around the mouth or loose stools—the worst thing to do may be to stop giving her that food.

First, let me quash the widely held notion that delaying the introduction of allergenic foods to babies is a good idea. That approach was based in part on the flawed notion that it's smart to let an infant's gastrointestinal and immune systems "mature" for a while so they can better handle allergenic foods, and some studies from the 1990s did support it. But then contradictory studies began flooding in, and scientists now believe that exposing the gastrointestinal system to an allergen early in life is unlikely to cause an allergy. It probably does the opposite. (More on that later.)

In light of the changing tide, back in 2008, the American Academy of Pediatrics published new recommendations that reversed its old dogma. "Although solid foods should not be introduced before 4 to 6 months of age," it wrote, "there is no current convincing evidence that delaying their introduction beyond this period has a significant protective effect." Unfortunately, a lot of pediatricians haven't gotten the memo and are still giving parents outdated advice, which may explain why everyone was so shocked by last month's trial results. Also, in 2012, the AAP confused things further when it started telling parents to wait until 6 months to feed babies *any* solid food, a recommendation that was designed to encourage mothers to breastfeed for longer.

Here's the thing, though: When it comes to preventing food allergies, research is starting to suggest that it may be better to give babies allergenic foods closer to 4 months than 6 months. You should never give babies *under* the age of 4 months solid food, and you also shouldn't force solid food on a baby who isn't showing signs of being ready. But once your infant does seem ready, you can go for it—give her eggs, peanut butter, strawberries, the works (though be sure to read the caveats below). One recent Finnish study found that babies introduced to solid foods such as oats, potatoes, and meat before the age of 6 months were less likely to develop food allergies. Another study by some of the same authors found that babies— particularly those with a family history of allergies—who were fed a larger variety of solid foods at 4 months developed fewer skin allergies than those fed a smaller variety at 4 months. Another study reported that babies who were fed cereal grains before they hit the 6-month mark were less likely to develop wheat allergies than babies who were first fed grains after 6 months. And a rather shocking and controversial 2010 study reported that newborns who were given cow's milk formula within two weeks of birth had 19 times lower odds of developing a cow's milk allergy compared with newborns who were not. "Solid food introduction from 4 months of age, including a wide range of healthy foods and potential food allergens such as eggs, peanuts, and fish, is our current best advice," says Debbie Palmer, head of the Childhood Allergy and Immunology Research team at the University of Western Australia, who has published extensively on the topic.

The American Academy of Allergy, Asthma & Immunology recently published detailed recommendations on this front, and its advice is basically this: Breastfeed your baby exclusively for the first 4 months of life; if you can't, and your baby has a family risk of allergy, consider using a hydrolyzed formula. Then, regardless of whether your baby has a family risk of allergy or not, feed your 4-to-6-month-old "complementary" foods first, one at a time, waiting a few days in between, while continuing to breastfeed or feed formula. These include rice and oat cereals, vegetables, fruits (including berries—they're fine), and certain meats. If your baby has tried and done well with a few of these, start giving her tastes of allergenic foods such as peanut products and eggs. (But before you start giving your baby Cracker Jacks, there are a few important caveats: Never feed babies whole peanuts, because they can choke on them. If your baby has a sibling with a food allergy, you may want to consult an allergist before giving her those same allergenic foods. And babies still shouldn't be given cow's milk as their main drink before their first birthday because it's too low in iron and may lead to anemia.)

So how does this approach work? After all, you have to be exposed to something repeatedly in order to become "sensitized" to it and develop an allergy. That's part of the established allergic cascade. So why would eating something repeatedly prevent allergies? As it turns out, *how* a person is exposed to an allergen really matters. Most scientists now believe, based on what is called the dual-allergen-exposure hypothesis, that a person becomes allergic to, say, peanuts by being exposed to peanut proteins through the skin. (If you have peanut eaters in your home, peanut proteins are probably all over your house, no matter how frequently you vacuum.) Eating peanuts, on the other hand, helps to promote tolerance to them, thereby decreasing allergy risk. The epidemiology of peanut allergies supports this idea. In countries where peanuts are not regularly consumed, such as in parts of Europe, peanut allergies are rare, because babies are less likely to become sensitized to peanut proteins through the skin. In the Middle East and Africa, where peanuts are regularly consumed by everyone but babies also eat peanuts at a young age, rates of peanut allergy are also low, because babies become sensitized to peanuts but also tolerant of them. It's really only in the countries where peanuts are a food staple and yet babies don't regularly eat them—such as in the U.S. and in Canada and in the U.K.—that peanut allergies are so common, because infants become sensitized but not tolerant. In other words, here in America, the old recommendation to "delay the oral introduction of peanuts and eggs was quite possibly the worst approach," Palmer says. Oops!

This theory suggests something else interesting too: People who are allergic to a food might become less allergic the more they eat it. And actually, this is one of the findings from last month's trial. At the beginning of the trial, researchers gave peanut allergy skin prick tests to all the enrolled infants. Even if the infants tested positive—indicating that they were probably allergic to peanuts—the researchers advised the parents to give their babies small amounts of peanut snacks regularly, as long as they did not have dangerous reactions to it in an initial food challenge, until their kids reached their fifth birthday. The researchers told a second group of parents whose babies had tested positive on these skin prick tests to avoid peanuts until age 5. Then, years later, the researchers gave allergy tests to all the 5-year-olds and found that those who had regularly consumed the peanuts were one-third as likely to be allergic to peanuts compared with the kids who had been told to avoid them.

These findings suggest that if your children have a mild reaction to a food—maybe it makes them break out in a mild rash or causes digestive troubles—then "they would be best to continue to include having small amounts on a regular basis," Palmer says. (Of course, you should consult an allergist too.) A number of other small studies support this idea, known as "immunotherapy," for overcoming various types of food allergies, but it's still unclear how long the effects last—it may be that people have to keep consuming the allergen regularly to avoid becoming allergic again—and exposing allergic individuals to their offending allergens can, of course, be risky. By the way, if you do suspect your kid has a food allergy, go get him tested—one study found that only 14 percent of parentally diagnosed food allergies are actual food allergies. Plus, those that do exist often resolve themselves over time, so consider getting your child retested once a year. There's certainly no reason to keep peanut butter out of the house if you don't have to.

Critical Thinking

1. Why have children's food allergies become more common?

2. Based on evidence in the article, are mothers good judges of their children's food allergies? What might cause mothers to "over-diagnose" their children's allergies?

3. If you were to design a new "baby food" campaign to distribute to new parents, what would it look like? How would your recommendations reflect the information presented in this article?

Internet References

KidsHealth.org
http://kidshealth.org/parent/general/body_basics/immune.html
NBC News
http://www.nbcnews.com/id/48489391/ns/health-childrens_health/t/ask-dr-ty-will-early-exposure-colds-boost-immunity/
Parents.com
http://www.parents.com/health/cold-flu/cold/boost-childs-immunity/
WebMD.com
http://www.webmd.com/parenting/features/immune-system

Wenner Moyer, Melinda. "Possibly the Worst Approach," *Slate.com*, March 2015. Copyright © 2015 by Slate Group. Reprinted by permission.

Prepared by: Chris J. Boyatzis, *Bucknell University*
Ellen N. Junn, *California State University, Dominguez Hills*

Article

The Talking Cure

The poorer parents are, the less they talk with their children. The mayor of Providence is trying to close the "word gap."

MARGARET TALBOT

Learning Outcomes

After reading this article, you will be able to:

- Describe the Providence Talks campaign—its goals, its method, and the challenges of implementing it.

- Describe the famous research by Hart and Risley on social class and language development. What were its major findings? How did it help inspire the Providence Talks campaign and others like it?

- Understand the role of poverty and stress on parents' ability to talk with their babies and children and hence understand why social class differences exist in language input to children.

One morning in September, Lissette Castrillón, a case-worker in Providence, Rhode Island, drove to an apartment on the western edge of town to visit Annie Rodriguez, a young mother, and her two-year-old daughter, Eilen. Castrillón and Rodriguez sat down on a worn rug and spoke about the importance of talking to very young children. They discussed ways to cajole a toddler into an extended conversation, and identified moments in the day when Rodriguez could be chatting more with Eilen, an ebullient little girl who was wearing polka-dot leggings.

"Whenever she's saying a few new words, it's important to tell her yes, and add to it," Castrillón told Rodriguez. "So if she sees a car you can say, 'Yes, that's a car. It's a big car. It's a blue car.'"

Eilen suddenly said, "Boo ca!"

Castrillón looked at her and said, "Right! Blue car! Good job!"

Rodriguez noted that Eilen had recently become so enthralled by an animated show, "Bubble Guppies," that she had become

"stuck on that word 'guppy.'" She went on, "Everything's 'guppy, guppy, guppy.' So when she refers to something as 'guppy' I try to correct it—like, 'No, that's not a guppy. That's a doll.'"

"Guppy?" Eilen said, hopefully.

Castrillón said, "Well, I think right now the important thing won't be so much telling her no but just adding words and repeating them, so she'll start repeating them on her own."

Rodriguez is enrolled in a program called Providence Talks, the most ingenious of several new programs across the country that encourage low-income parents to talk more frequently with their kids. Once a month, Eilen wears a small recording device for the day, and the recording is then analyzed. An algorithm tallies all the words spoken by adults in her vicinity, all the vocalizations Eilen makes, and all the "conversational turns"—exchanges in which Eilen says something and an adult replies, or vice versa. The caseworker who visits Rodriguez's home gives her a progress report, which shows in graph form how many words Eilen has been hearing, and how they peak and dip throughout the day.

Castrillón presented Rodriguez with the month's report. She leaned over her shoulder and said, "See, this shows the percentage of adult words. There were over fifteen thousand words spoken in that day."

"Wow!" Rodriguez said.

Castrillón noted that significantly more conversation took place when the TV was off, and that it had been off more that month than the previous one. "There was pretty high electronic sound last time," she said. "This time, there was very little." Rodriguez nodded, studying the printout.

In the nineteen-eighties, two child psychologists at the University of Kansas, Betty Hart and Todd Risley, began comparing, in detail, how parents of different social classes talked with their children. Hart and Risley had both worked in preschool programs designed to boost the language skills of low-income kids, but they had been dissatisfied with the results of such efforts: the achievement gap between rich and poor had continued to widen. They decided to look beyond the classroom and examine what went on inside the home. Hart and Risley recruited forty-two families: thirteen upper, or "professional," class, ten middle class, thirteen working class, and six on welfare. Each family had a baby who was between seven and twelve months old. During the next two and a half years, observers visited each home for an hour every month, and taped the encounters. They were like dinner guests who never said much but kept coming back.

In all, Hart and Risley reported, they analyzed "more than 1,300 hours of casual interactions between parents and their language-learning children." The researchers noticed many similarities among the families: "They all disciplined their children and taught them good manners and how to dress and toilet themselves." They all showed their children affection and said things like "Don't jump on the couch" and "Use your spoon" and "Do you have to go potty?" But the researchers also found that the wealthier parents consistently talked more with their kids. Among the professional families, the average number of words that children heard in an hour was twenty-one hundred and fifty; among the working-class families, it was twelve hundred and fifty; among the welfare families, it was six hundred and twenty. Over time, these daily differences had major consequences, Hart and Risley concluded: "With few exceptions, the more parents talked to their children, the faster the children's vocabularies were growing and the higher the children's I.Q. test scores at age 3 and later."

Hart and Risley's research has grown in prominence, in part because large-scale educational reforms like No Child Left Behind have proved disappointing. Addressing the word gap by coaching new parents sounds like a simpler intervention. Last year, Hillary Clinton announced a new initiative, Too Small to Fail, that emphasizes the importance of talking to infants and young children; in the fall, President Barack Obama convened a White House conference whose goal was to "bridge the word gap and put more young people on the path to success." Other cities, including Cambridge, Massachusetts, have initiated programs similar to the one in Providence, and still others have begun public-awareness campaigns with radio spots and bus-shelter signs reminding parents to talk frequently to their kids. The notion of the word gap even turned up on "Orange Is the New Black," when one of the inmates urged her boyfriend to talk with their new daughter, because "there's all these studies that say that if you don't talk to the baby they end up, like, fucked by the time they're five."

The way you converse with your child is one of the most intimate aspects of parenting, shaped both by your personality and by cultural habits so deep that they can feel automatic. Changing how low-income parents interact with their children is a delicate matter, and not especially easy. Lissette Castrillón was sensitive to the challenge, and she had an appealing informality: she listened carefully to Rodriguez, praised her efforts, and said admiring things about Eilen, all while sitting cross-legged on the floor. But, perhaps inevitably, there was an awkward moment.

Castrillón had brought an iPad with her, and she played for Rodriguez a video of a mother shopping at the grocery store while her toddler sat in the cart—just to show, Castrillón explained, that you could "talk aloud when you're pretty much doing anything." The mother onscreen was blond and fit, and wore white jeans; she looked like a character in a Nancy Meyers movie, and her patter was so constant that it became wearying. "Here's our crunchy peanut butter, sweetheart!" she trilled, scanning an aisle filled with organic food. "Here's the Wild Oats one. Roasted almond butter. Crunchy. Let's get crunchy, Bubba." The cart was piled high, and the items looked expensive. "Bubba, we're running out of room. What are we going to do? Did Mommy buy too many groceries today? I think we should get the creamy, too, because Murphy does *not* like when I get that crunchy. And we like to have the peanut butter because peanut butter's good for *you*. It's got protein."

Rodriguez watched the video with a serious expression. It was hard to imagine her holding forth with such preening gusto in the organics aisle. Castrillón said, "Well, you know, just—whatever the food is you're buying, you can talk about color, shape, and texture."

In 2012, the mayor of Providence, Angel Taveras, heard about the Mayors Challenge, a new competition being offered to cities that proposed a bold idea for making urban life better. The prize was to be given by Bloomberg Philanthropies, the foundation started by Michael Bloomberg, the former New York mayor, on the premise that cities are "the new laboratories of democracy." The city that won the grand prize would receive five million dollars to realize its project, and four other cities would be given a million each. As Taveras recalled, "They announced that challenge on Twitter, and right away I said, 'We're going to go for it.' And I didn't know exactly what it would be at the time, but I knew it was going to be on early childhood education."

Taveras's focus was not unusual: these days, everyone from preschool teachers to politicians talks about infant brain development, and toy companies tap into parental anxiety about it. But Taveras had a personal investment in the subject. He is the son of immigrants from the Dominican Republic, neither of whom went beyond the eighth grade. He grew up in Providence, and his mother, Amparo, who raised him largely on her own, worked factory jobs to support him and his two siblings. When he was four, Amparo enrolled him in a local Head Start program, and he felt that it had made a decisive difference in his life. He went on to Providence public schools, and then attended Harvard University and Georgetown law school. Taveras calls himself the "Head Start to Harvard" mayor, and he still has his graduation picture from the program. "I wore a cap and gown, and it was so special for me," he recalled.

In 2010, at the age of forty, Taveras became the first Latino mayor of Providence, a city that is nineteen percent Latino, mostly Dominican. Tall and skinny, with rimless eyeglasses, Taveras is nerdier and nicer than you might expect of a Providence mayor. One of his predecessors, Buddy Cianci, was twice convicted of felonies while in office: once for racketeering, and once for assaulting a man—using a lit cigarette and a fireplace log—who was dating his ex-wife. Taveras, by contrast, wrote a children's book called "How to Do Well in School" and seems genuinely to enjoy mayoral duties like dropping in for "story time" at a local library.

One day, while Taveras was mulling over what to propose for the Bloomberg competition, his policy director, Toby Shepherd, told him about Hart and Risley's research—including their calculation that a poor four-year-old has heard thirty million fewer words from his parents than a wealthy one has.

That number had attracted a lot of attention in the press—to the point that Hart and Risley's study was sometimes faulted for an overemphasis on the sheer quantity of words. But Taveras learned that Hart, who died in 2012, and Risley, who died in 2007, had also identified important differences in *kinds* of talk. In the recordings of the professional families, they found a "greater richness of nouns, modifiers, and past-tense verbs," and more conversations on subjects that children had initiated. Catherine Snow, a professor at Harvard's Graduate School of Education, who studies children's language development, told me that these findings made sense, since quantity was often a proxy for quality. "Families that talk a lot also talk about more different things," Snow said. "They use more grammatical variety in their sentences and more sophisticated vocabulary, and produce more utterances in connected chains." Such parents, she noted, "don't just say, 'That's a teapot.' They say, 'Oh, *look*, a teapot! Let's have a tea party! There's Raggedy Ann—do you think she wants to come to our tea party? Does she like sugar in her tea?'" Parents who talk a lot with their young children ask them many questions, including ones to which they know the answer. ("Is that a ducky on your shirt?") They reply to those devilish "Why?" questions toddlers love with elaborate explanations. Erika Hoff, a developmental psychologist at Florida Atlantic University, has published studies about early language development whose results are similar to those of Hart and Risley. She recalled marvelling at "the young professor mothers" at a university childcare center: *Everything* was a topic of conversation. If they had to get out of the building in case of a fire, they'd be so busy discussing the pros and cons with their toddlers that I kind of wondered if they'd make it."

Among the more affluent families studied by Hart and Risley, a higher proportion of the talk directed at children was affirming, which was defined to include not just compliments like "Good job!" but also responses in which parents repeat and build on a child's comments: "Yes, it is a bunny! It's a bunny eating a carrot!" In those families, the average child heard thirty-two affirmations and five prohibitions ("Stop that"; "That's the wrong way!") per hour—a ratio of six to one. For the kids in the working-class families, the ratio was twelve affirmatives to seven prohibitions, and in the welfare families it was five affirmatives to eleven prohibitions. Hart and Risley included one extended description of a mother from the poorest group, at home with her twenty-three-month-old daughter, Inge:

> The mother returns; Inge sits on the couch beside her to watch TV and says something incomprehensible. Mother responds, "Quit copying off of me. You a copycat." Inge says something incomprehensible, and her mother does not respond. Inge picks up her sister's purse from the couch. Her mother initiates, "You better get out of her purse." Inge continues to explore the purse and her mother initiates, "Get out of her purse." Inge does not answer; she begins to take coins out of the purse and put them on the coffee table. Her mother initiates, "Give me that purse." Inge continues to put coins on the table. Her mother initiates, "And the money." Inge does not answer but gives her mother the purse.

Hart and Risley noted that the mother was "concerned" and "affectionate" toward her child. Inge was dressed in nice clothes and fed consistently, and she was toilet trained; at one point, the mother picked her up and kissed her. But she made "few efforts to engage the child in conversation," and did not "re-direct" Inge when she wanted her to stop doing something, or treat exploratory misbehavior as a sign of curiosity rather than defiance. Most of what the mother said to Inge was "corrective or critical."

Hart and Risley also provided examples of various kinds of conversation—mostly, but not exclusively, among the professional families—in which parents prompted and encouraged children to talk:

> The mother initiates, asking Calvin (24 months), "What did we do on Halloween? What did you put on your head and on your body? What did you look like?" When Calvin does not answer, she tells him, "You were a kitty cat." Calvin says, "Wanna get. Where go?" His mother says, "What are you looking for? I know what you're

looking for. What used to be on the door handle?" Calvin says, "Where?" His mother says, "The trick-or-treat bag. We ate up all the candy already." Calvin says, "Where the candy go?" His mother says, "It's all gone in your tummy." Calvin says, "Want some."

Mayor Taveras thought that such conversational strategies could be taught to new parents, and decided to address the word-gap problem with the Mayors Challenge. "Head Start is awesome," he told me. "But we've gotta do something even *before* Head Start." At the time, his wife was pregnant with their first child, and he "was reading and talking to my daughter in utero. I decided it can't hurt. I'd come home and say, 'It's Daddy,' and 'How are you?,' and everything else."

Even though the Hart and Risley study had encompassed just a few dozen families, the transcribing and coding of all those tapes had been laborious. New technology, Shepherd told him, could make counting words much easier. In 2005, a research foundation named LENA (for Language Environment Analysis) had developed a small digital device that could record for sixteen hours and recognize adult words, child vocalizations, and conversational turns. Such distinctions were important, because researchers had determined that merely overheard speech—a mother holding a child on her lap but talking on the phone, for instance—contributed less to language development. The LENA recorder could also distinguish between actual people speaking in a child's earshot and sounds from TVs and other electronic devices; children under the age of two appear to learn language only from other humans. The device was about the size of an iPod, and it fit into the pocket of a specially designed vest or pair of overalls. (Children soon forgot about the devices, though they occasionally ended up in the toilet or in the dog's bed.)

LENA's device had been used in academic research on language development and in interventions for hard-of-hearing, autistic, and developmentally delayed children. In 2009, a Chicago surgeon named Dana Suskind, who specializes in cochlear-implant surgery for deaf children, began using LENA's technology in a program called the Thirty Million Words Initiative, which includes a study on the effects of encouraging low-income parents to talk more with their children. Suskind had come across Hart and Risley's research after noticing divergent outcomes for her young patients. "Cochlear implants are truly a modern medical miracle," she said. "But, after the implantation surgery, some of the kids we saw were reading and speaking on grade level, and others were much slower to communicate. The difference almost always had to do with socioeconomic status."

Taveras named his proposed project Providence Talks, and decided that technology would be supported with counselling. During home visits with low-income parents, caseworkers would discuss the science of early brain development. They'd advise parents to try to understand better what their kids were

feeling, instead of simply saying no. Parents would be told that, even when they were bathing a child or cooking dinner, they could be narrating what was going on, as well as singing, counting, and asking questions. The caseworkers would bring books and demonstrate how to read them: asking children questions about what was going to happen next and livening up the dialogue with funny, high-pitched voices and enthusiastic mooing and woofing.

For the mayor, it was important that Providence Talks did not seem exclusive. "I love it that you can do this in Spanish or any other language," he said. "I love it that you can do it even if you're not literate. Even if you can't read them a book. You can still talk to them about what an apple is: 'This is a red apple, this is a green apple, this is how you cut it.' Just talking and engaging and having a conversation."

In March of 2013, Taveras learned that Providence Talks had won the Mayors Challenge grand prize. The Bloomberg committee praised the city for its "direct, simple, and revolutionary approach." Taveras wanted to jump up and down and scream, but, fearing that this wasn't mayoral, he contented himself with fist-bumping Toby Shepherd and the rest of his staff.

A big part of the program's appeal lay in its technology. Using LENA devices, caseworkers could show parents how much they'd been talking at various times of the day. Crucially, parents found the gadgets fun: they were like Fitbits for conversation. Andrea Riquetti, the director of Providence Talks, told me, "The fact that we have this report, in a graph form, makes it nonjudgmental." Parents were likely to resist, she felt, if the program seemed scolding. "We can say, look, here's the data. Look how much you were talking at eleven o'clock! How can we do this for another half hour? As opposed to a home visitor telling a parent, 'You're not talking to your child enough.'"

Providence Talks had its critics, some of whom thought that the program seemed too intrusive. The A.C.L.U. raised questions about what would happen to the recordings, and one of the organization's Rhode Island associates, Hillary Davis, told *National Journal,* "There's always a concern when we walk in with technology into lower-income families, immigrant populations, minority populations, and we say, 'This will help you.'" She continued, "We don't necessarily recognize the threat to their own safety or liberty that can accidentally come along with that."

Others charged that Providence Talks was imposing middle-class cultural values on poorer parents who had their own valid approaches to raising children, and argued that the program risked faulting parents for their children's academic shortcomings while letting schools off the hook. Nobody contested the fact that, on average, low-income children entered kindergarten with fewer scholastic skills than kids who were better off, but there were many reasons for the disparity, ranging from poor nutrition to chaotic living conditions to the absence of a preschool education. In a caustic essay titled "Selling the Language Gap," which was published in *Anthropology News,* Susan Blum, of Notre Dame, and Kathleen Riley, of Fordham, called Providence Talks an example of "silver-bullet thinking," the latest in a long history of "blame-the-victim approaches to language and poverty."

To some scholars, the program's emphasis on boosting numbers made it seem as though the quality of conversation didn't matter much. As James Morgan, a developmental psycholinguist at Brown University, put it, obsessive word counting might lead parents to conclude that "saying 'doggy, doggy, doggy, doggy' is more meaningful than saying 'doggy.'" Kathy Hirsh-Pasek, a psychologist at Temple University, told me that Hart and Risley had "done a very important piece of work that pointed to a central problem"; nevertheless, their findings had often been interpreted glibly, as if the solution were to let words "just wash over a child, like the background noise of a TV." Her own research, including a recent paper written with Lauren Adamson and other psychologists, points to the importance of interactions between parents and children in which they are both paying attention to the same thing—a cement mixer on the street, a picture in a book—and in which the ensuing conversation (some of which might be conducted in gestures) is fluid and happens over days, even weeks. "It's not just serve and return," Hirsh-Pasek said. "It's serve and return—and return and return."

The original Hart and Risley research, whose data set had only six families in the poorest category, was also called into question. Mark Liberman, a linguist at the University of Pennsylvania, said, "Do low-income people talk with their kids less? Well, that's a question about *millions* of people. Think of people in the survey business, trying to predict elections or develop a marketing campaign. They would find it laughable to draw conclusions without a large randomized sample." Encouraging adults to talk more to children was all to the good, Liberman said, but it was important to remember that "there are some wealthy people who don't talk to their children much and some poor people who talk a lot."

Indeed, recent research that supports Hart and Risley's work has found a great deal of variability *within* classes. In 2006, researchers at the LENA Foundation recorded the conversations of three hundred and twenty-nine families, who were divided into groups by the mothers' education level, a reasonable proxy for social class. Like Hart and Risley, the LENA researchers determined that, on average, parents who had earned at least a B.A. spoke more around their children than other parents: 14,926 words per day versus 12,024. (They attributed Hart and Risley's bigger gap to the fact that they had recorded families only during the late afternoon and the evening—when families talk most—and extrapolated.) But the LENA team also found

that some of the less educated parents spoke a lot more than some of the highly educated parents.

Anne Fernald, a psychologist at Stanford, has published several papers examining the influence of socioeconomic status on children's language development. In one recent study, Fernald, with a colleague, Adriana Weisleder, and others, identified "large disparities" among socioeconomic groups in "infants' language processing, speech production, and vocabulary." But they also found big differences among working-class families, both in terms of "the children's language proficiency and the parents' verbal engagement with the child." Fernald, who sits on the scientific advisory board for Providence Talks, told me, "Some of the wealthiest families in our research had low word counts, possibly because they were on their gadgets all day. So you can see an intermingling at the extremes of rich and poor. Socioeconomic status is *not* destiny."

In response to the privacy concerns, Mayor Taveras and his team volunteered their own households to be the first ones recorded. They also guaranteed that the LENA Foundation's software would erase the recordings after the algorithm analyzed the data. Though this probably reassured some families, it also disappointed some scholars. "That's a huge amount of data being thrown out!" James Morgan, of Brown, told me. "There were real concerns whether families would participate otherwise. But as a scientist it breaks my heart."

To those who argued that Providence Talks embodied cultural imperialism, staff members responded that, on the contrary, they were "empowering" parents with knowledge. Andrea Riquetti, the Providence Talks director, told me, "It really is our responsibility to let families know what it takes to succeed in the culture they live in. Which may not necessarily be the same as the culture they have. But it's their choice whether they decide to. It's not a case of our saying, 'You *have* to do this.'" Riquetti grew up in Quito, Ecuador, came to America at the age of seventeen, and worked for many years as a kindergarten teacher in Providence schools. In Latino culture, she said, "the school is seen as being in charge of teaching children their letters and all that, while parents are in charge of discipline—making sure they listen and they're good and they sit still. Parents don't tend, overall, to give children a lot of choices and options. It's kind of like 'I rule the roost so that you can behave and learn at school.'" The Providence Talks approach "is a little more like 'No, your child and what they have to say is really important.' And having them feel really good about themselves as opposed to passive about their learning is important, because that's what's going to help them succeed in this culture."

Riquetti and the Providence Talks team didn't seem troubled by the concerns that Hart and Risley's data set wasn't robust enough. Although no subsequent study has found a word gap as large as thirty million, several of them have found that children in low-income households have smaller vocabularies than kids in higher-income ones. This deficit correlates with the quantity *and* the quality of talk elicited by the adults at home, and becomes evident quite early—in one study, when some kids were eighteen months old. Lack of conversation wasn't the only reason that low-income kids started out behind in school, but it was certainly a problem.

The biggest question was whether Providence Talks could really change something as personal, casual, and fundamental as how people talk to their babies. Erika Hoff, of Florida Atlantic University, told me, "In some ways, parenting behavior clearly can change. I have a daughter who has a baby now and she does everything differently from how I did it—putting babies to sleep on their backs, not giving them milk till they're a year old. But patterns of *interacting* are different. You're trying to get people to change something that seems natural to them and comes from a fairly deep place. I don't know how malleable that is."

After decades of failed educational reforms, few policymakers are naïve enough to believe that a single social intervention could fully transform disadvantaged children's lives. The growing economic inequality in America is too entrenched, too structural. But that's hardly an argument for doing nothing. Although improvements in test scores associated with preschool programs fade as students proceed through elementary school, broader benefits can be seen many years later. A few oft-cited studies have shown that low-income kids who attended high-quality preschool programs were more likely to graduate from high school and less likely to become pregnant as teen-agers or to be incarcerated; they also earned more money, on average, than peers who were not in such programs. Such data suggest that a full assessment of Providence Talks will take decades to complete.

On a cool, rainy morning in April, I went on a home visit with a young caseworker named Stephanie Taveras (no relation to the mayor), who had been assigned to Providence Talks. Two months earlier, the program had begun with fifty-eight families; the plan was to start adding many more families in the fall, with a projected, if optimistic, enrollment of two thousand families. The monthly recording and coaching visits would go on for two years. On earlier visits, Taveras had discussed a baby's cognitive development by bringing a little wax model of a brain with her.

The family lived in an apartment in Southside, on a block of small, scrubby lawns, chain-link fences, and two-story wooden houses. It was a predominantly Latino neighborhood, where a third of the families have incomes below the poverty line. On a nearby street, there was a corner shop, Perla del Caribe, and a meat market, El Vecinos, but there was no one out on the street that morning, and it felt a little desolate.

Inside, Taveras greeted a seven-month-old girl, Skylah, who was smiling and gurgling while propped up in an ExerSaucer. Skylah's parents, Maranda Raposo and Nicholas Mailloux, were seated on a couch in a gray-carpeted living room whose walls were mostly bare. In one corner, a cat was curled up. In another, a TV was showing an episode of "Law & Order: Special Victims Unit."

Raposo, who was twenty-one, had long, magenta-tinted hair pulled back in a ponytail. She smiled sweetly but was soft-spoken and reticent with her guests. She had dropped out of high school when she was a freshman, after she got pregnant with her first child, Isabella, who was now five. Raposo was hoping to get her G.E.D., but in the meantime she was working two part-time jobs as a cashier, at Party City and at Sears. Mailloux, who was twenty-five and had a five-year-old son by a former girlfriend, was staying home with the kids. Raposo told me later that she had been willing to try Providence Talks because "it was something we could experience with Skylah—it could bring us closer as a family." Just as she and Mailloux wanted to help Skylah stand out by giving her a name with an unusual spelling, they wanted to feel that the time they spent with her was special. "Some people don't even bother talking to their kids," Raposo said. "We talk to her." Nevertheless, before enrolling in the program she hadn't known "exactly how important that is."

Taveras plopped down on the floor and, like Mary Poppins with her carpet bag, started pulling items out of her satchel. She handed Mailloux a board book, "Peek-a Who?," and he put Skylah on his lap and started reading it to her: "Who do you think it's gonna be?" Skylah patted the book and giggled.

Taveras showed them graphs generated by the previous month's recording, noting that their words and conversational turns had gone down a bit. "I went to the nail salon that day," Raposo recalled. "Everybody was talking to her, but she was just, like, staring."

"She wasn't in a talking mood that day," Mailloux added.

"That happens," Taveras reassured them. "What's important is that you challenge yourself to do better the next time." At one point, she asked, "Are there particular times of the day when you read to her? How many times a day, would you say?"

Both parents seemed a little vague on this point. After a moment, Raposo said, "We try to do it more than once."

Taveras asked them what they thought Skylah was learning when they read to her.

"Colors, shapes, animals," Raposo said.

"Yes, and also she's learning about relationships," Taveras said. "You're teaching her that she's important to you. You're making her feel good about herself." Both parents nodded. "And educational skills, too. When she gets to school, she's gonna already be used to sitting still and paying attention."

Taveras told them, "Babies at this age like books with large photos, bright pictures, simple drawings, and familiar things." She recommended board books, noting, "Paper books she's gonna want to tear and chew."

Taveras then offered some thoughts on how to read a book to a baby: "It's a four-part interaction. Get your book, point to something in the book—'Look, Skylah, a ball!'—ask a labelling question—'What's that? That's a cow! Moo! Can you say moo?'—and acknowledge her response. Like, if she babbles or makes a noise, make it back to her, so she knows you heard her. And, if you correct, do it positively. If you say, 'What's that?,' and she says, 'A dog,' you could say, 'It looks like a dog,' or 'It's brown like the dog, but it's a monkey!' That makes her feel good. Not just 'No,' or 'No, that's a monkey.'"

Raposo nodded again, but she seemed most comfortable quietly watching Taveras, who remained on the floor, singing and clapping with Skylah.

Though cultural factors may well explain why some low-income parents talk relatively little with their toddlers, the most obvious explanation is poverty itself. When daily life is stressful and uncertain and dispiriting, it can be difficult to summon up the patience and the playfulness for an open-ended conversation with a small, persistent, possibly whiny child. In 2007, Richard Weissbourd, a senior lecturer at the Harvard Graduate School of Education, helped establish a campaign in Boston that urged parents to talk to their kids, and he organized focus groups with low-income parents. "You had some people working three jobs or dealing with the steady drizzle of helplessness and hopelessness," he recalled. "That makes it hard to have vibrant conversations with a baby. They'd say, 'Look, when I get home I have to clean and cook and do the laundry.' They're exhausted. They'd say, 'Sometimes we have to put our kids in front of the TV.'" Weissbourd said of interventions like Providence Talks, "Maybe we have the model wrong. Maybe what we need to do is come in and bring dinner and help with laundry and free up a parent to engage in more play with their child."

Patricia Kuhl, a co-director of the Institute for Learning and Brain Science at the University of Washington, has studied "motherese," the brightly inflected talk that mothers, whatever their native language, direct at their babies, and that babies love. (Fathers and other adults, of course, are equally capable of saying "Sooooo big!" in a singsong voice.) Kuhl told me, "Motherese, when you combine that with being one on one with a baby, is dynamite for language development." Parents are paying full attention, speaking in that high, lilting voice for maximum reaction, giving babies a chance to babble and coo back. But, Kuhl added, "Motherese is, by nature, happy talk. If you're stressed or depressed, it can be hard to get into that mode."

Then, too, some parents may not see the point of talking to babies, who can't yet speak, or even of talking much to toddlers,

who do, but sometimes unintelligibly. Andrea Riquetti told me, "I think educated people are more aware of the importance of communication and interaction and language." In some families, she said, "if a baby's really 'good' they get to spend a lot of time alone in their crib."

When I asked myself why I had talked a lot with my babies—and had read aloud favorite picture books to the point that I could recite them from memory—I realized that I hadn't been driven mainly by knowledge of brain development or by pedagogical intent. It was just that talking made the daily labor of mothering more interesting. Long stretches of time with toddlers can be boring, and the unavoidable moments when you admonished and corrected them were, to me, the dullest. It was more fun if you satisfied your own intellectual curiosity along with theirs: reading books about African animals or Chinese New Year celebrations; trying to remember why the sky is blue; honing age-appropriate arguments for eating your carrots.

When a family places a very high value on discipline and respect for parental authority, there is often disapproval of talking back, which can inhibit conversation in general. To some extent, this attitude tracks with class, perhaps because many working-class parents, consciously or not, are preparing children for jobs and lives in which they will not have a lot of power or autonomy. The sociologist Annette Lareau, in her classic 2003 study, "Unequal Childhoods," interviewed the parents of eighty-eight nine- and ten-year-old children, then closely followed twelve of these families in order to compare the child-rearing styles of middle-class parents with those of poor and working-class parents. The middle-class families she observed practiced what she called "concerted cultivation": enrolling kids in various organized activities led by adults, but also engaging even young kids in a lot of back-and-forth conversation with adults. Working-class and poor families favored an "accomplishment of natural growth" approach. Their children's lives were less customized to their preferences or to their parents' notions of how to develop their particular talents; discipline came in the form of directives and, sometimes, threats of physical punishment; talk was less extensive and less geared toward drawing out a child's opinions.

When I asked Lareau, who teaches at the University of Pennsylvania, about the language aspect of her research, she said, "The class differences in the amount of speech inside the families really surprised me." She recalled that a white working-class girl in her study once brought up a weighty spiritual matter with her parents: "We were sitting in their completely comfortable, pleasant living room. The girl was all excited. She said, 'Do you know what a mortal sin is?' The parents said, 'You tell us.' They listened to her answer, said nothing in reply, and went back to watching TV."

In middle-class families, Lareau frequently witnessed the kind of verbal jousting between parents and children that gives kids a certain intellectual confidence. One upper-middle-class African-American family she spent time with—Terry, a trial lawyer; his wife, Christina, a corporate executive; and their nine-year-old son, Alexander—was especially fond of these kinds of debate. In one conversation, Terry playfully challenged his son to defend his list of favorite cars: "Last time, you said the Miata, the Mercedes, and the Bugatti. Which one is it?" Alex replied, "This is America. It's my prerogative to change my mind if I want to."

Lareau did not see the middle-class approach as inherently superior. "The amount of talk in those households is exhausting," she said. "It involves a lot of labor on the parents' part, and sometimes parents are really not enjoying it. Sometimes kids use their verbal acuity to be really mean to each other." She often found the kids in poor and working-class families to be more polite to their elders, less whiny, more competent, and more independent than their middle-class counterparts. Still, Lareau concluded, the kind of talk that prevailed in middle-class households offered better preparation for success in school and in professional careers. It taught children to debate, extemporize, and advocate for themselves, and it helped them develop the vocabulary that tends to reap academic rewards.

James Morgan, the Brown University linguist, told me, "If you're mainly confined to 'Eat your food,' 'Chew every bite,' there are going to be fewer words heard at the dinner table. As opposed to starting a conversation with 'Hey, did you hear the blue whales are making a comeback off California?,' or 'Oh, they just discovered a huge new dinosaur.' And, after all, almost all little kids are interested in subjects like that."

Asking such questions often depends on having an education. But it's not just the topics—it's the mode of inquiry. Anne Fernald said, "As an educated mother, you have more experience with teacher talk, which is necessarily more abstract, because kids don't share common ground when they come to school. Education helps you learn how to make yourself clear to people who are outside your point of view."

Last summer, I returned to Providence to see how the campaign was working for the families I'd met in April. Andrea Riquetti, the program director, and Stephanie Taveras, the caseworker, took me back to the home of Maranda Raposo and Nicholas Mailloux. Skylah was now ten months old, and even more adorable, but the latest data were disappointing: the number of conversational turns and the over-all word count weren't as high as Taveras would have liked to see.

Mailloux told her, "As soon as that vest goes on, she quiets down."

"Are you onto us, Skylah?" Taveras asked, smiling.

Mailloux pointed to an uptick on the chart. "I sang to her at ten o'clock."

"Look at that!" Taveras said.

Raposo's older daughter, Isabella, was sitting on Mailloux's lap, watching the Disney Channel. Skylah crawled over to her and bopped her gleefully with the remote control.

"Stop being so mean!" Raposo told her.

Riquetti stepped in to offer a benign interpretation of Skylah's behavior: "She's saying, 'Pay attention to me.'" Soon afterward, Skylah, grinning, dropped the remote control, and the batteries rolled under the couch. "This is the age where they're trying to see how gravity works," Riquetti explained. The remote was put back together and the TV was turned off. "It's cause and effect. She's trying to make you—"

"*Work,*" Raposo said.

Riquetti laughed sympathetically, then asked her how much time they spent reading with Skylah. Raposo answered firmly: thirty minutes a day.

The TV was back on again. Riquetti had told me that asking families to leave the set off could seem intrusive and high-handed. The staff at Providence Talks had hoped that, once parents saw data showing how much less conversation took place when the TV was on, they would leave it off more often. But the habit wasn't so easy to break.

On this visit, both parents seemed more attuned to Skylah's efforts to express herself, and more confident in their efforts to guide her. It was hard to say if this was because Skylah was older and more vocal or because Providence Talks had taught them to interact with her in richer ways. When I asked them about the change, Mailloux gave the program credit. "It helps us learn more of how she understands things and reacts to them," he said. "And . . ." He paused, flustered. "I don't know how to put it into words. It's in my head, but it won't come out."

As part of the visit, Taveras was going through a developmental checklist for Skylah. One of the questions was "Does she express pleasure and displeasure?"

Both parents nodded vigorously. "If there's something she doesn't want, she screams and throws it," Raposo said. "It's so funny."

"Does she play with sounds, like vocal play?" Taveras asked. They nodded.

"What do you do when she does that?"

"Copy it," Mailloux said.

"Perfect."

Raposo picked up a board book that contained pictures of animals. "Where's the mouse?" She took Skylah's finger and gently placed it on the correct image. "Right there!" she said, in motherese.

Mailloux pointed to a picture of a messy room in the book. "That looks like your brother and sister's room, doesn't it?" he joked.

Riquetti said, "You're pointing and labelling and talking to her constantly. It's great. It's so important that you do what you do. You're making her smart when you talk to her."

Mailloux looked a little sheepish. "It's out of respect," he told Riquetti. "You guys do your part, and we gotta do ours."

In Angel Taveras's proposal to Bloomberg Philanthropies, he promised that Providence Talks would have a research component. Its results would be monitored and studied by a Brown University professor of educational policy, Kenneth Wong. The results of that study won't be published for some time, since the interventions are supposed to last for two years, and Providence Talks is only now expanding from its original pilot study of fifty-eight families. But there had been some analysis of the data from the first families, and Rob Horowitz, a spokesman for Providence Talks, told me, "We are seeing early but promising preliminary results. More specifically, families that started with low word counts are showing increases of about fifty percent in daily word counts and thirty per cent in conversational turns. The improvement is not as marked for families that began the program with above-average word counts."

Of course, the hard numbers are only part of what you'd want to know: to assess how successful an intervention like Providence Talks had been, you'd have to look at whether the kids in the program entered kindergarten readier to learn, with bigger vocabularies than those of children in a control group. Wong and his team are looking at these questions.

The caseworkers at Providence Talks had impressed me with their sunny, gentle directives, but I wasn't sure if they could effect sweeping changes in the children's lives. Many of the core aspects of a parent's conversational style would be hard to alter, from grammar to vocabulary. And it didn't seem easy to revise, say, a parent's relationship to books. Riquetti had told me about a mother in the program who came to her crying because she had never read a book to her toddler. Since the child couldn't read, she hadn't seen the point of turning the pages together, looking at the pictures. Now she would try it, but she wouldn't be drawing on what the linguistic anthropologist Shirley Brice Heath had described to me as the "romantic memory, the nostalgia, of books being read to you when you were a child." Even if you succeeded in getting such parents to read books regularly, the effect of the intervention would be minimal compared with, say, helping somebody like Maranda Raposo go back and finish her education. The last time I spoke with Raposo, she told me that, with two jobs and her kids to care for, she didn't have time to study for her G.E.D. When I tried, on several occasions, to contact the family again, I couldn't reach them—their phones didn't seem to be working—and Stephanie Taveras thought that they might have moved.

Providence Talks had more obvious value if you saw it as the beginning of a series of sustained interventions. Some of the children will likely attend preschool programs that will help them build on any language gains. Providence Talks will also help identify kids who could benefit from speech therapy and

other support. Mayor Taveras told me he hopes that this integrated approach will become a model for the rest of the country.

The word "empowering" is overused, but a clear strength of Providence Talks is that it seemed to instill confidence in parents. Those rising graphs promised that parents could make a demonstrable difference in their children's lives. The parents I met did not seem to feel chided by the data, and they liked the idea of competing with their partners or themselves to log higher word counts.

One night in Providence, I had dinner with Andrea Riquetti and Toby Shepherd, the official who had first told Mayor Taveras about the word-gap problem. "Providence Talks is not a panacea," Shepherd said. "These families face all kinds of challenges—unemployment or whatever it is. My hope is that it's a helpful tool."

Riquetti said, "It's a chance to talk with parents about how they can positively interact with their kids. Sometimes in their busy lives, their stressful lives, they miss out on that." The goal, she said, was to help parents "feel they can make a difference when everything else kind of sucks."

Critical Thinking

1. The article presents ample evidence of social class differences in parents' language to their children. But why do such differences exist? What is it about social class and culture that affects how parents speak to their babies and children?

2. Based on the research and the accounts of actual families in the article, what are two or three recommendations you would give to the mayor of Providence (or other cities) to design the best possible community intervention to help parents speak in ways that could promote their children's language and intellectual development?

3. The purpose of these interventions is to help working-class parents learn to speak more often and at richer levels with their children. Is there a possible class bias in this assumption? What values does this assumption reflect? Does it imply that middle- and upper-class parents and children are "better" in some way than working-class families?

Internet References

American Speech-Language-Hearing Association
http://www.asha.org/public/speech/development/Parent-Stim-Activities.htm

ParentingLiteracy.com
http://parentingliteracy.com/parenting-a-z/45-mental-development/97-infant-language-development

ParentingScience.com
http://www.parentingscience.com/baby-talk.html

PBS.org

http://www.pbs.org/parents/education/reading-language/reading-milestones/baby-language-development-milestones/baby-talking/

Providence Talks Language Log

http://languagelog.ldc.upenn.edu/nll/?p=4514

Zero To Three.org

http://www.zerotothree.org/early-care-education/early-language-literacy/communication-skills.html?referrer=http://www.bing.com/search?q=parents%20and%20infant%20verbal%20language&pc=cosp&ptag=A9BE876E986&form=CONBDF&conlogo=CT3210127

Talbot, Margaret. "The Talking Cure," originally published in *The New Yorker.* Copyright © 2015 by Margaret Talbot, used by permission of The Wylie Agency LLC.

Article

Prepared by: Chris J. Boyatzis, *Bucknell University*
Ellen N. Junn, *California State University, Dominguez Hills*

Good Thinking!
Fostering Children's Reasoning and Problem Solving

JESSICA VICK WHITTAKER

Learning Outcomes

After reading this article, you will be able to:

- Understand how critical thinking and problem solving develop across childhood and appear even in very young children's thinking.

- Describe different research approaches to studying young children's critical thinking and problem solving.

- Evaluate teaching practices for how well they promote problem solving and reasoning in preschool children.

Sandy teaches 3- and 4-year-old children in a Head Start classroom. She often asks children to be investigators and to solve problems or questions that arise. For example, during outside time one day, Sandy notices Keira and Amir playing on the slide. Sandy hears Keira say, "Hey, Amir, you're going really fast down that slide! How come I'm not going so fast?" Sandy comments, "Keira, you made a really interesting observation. You noticed that Amir is going down the slide faster than you. Why do you think that might be?" "Well," Keira says thoughtfully, "maybe because his pants are more slippery than mine." Sandra responds, "That is really good thinking! You've made a guess, a hypothesis. Can you think of some way we could test out whether Amir's clothing is making him go faster?"

Keira decides that she can test whether clothing makes a difference by using clothes from the dramatic play area. She finds two pairs of pants: one pair from a wizard outfit that is very shiny and made of what Keira calls "slippery" material, and the other a pair of jeans from the construction worker outfit. They look rough and less slippery. Sandy times Keira as she goes down the slide to see whether the slippery pants make her go faster. They find that Keira can indeed slide faster with the slippery pants on.

From this experience Keira learns several things. She learns, for example, that the texture of a material—whether it is smooth or rough—affects how quickly or slowly an object (in this case, a person) moves down a ramp. She learns that if she doesn't know the answer to a question she can make a guess and then test that guess to determine if it is correct (she also discovers that another word for *guess is hypothesis*). If something puzzles Keira, she now knows that she can ask her teacher for help and information.

If asked, Sandy could identify particular content areas she supported during this interaction. She could respond that she fostered Keira's knowledge about the physical world and how things work (science), encouraged her thinking about inclined planes (mathematics), and expanded her communication skills by teaching her new words and how to explain her thinking (language). As important as these skills are, however, there was more to this learning experience than just science, mathematics, and language. In this interaction, Sandy encouraged Keira to construct a possible explanation, a hypothesis, and then test that explanation to better understand cause-and-effect relationships. Sandy promoted "good thinking," the ability to logically think and reason about the world.

Critical thinking skills span multiple domains. They include focusing to pursue knowledge, using self-control to define a problem and determine goals, making connections to brainstorm solutions, and communicating to justify actions and share evaluations (Galinsky 2010).

Forty-four percent of the preschool day is spent on learning activities, primarily literacy and writing activities (Early et al. 2005). Too often, such activities focus on skill attainment and not on the critical thinking, reasoning, and problem solving that are foundational to learning and development. Such skills warrant attention, and it is important that teachers foster them *intentionally*. This article summarizes research on the development of preschool children's critical thinking skills and suggests practical, research-based strategies for supporting them.

Reasoning and Problem-Solving Skills

Definitions of critical thinking skills vary, although nearly all include reasoning, making judgments and conclusions, and solving problems (Willingham 2008; Lai 2011). Although it was previously believed that these were higher-order thinking skills that developed only in older children and adults (Piaget 1930), research demonstrates that children reason and problem solve as early as infancy (e.g., Woodward 2009). Between ages 3 and 5, children form complex thoughts and insights, and during the preschool years their cognitive abilities—including logical thinking and reasoning—develop substantially (Amsterlaw & Wellman 2006). These skills enable children to recognize, understand, and analyze a problem and draw on knowledge or experience to seek solutions to the problem (USDHHS 2010). Some researchers conclude that reasoning and problem-solving skills are domain specific (e.g., reasoning skills in science do not necessarily transfer to mathematics); others, however, argue that teachers can foster young children's general critical thinking skills (see Lai 2011 for a review).

Reasoning and problem-solving skills are foundational for lifelong learning. Analyzing arguments, making inferences, reasoning, and implementing decisions to solve problems are important skills across all content areas and thus critical for school success. The ability to efficiently gather, understand, analyze, and interpret information is increasingly necessary to function in school and in the workplace (Schneider 2002). Educators and policy makers, now more than ever, recognize the need to foster critical thinking skills in young children. This is evidenced in the Common Core State Standards, which emphasize the importance of reasoning and problem-solving skills in preparing children for "college, workforce training, and life in a technological society" (NGA Center & CCSSO 2010, 4).

Key Ideas about Children's Thinking

Three key ideas emerge from the research on young children's thinking:

1. Young children are capable of developing reasoning and problem-solving skills.
2. Children's early reasoning and problem-solving skills support their later development and learning.

3. Early childhood educators can foster children's reasoning and problem solving.

Research suggests how these ideas relate to everyday practice.

Young Children can Develop Reasoning and Problem-Solving Skills

Scholars long believed that true logical reasoning does not develop until adolescence (Piaget 1930). However, recent research suggests that logical thinking and reasoning begin in infancy and develop gradually throughout childhood (Gopnik et al. 2004; Hollister Sandberg & McCullough 2010). From infancy on, children pay attention to people's intentions and goals, and infants as young as 6 months old demonstrate rudimentary reasoning skills (Woodward 2009).

Early reasoning skills

Woodward and her colleagues explored how infants make sense of their physical and social worlds and develop reasoning skills (e.g., Hamlin, Hallinan, & Woodward 2008; Cannon & Woodward 2012). The researchers tested whether 7-month-olds would copy an experimenter's actions if they understood the experimenter's intention (Hamlin, Hallinan, & Woodward 2008). Infants were shown two toys, and then they watched as the experimenter reached for one of the toys and grasped it. The experimenter pushed the toys within reach of the infants and said, "Now it's your turn!" Infants reliably touched the same object the experimenter had grasped. This was not the case when the experimenter simply brushed the toy with the back of her hand rather than grasped it (suggesting that the touch was unintentional, not goal directed). In both cases the experimenter's actions drew attention to the object, but infants responded only when they interpreted the experimenter's actions as goal directed. These results, along with others from a series of studies Woodward and colleagues conducted, demonstrate that infants as young as 7 months old can analyze others' intentions and use this information to reason about things in their world (Woodward 2009).

Understanding of causality

Between 9 and 12 months, infants begin to understand that one event or behavior causes another (Woodward 2009), and 2-year-olds are adept at using causality in their thinking (McMullen 2013). Gopnik and colleagues (2000; 2001) designed a series of experiments to explore how young children construct and test explanations for events. They showed children a "magical" light box that glowed when it was activated. Although the experimenter controlled the box, the box appeared to be activated by placing a block on top of it. The experimenter showed

2- to 4-year-old children different blocks, some that turned the box on (the experimenter called these *blickets*) and some that did not (not blickets). The children were asked which block was the blicket. Children as young as 2 were able to draw causal conclusions about which object was the blicket, correctly choosing the block that had "activated" the light. In another experiment with 3- and 4-year-old children, the task was modified so two blocks were placed on the machine and children were asked which block to remove to make the machine stop lighting up. Children correctly predicted which object they should remove from the box to make it stop.

The blicket studies are important because they demonstrate that very young children understand how one thing affects another and that as children get older, their reasoning skills are more sophisticated. Children are increasingly able to generate theories about the causal effects of objects and to test those theories by asking questions and making predictions.

Inductive and deductive reasoning

Understanding cause and effect is an important component of both inductive and deductive reasoning, which develop between the ages of 3 and 6 (Schraw et al. 2011). Young children use *inductive reasoning* when they generalize the conclusions they draw from the consequences of their own behaviors or experiences. *Deductive reasoning* is the process by which individuals use facts or general rules to draw a conclusion, being able to understand the premise "If *P* happens, then *Q* will too" (Schraw et al. 2011).

Three-year-old Maya has a fireplace at home and has learned through experience that fires are hot and should not be touched. When she sees the flame on a gas stove in the kitchen at her early childhood program, she reasons that the stove is also hot and should not be touched. "Hot," she says to her friend. "Don't touch!" Maya uses inductive reasoning in this situation, generalizing and extending her knowledge about fire and heat to a new situation.

Although young children's deductive reasoning becomes more sophisticated with age, their development of this reasoning is complex.

Three-year-old Brandon knows that if it is nighttime, it is time for him to take a bath (if *P*, then *Q*). Through repeated experiences—nighttime (P), then bath (Q)—Brandon connects these two events using deductive reasoning, the basis for making predictions. Inductive and deductive reasoning skills grow

substantially during the preschool years as a result of children's increasing knowledge and varied experiences and interactions with the world around them.

Analogical reasoning

Goswami and Pauen (2005) have spent many years researching how *analogical reasoning*, a form of inductive reasoning that involves making and understanding comparisons, develops in young children (Goswami 1995; Goswami & Pauen 2005). In a series of three experiments, they tested the ability of 3- and 4-year-olds to make comparisons, or relational mappings, based on size (Goswami 1995). An experimenter read *Goldilocks and the Three Bears* to a child, and then said they were going to play a game about choosing cups. The experimenter said, "We are each going to have a set of cups, a daddy-bear-size cup, a mummy-bear-size cup, and a baby-bear-size cup, and you have to choose the same cup from your set that I choose from mine." The experimenter named the cups in her set (e.g., "I'm choosing the Mummy cup") but not in the child's set. To choose the correct cup, the child had to work out the size relationship between the two sets of cups using one-to-one correspondence. Not only did 3- and 4-year-old children choose the correct cup, they could do so even when the positions and colors of their cups were different from those of the experimenter's cups.

However, when experimenters asked 3- and 4-year-olds to make analogies (comparisons) involving concepts rather than physical characteristics (e.g., *A* is hotter than *B* is hotter than *C*, or *A* is louder than *B* is louder than *C*), only the 4-year-olds were successful (Goswami 1995; Goswami & Pauen 2005). Goswami concluded that children as young as 3 can use analogies as a basis for reasoning only if the analogy is based on a familiar structure, such as the characters in *Goldilocks*. This skill develops and becomes more sophisticated over time, doing so rather rapidly during the brief time between ages 3 and 4.

Reasoning with abstract ideas

Research demonstrates that although young children's deductive reasoning becomes more sophisticated with age and that 4-year-olds can reason using abstract ideas, their development of this reasoning is complex. For example, a teacher is working with a small group of children. She says, "We're going to think about some silly stories together. Some of the stories may sound funny, but I want you to think carefully about them. For each story, I'm going to ask you to use your imagination and make a picture in your head. In this story, all cats bark. So the cats that are in your head, are they barking? Are they meowing? Now, Jeremy is a cat. Is Jeremy barking? Is Jeremy meowing? How do you know?" Problems like this actually get more difficult for children as they get older and acquire more real-world experience, because they are more likely to know of counterexamples ("I know a cat that can't 'meow'!"). However, children eventually overcome this and draw the correct conclusions from complex, even absurd, premises (Hollister Sandburg & McCullough 2010).

Children's Early Reasoning and Problem-Solving Skills Support their Later Development and Learning
Cognitive learning

Children's reasoning and problem-solving skills are associated with a range of important literacy learning (e.g., Tzuriel & Flor-Maduel 2010) and mathematics outcomes (Grissmer et al. 2010). In an analysis of six longitudinal data sets, researchers found that general knowledge at kindergarten entry was the strongest predictor of children's science and reading skills and a strong predictor of math skills (Grissmer et al. 2010). General knowledge includes children's thinking and reasoning skills, in particular their ability to form questions about the natural world, gather evidence, and communicate conclusions (USDOE 2002).

Social-emotional learning

Children's reasoning and problem-solving skills are also important components of social and emotional competence. Social problem-solving skills include generating a number of alternative solutions to a conflict and understanding and considering the consequences of one's behaviors (Denham & Almeida 1987; Denham et al. 2012). These skills are linked to children's long-term behavioral outcomes (Youngstrom et al. 2000), school adjustment (Bierman et al. 2008), and academic success (Greenberg, Kusché, & Riggs 2001).

To see how reasoning and problem solving apply to the social-emotional domain, let's return to Sandy's classroom a couple of months after Keira's first experience with creating an experiment to test a hypothesis:

> Keira notices Andy and Eric creating a zoo with animals and blocks in the block area and asks, "Can I play with you?" Andy responds, "No, there's not enough animals for three people!" Upset, Keira says to her teacher, Sandy, "Andy won't play with me because I'm a girl." Sandy bends down to Keira's eye level and says, "Are you sure? I saw you and Andy playing together just this morning on the playground. Can you think of any other reasons Andy might not want to play with you right now?" Keira says, "Well, maybe because there aren't enough animals for me too." Sandy asks Keira where she might find some other animals to add to the zoo. Keira finds several animal puppets in the book area and takes them to the block area.

As this situation demonstrates, children's daily experiences offer opportunities to construct explanations about cause and effect. When teachers provide enriching experiences and materials and support children's interactions with each other, they enable children to develop their reasoning and problem-solving skills. In both scenarios with Keira, Sandy encouraged her to think and to generate hypotheses to solve her questions and problems. In the second scenario, Sandy pointed out that evidence did not support Keira's initial hypothesis and encouraged Keira to problem solve to find a solution. Further, Keira's response provided Sandy insight into Keira's concept of herself in social situations, in particular those involving playing with boys and playing in the block area. From this experience, Keira may begin to learn the importance of producing alternative solutions to interpersonal problems, a key social problem-solving skill (Youngstrom et al. 2000).

Checklist of Teaching Practices and Strategies to Support Preschool Children's Problem Solving and Reasoning

- **Facilitate children's play.** Support children's exploratory play experiences by providing challenging, varied materials that appeal to all of the senses—sight, sound, smell, touch, and taste. Encourage communication during play by extending children's language with their peers and with you. Ask them to talk about their play both during and after their play experiences.
- **Help children understand the difference between guessing and knowing.** A guess, or hypothesis, needs to be tested. Assist children with simple experiments in which they make predictions based on their hypotheses, gather evidence by making observations that they document (e.g., through pictures, dictated stories, graphs), and seek information to help them support or reject their original hypotheses and make conclusions. Do they prove their hypotheses, or do they need to do additional experimenting?
- **Foster categorization skills.** Provide materials that allow children to explore, compare, and sort by a variety of attributes (size, shape, sound, taste, etc.). With younger children, use objects that differ in just one attribute (e.g., balls of different colors). Ask children to describe the similarities and differences and to put the objects into categories. Use and reinforce vocabulary that helps children describe their comparisons (e.g., *short, round, loud, quiet, blue, red,*

smooth, bumpy) and use problem-solving language (e.g., *hypothesis, compare, observe, interpret).* During play, notice how children use materials. Do they sort them? Do they comment on similarities and differences?

- **Encourage children to think before responding.** Help children learn to freeze—to take a moment before answering a question to think about their best or most reasonable response to a problem and how they would test it. With a group of children, discuss different ways they solved a problem to demonstrate that there is often more than one way to do so. Point out that children sometimes think about and approach things differently, but that everyone's ideas should be respected.
- **Model and promote scientific reasoning, using the language of problem solving.** Teachers demonstrate good habits of problem solvers when they encourage children to use their senses to observe the world around them, help children form questions about what they observe and make predictions, share their own thinking and problem-solving processes aloud with children, model and conduct experiments to test predictions, and facilitate discussion about the results of children's experiments.

Early Childhood Educators can Foster Children's Reasoning and Problem Solving

Although children are naturally curious and like to explore, they need adult support to make sense of the world around them. Early childhood educators can foster children's reasoning and problem-solving skills in the context of the developmentally appropriate practices in which they already engage. For example, teachers can provide experiences and materials and engage in interactions that build on children's natural curiosity.

Facilitate children's play

As stated in NAEYC's (2009) position statement on developmentally appropriate practice, "play is an important vehicle for developing self-regulation as well as for promoting language, cognition, and social competence" (14). Play also supports children's reasoning and problem solving (Schulz & Bonawitz 2007; Ramani 2012). Through play, children actively explore their environments, manipulate objects and interact with others, construct knowledge about the way the world works, and learn vital concepts such as cause and effect. Play also provides children opportunities to plan, negotiate, and develop social

perspective-taking skills by considering others' points of view. In the previous scenario, Sandy helped Keira understand why Andy might be hesitant to allow her to join their play and to negotiate a possible solution. Like Sandy, all teachers have an important role in supporting, yet not interfering with, children's play experiences not only by providing materials and opportunities but also by offering suggestions for solving problems.

Scaffold children's understanding of the difference between guessing and knowing

Teachers scaffold children's learning by providing hints, offering a range of answers, and encouraging children to use additional resources. These strategies help children understand the difference between guessing and knowing—and realize that guessing requires testing. The ability to distinguish when there is and is not enough evidence to draw conclusions is fundamental to good problem solving. The more information children have about a particular topic, the better able they are to form reasoned theories and to be confident that those theories are correct. Young children need to learn to find and use evidence to confirm hypotheses, identify trustworthy sources, and reject hypotheses that cannot be supported by evidence.

In addition to these general teaching practices, there are specific strategies that promote preschool children's reasoning and problem-solving skills. These strategies, described in detail in the following three sections, promote "thoughtful decision making" by developing children's planning and reflecting skills (Epstein 2014). (See "Checklist of Teaching Practices and Strategies to Support Preschool Children's Problem Solving and Reasoning" for further explanation of strategies.)

Foster categorization skills

Understanding how to compare and contrast, categorize, and sort enables children to generalize information from one category or situation to another—to reason inductively (Hollister Sandberg & McCullough 2010). Generalizing helps children determine how to approach new objects or events with confidence. For example, 4-year-old Justin was once bitten by a dog and now is afraid of all dogs. During neighborhood walks, his parents have helped him categorize dogs by watching for behavioral signs: a dog with a wagging tail and relaxed demeanor is most likely friendly, but a dog that is barking and has its ears pinned back and teeth bared should be given some space. When they visit the park, Justin generalizes the information he learned about which dogs he can feel safe with based on how he categorizes their behavior.

To promote categorizing, provide children with objects or sets of objects that have contrasting qualities and encourage them to explain how the objects are alike and not alike (Loewenstein & Gentner 2001; Mix 2008; Christie & Gentner

Sample Lesson Plan: Sink or Float

Learning domain: Science Knowledge & Skills, Physical Science (Properties of Materials)

Learning objectives: Children will develop initial understandings of the concept of buoyancy, and will observe and predict whether objects sink or float and classify them accordingly. Children will observe and describe the ways sinking objects can be made to float and floating objects can be made to sink.

Activity setting: Small group

Materials:

- Plastic bottle cap (one per group)
- Cups of water (one per teacher and one per child)
- Objects that float (three to five per group—foam peanuts, plastic bears, etc.)
- Objects that sink (three to five per group—coins, pebbles, solid rubber balls, balls of clay, etc.)
- Pennies (three per group, not plastic)
- Large transparent container of water, such as a glass bowl or an aquarium
- Paper towels

Big idea: The concept of floating and sinking is a tricky one! It is hard to accurately describe the characteristics of an item that will float or sink because the concept of buoyancy may be too advanced for most preschoolers. The goal of the activity is for children to make predictions and then to experiment with, observe, and describe items that float or sink. It is not necessary or appropriate to draw conclusions about buoyancy as a result of this activity.

Planned activity:

1. Say, "Today we are going to learn about objects that float and sink."
2. Demonstrate how to make a floating object sink.
   - Fill a large, transparent container with water. Float an upturned plastic bottle cap in the water. Ask the children to predict what will happen as pennies are placed into the bottle cap "boat." Ask children to describe what happens as each penny is added.
3. Encourage children to experiment with materials that float or sink.
   - Give children cups of water and objects that float or sink.
   - Ask children to describe each object's shape, weight (heavy/light), and material.

- Ask children to predict whether each object will float or sink.
- Ask children to place the objects in the water to see if they float or sink.
- Ask children to group the objects according to whether they float or sink.

Foster categorization skills: The teacher encourages children to sort items according to whether they float or sink.

4. Experiment to make floating items sink and sinking items float.
   - Encourage children to describe the objects that floated.
   - Challenge children to see if they can make those objects sink.
   - As a group, brainstorm ways to make an object float or sink using classroom materials. For example, attach an object that sinks to a foam peanut or shape the clay ball into a boat to make it float; add small blocks or pennies to make a floating object sink.
   - Test the modifications, revising as children offer other ideas.

Model and promote scientific reasoning: Ask children to brainstorm ways to make an object float or sink and then encourage them to test those hypotheses.

5. Say: "Today we learned about things that float and sink." Ask questions such as the following:
   - "Were we able to make something that floated sink? How did we do it? Why do you think that worked?"
   - "Can anyone think of a way we made something that sank be able to float? How?" (e.g., changing a ball of clay or foil into a boat shape can allow it to float)
   - "What was the same or different about the items that were able to float? What was the same or different about the items that were able to sink? Was that *always* the case?"

Scaffold children's understanding of the difference between guessing and knowing: Review with children what was the same or different about the items that floated. Scaffold their understanding of whether there was enough evidence to conclude that the characteristics they identified *always* made the items float or sink.

Adapted, by permission, from M. Kinzie, R.C. Pianta, J. Vick Whittaker, M.J. Foss, E. Pan, Y Lee, A.P. Williford, & J.B. Thomas, *MyTeachingPartner—Math/Science* (Charlottesville: University of Virginia, Curry School of Education, The Center for Advanced Study of Teaching and Learning, 2010), 258–9.

2010). Challenge children to categorize by attributes beyond size and shape; for example, ask them to group objects according to color, width, or function (e.g., "find tools that can cut") (Kemler Nelson, Holt, & Egan 2004). Also, notice how children spontaneously categorize during play; what attributes are they using to categorize in sets they create?

Teachers also foster categorization skills by modeling strategies for children. Children as young as 3 can understand and imitate categorization strategies they see a teacher use without the teacher explicitly stating the strategies (Williamson & Markman 2006; Williamson, Meltzoff, & Markman 2008; Williamson, Jaswal, & Meltzoff 2010). For example, with a group of children watching, Sandy arranges several toys in front of her. Some of the toys make noise and some do not. Without telling children what characteristic she is using to sort, she carefully picks up each toy, shakes it and listens to it, and then puts the toy in the appropriate group. For the last few unsorted toys, she picks them up one at a time and says to a child, "Sort the toys the way I did." To do so, the child must have attended to what Sandy did, understood her goal, and learned her sorting rule as she modeled the strategy (shaking the toys and listening). This requires deeper-level mental processes and more complex problem solving than if Sandy had simply told the children her sorting rule.

Encourage children to brainstorm multiple solutions to problems

Young children tend to act on their first impulse in a situation or on the first thing that comes to mind. But to be good thinkers, they need to develop *inhibitory control,* "the ability to ignore distractions and stay focused, and to resist making one response and instead make another" (Diamond 2006). Inhibitory control helps children regulate their emotions and behavior and problem solve more effectively. Teachers can help children learn this important skill by encouraging them to pause before acting; consider multiple solutions to questions, tasks, or problems; and then choose a solution to try out.

Model and promote scientific reasoning

Scientific reasoning involves constructing hypotheses, gathering evidence, conducting experiments to test hypotheses, and drawing conclusions (Hollister Sandberg & McCullough 2010). It requires children to distinguish between various explanations for events and determine whether there is evidence to support the explanations. Although this is a complex type of reasoning for young children, teachers can support it through modeling and scaffolding. For example, after encouraging children to construct multiple reasonable explanations for events (hypotheses), teachers can help children talk through the steps they will take to test their hypotheses, as Sandy did in

the first scenario with Keira and the slide. As children test their hypotheses, teachers should encourage them to use their senses (i.e., smell, touch, sight, sound, taste) to observe, gather, and record data (e.g., through pictures or charts). Finally, teachers can help children summarize the results of their investigation and construct explanations (i.e., verbalize cause and effect) for their findings. When teachers ask children questions such as "Why do you think that?" or "How do you know?," they help children become aware of their own thinking processes, reflect on the results of their experiments, and evaluate outcomes. (See the sample lesson plan for an example of how teachers support scientific reasoning.)

Conclusion

Children's ability to problem solve and reason is integral to their academic as well as social success. Each day, early childhood teachers support these skills in numerous ways—for example, by facilitating children's play, scaffolding learning, and offering interesting and challenging experiences. With a better understanding of how young children's reasoning and problem-solving skills develop, and a plan for implementing strategies to support them, teachers will become more intentional in helping children become good thinkers.

References

Amsterlaw, J., & H.M. Wellman. 2006. "Theories of Mind in Transition: A Microgenetic Study of the Development of False Belief Understanding." *Journal of Cognition and Development* 7(2): 139–72.

Bierman, K.L., C.E. Domitrovich, R.L. Nix, S.D. Gest, J.A. Welsh, M.T. Greenberg, C. Blair, K.E. Nelson, & S. Gill. 2008. "Promoting Academic and Social-Emotional School Readiness: The Head Start REDI Program." *Child Development* 79(6): 1802–17. www.ncbi.nlm.nih.gov/pubmed/19037591.

Cannon, E.N., & A.L. Woodward. 2012. "Infants Generate Goal-Based Action Predictions." *Developmental Science* 15(2): 292–98. www.ncbi.nlm.nih.gov/pubmed/22356184.

Christie, S., & D. Gentner. 2010. "Where Hypotheses Come From: Learning New Relations by Structural Alignment." *Journal of Cognition and Development* 11(3): 356–73.

Denham, S.A., & C.M. Almeida. 1987. "Children's Social Problem-Solving Skills, Behavioral Adjustment, and Interventions: A Meta-Analysis Evaluating Theory and Practice." *Journal of Applied Developmental Psychology* 8(4): 391–409. http://nichcy.org/research/summaries/abstract29.

Denham, S.A., H.H. Bassett, M. Mincic, S. Kalb, E. Way, T. Wyatt, & Y Segal. 2012. "Social-Emotional Learning Profiles of Preschoolers' Early School Success: A Person-Centered Approach." *Learning and Individual Differences* 22(2): 178–89. www.ncbi.nlm.nih.gov/pmc/articles/PMC3294380.

Good Thinking! Fostering Children's Reasoning and Problem Solving by Jessica Vick Whittaker

33

Diamond, A. 2006. "The Early Development of Executive Functions." Chap. 6 in *Lifespan Cognition: Mechanisms of Change,* eds. E. Bialystok & F.I.M. Craik, 70–95. New York: Oxford University Press.

Early, D., O. Barbarin, D. Bryant, M. Burchinal, F. Chang, R. Clifford, G.M. Crawford, C. Howes, S. Ritchie, M.E. Kraft-Sayre, R.C. Pianta, W.S. Barnett, & W. Weaver. 2005. "Pre-Kindergarten in Eleven States: NCEDL's Multi-State Study of Pre-Kindergarten & Study of State-Wide Early Education Programs (SWEEP): Preliminary Descriptive Report." NCEDL working paper. National Center for Early Development & Learning. http://fpg.unc.edu/sites/fpg.unc.edu/files/resources/reports-and-policy-briefs/NCEDL_PreK-in-Eleven-States_Working-PaperJ005.pdf.

Epstein, A.S. 2014. *The Intentional Teacher: Choosing the Best Strategies for Young Children's Learning.* Rev. ed. Washington, DC: NAEYC.

Galinsky, E. 2010. *Mind in the Making: The Seven Essential Life Skills Every Child Needs.* New York: HarperCollins. Available from NAEYC.

Gopnik, A., C. Glymour, D.M. Sobel, L.E. Schulz, T. Kushnir, & D. Danks. 2004. "A Theory of Causal Learning in Children: Causal Maps and Bayes Nets." *Psychological Review* 111(1): 3–32. www.ncbi.nlm.nih.gov/pubmed/14756583.

Gopnik, A., & D.M. Sobel. 2000. "Detecting Blickets: How Young Children Use Information About Novel Causal Powers in Categorization and Induction." *Child Development* 71(5): 1205–22. www.ncbi.nlm.nih.gov/pubmed/11108092.

Gopnik, A., D.M. Sobel, L.E. Schulz, & C. Glymour. 2001. "Causal Learning Mechanisms in Very Young Children: Two -, Three-, and Four-Year-Olds Infer Causal Relations From Patterns of Variation and Covariation." *Developmental Psychology* 37(5): 620–9. www.ncbi.nlm.nih.gov/pubmed/11552758.

Goswami, U. 1995. "Transitive Relational Mappings in Three- and Four-Year-Olds: The Analogy of Goldilocks and the Three Bears." *Child Development* 66(3): 877–92.

Goswami, U., & S. Pauen. 2005. "The Effects of a 'Family' Analogy on Class Inclusion Reasoning by Young Children." *Swiss Journal of Psychology/Schweizerische Zeitschrift für Psychologie/Revue Suisse de Psychologie* 64(2): 115–24.

Greenberg, M.T., C.A. Kusché, & N. Riggs. 2001. "The P(romoting) A(lternative) TH(inking) S(trategies) Curriculum: Theory and Research on Neurocognitive and Academic Development." *The CEIC Review* 10(6): 22–23, 26. http://files.eric.ed.gov/fulltext/ED455318.pdf.

Grissmer, D., K.J. Grimm, S.M. Aiyer, W.M. Murrah, & J.S. Steele. 2010. "Fine Motor Skills and Early Comprehension of the World: Two New School Readiness Indicators." *Developmental Psychology* 46(5): 1008–117. http://curry.virginia.edu/uploads/resourceLibrary/Research_Brief-Readiness_Indicators.pdf.

Hamlin, J.K., E.V. Hallinan, & A.L. Woodward. 2008. "Do as I Do: 7-Month-Old Infants Selectively Reproduce Others' Goals." *Developmental Science* 11(4): 487–94. www.ncbi.nlm.nih.gov/pubmed/18576956.

Hollister Sandberg, E., & M.B. McCullough. 2010. "The Development of Reasoning Skills." Chap. 10 in *A Clinician's Guide to Normal Cognitive Development in Childhood,* eds. E. Hollister Sandberg & B.L. Spritz, 179–98. New York: Routledge.

Kemler Nelson, D.G., M.B. Holt, & L.C. Egan. 2004. "Two- and Three-Year-Olds Infer and Reason About Design Intentions in Order to Categorize Broken Objects." *Developmental Science* 7(5): 543–9. www.ncbi.nlm.nih.gov/pubmed/15603287.

Lai, E.R. 2011. "Critical Thinking: A Literature Review." Research report. San Antonio, TX: Pearson. http://images.pearsonassessments.com/images/tmrs/criticalthinkingreviewfinal.pdf.

Loewenstein, J., & D. Gentner. 2001. "Spatial Mapping in Preschoolers: Close Comparisons Facilitate Far Mappings." *Journal of Cognition and Development* 2(2): 189–219. http://groups.psych.northwestern.edu/gentner/papers/LoewensteinGentner01.pdf.

McMullen, M.B. 2013. "Understanding Development of Infants and Toddlers." Chap. 3 in *Developmentally Appropriate Practice: Focus on Infants and Toddlers,* eds. C. Copple, S. Bredekamp, D. Koralek, & K. Charner, 23–49. Washington, DC: NAEYC.

Mix, K.S. 2008. "Children's Numerical Equivalence Judgments: Cross-mapping Effects." *Cognitive Development* 23(1): 191–203. www.ncbi.nlm.nih.gov/pmc/articles/PMC2719857.

NAEYC. 2009. "Developmentally Appropriate Practice in Early Childhood Programs Serving Children From Birth Through Age 8." Position statement. Washington, DC: NAEYC. www.naeyc.org/files/naeyc/file/positions/PSDAP.pdf.

NGA Center (National Governors Association Center for Best Practices) & CCSSO (Council of Chief State School Officers). 2010. *Common Core State Standards for English Language Arts and Literacy in History/Social Studies, Science, and Technical Subjects.* Washington, DC: NGA Center & CCSSO. www.corestandards.org/assets/CCSSI_ELA%20Standards.pdf.

Piaget, J. 1930. *The Child's Conception of Physical Causality.* Trans. M. Gabain. New York: Harcourt, Brace.

Ramani, G.B. 2012. "Influence of a Playful, Child-Directed Context on Preschool Children's Peer Cooperation." *Merrill-Palmer Quarterly* 58 (2): 159–90.

Schneider, V. 2002. "Critical Thinking in the Elementary Classroom: Problems and Solutions." Educators Publishing Service. www.eps.schoolspecialty.com/downloads/articles/Critical_Thinking-Schneider.pdf.

Schraw, G., M.T. McCrudden, S. Lehman, & B. Hoffman. 2011. "An Overview of Thinking Skills." In *Assessment of Higher Order Thinking Skills,* eds. G. Schraw & D.H. Robinson, 19–46. Charlotte, NC: Information Age Publishing.

Schulz, L.E., & E.B. Bonawitz. 2007. "Serious Fun: Preschoolers Engage in More Exploratory Play When Evidence Is Confounded." *Developmental Psychology* 43(4): 1045–50. www.ncbi.nlm.nih.gov/pubmed/17605535.

Tzuriel, D., & H. Flor-Maduel. 2010. "Prediction of Early Literacy by Analogical Thinking Modifiability Among Kindergarten Children." *Journal of Cognitive Education and Psychology* 9(3): 207–26.

USDHHS (US Department of Health and Human Services). 2010. "The Head Start Child Development and Early Learning Framework: Promoting Positive Outcomes in Early Childhood Programs Serving Children 3–5 Years Old." www.eclkc.ohs.acf .hhs.gov/hslc/tta-system/teaching/eecd/Assessment/Child%20 Outcomes/HS_Revised_Child_Outcomes_Framework(rev-Sept2011).pdf.

USDOE (US Department of Education). 2002. "Early Childhood Longitudinal Study—Kindergarten Class of 1998–99 (ECLS-K), Psychometric Report for Kindergarten Through First Grade." Working paper. www.nces.ed.gov/pubs2002/200205.pdf.

Williamson, R.A, V.K. Jaswal, & A.N. Meltzoff. 2010. "Learning the Rules: Observation and Imitation of a Sorting Strategy by 36-Month-Old Children." *Developmental Psychology* 46 (1): 57–65. http://ilabs.washington.edu/meltzoff/pdf/10Williamson_Jaswal_Meltzoff_Rule_Imitation.pdf.

Williamson, R.A., & E.M. Markman. 2006. "Precision of Imitation as a Function of Preschoolers' Understanding of the Goal of the Demonstration." *Developmental Psychology* 42 (4): 723–31. http://bingschool.stanford.edu/pub/emarkman/8.%20 Williamson-Precision%20of%20Imitation.pdf.

Williamson, R.A., A.N. Meltzoff, & E.M. Markman. 2008. "Prior Experiences and Perceived Efficacy Influence 3-Year-Olds' Imitation." *Developmental Psychology* 44 (1): 275–85. www. ncbi.nlm.nih.gov/pubmed/18194026.

Willingham, D.T. 2008. "Critical Thinking: Why Is It So Hard to Teach?" *Arts Education Policy Review* 109 (4): 21–32. www. uvm.edu/~facsen/generaleducation/Critical%20Thinking%20 Article%20-%20Willingham.pdf.

Woodward, A.L. 2009. "Infants' Grasp of Others' Intentions." *Current Directions in Psychological Science* 18 (1): 53–7. http://web.mit.edu/course/other/i2course/www/devel/wco.pdf.

Youngstrom, E., J.M. Wolpaw, J.L. Kogos, K. Schoff, B. Ackerman, & C. Izard. 2000. "Interpersonal Problem Solving in Preschool and First Grade: Developmental Change and Ecological Validity." *Journal of Clinical Child Psychology* 29 (4): 589–602. www. ncbi.nlm.nih.gov/pubmed/11126636.

Critical Thinking

1. How might preschools do a better job of balancing knowledge development and skills with the cultivation of critical thinking and problem solving?

2. Read the sample lesson plan and critique it: What aspects might work better than others, and why? If you are volunteering or working at an early childhood setting, try to implement small parts of the plan and then share your experience with your class and teacher.

3. There has recently been increased emphasis on academics in preschool settings. Is this good for children? How do the activities described in this article seem to integrate development of critical thinking and problem solving with children's natural play?

Internet References

AboutKidsHealth.com
http://www.aboutkidshealth.ca/En/HealthAZ/LearningandEducation/LiteracyandNumeracy/Pages/spatial-skills-children.aspx

Everydaylife.globalpost
http://everydaylife.globalpost.com/reasoning-activities-preschoolers-45782.html

Jump Start
http://www.jumpstart.com/parents/activities/critical-thinking-activities

National Association for the Education of Young Children
https://www.naeyc.org/files/yc/file/200309/Planning&Reflection.pdf

ParentingScience.com
http://www.parentingscience.com/teaching-critical-thinking.html

Vick Whittaker, Jessica. "Good Thinking! Fostering Children's Reasoning and Problem Solving," *Young Children*, July 2014. Copyright © 2014 by Jessica Vick Whittaker. Reprinted by permission.

Prepared by: Chris J. Boyatzis, *Bucknell University*
Ellen N. Junn, *California State University, Dominguez Hills*

Article

The Preschool Puzzle

Politicians are promoting the idea of universal preschool. Psychologists are helping to illuminate what works.

KIRSTEN WEIR

Learning Outcomes

After reading this article, you will be able to:

- Evaluate research evidence on the benefits of pre-K education.

- Describe the political and scientific arguments for pre-K education.

- Distinguish between Head Start programs and other kinds of preschool programs.

Preschool has never been more popular. In his 2013 State of the Union address, President Obama introduced a plan to provide universal preschool for all 4-year-olds from low-income and moderate-income families. During his successful run for New York City mayor last year, Bill de Blasio made universal preschool a cornerstone of his campaign.

Even before those proposals, preschool was having a heyday. State funding for pre-K more than doubled, from $2.4 billion in 2002 to $5.4 billion in 2010, according to a 2011 report from The Pew Charitable Trusts. In 2000, some 700,000 children in the United States had access to pre-K, compared with 1.3 million in 2011.

But in many ways, the national conversation about early education is just getting started. The top question about universal pre-K—whether it is worth the cost to taxpayers—remains up for debate. That's partly because studies of early education have found mixed results.

While psychologists have long been involved in studies of preschool, much of the focus lately has focused on economic cost-benefit analyses of early education. But now more than ever, psychologists are crucial in helping to explain how, why, when and for whom some preschool investments work while others fall flat. Though plenty of questions remain, these early education researchers are adding important shades of gray to the conversation.

"Whether universal pre-K is a good idea is a political question," says Daniel Willingham, PhD, a psychologist at the University of Virginia. "The scientific question would be: Is it likely that you could construct pre-K programs that would benefit kids academically and socially? And I think the answer is yes."

The Long View

When politicians discuss the benefits of early education, they often point to two influential long-term studies: The Abecedarian Project and the Perry Preschool Project.

The Abecedarian Project, led by psychologists at the University of North Carolina at Chapel Hill, targeted children from low-income, mostly African-American families in North Carolina. Between 1972 and 1977, investigators randomly assigned four cohorts of infants to an intensive, full-time early education program from birth to age 5, or to a control group that didn't receive services. Then the researchers followed the children into adulthood.

The investigators found that children who participated in the program scored higher on tests of cognitive functioning from toddlerhood through early adulthood. They had greater academic achievement from the primary grades through young adulthood, and were more likely to go to college.

The Perry Preschool Project had a similar design, but quite different findings. It began in 1962, when David P. Weikart, PhD, a psychologist for the Ypsilanti, Mich., school district, and colleagues randomly assigned low-income African-American children to an intensive two-year preschool program or to a control group that didn't attend preschool. The researchers followed those participants into their 40s.

Initially, the results didn't seem promising. Although children who attended the program scored higher on intelligence tests than the control group right after preschool, those intelligence gains disappeared by elementary school. However, other benefits materialized in early adulthood. The program appeared to have positive effects on high-school graduation rates, adult earnings and crime reduction.

The Perry study seemed to support a view first championed by Nobel laureate and economist James Heckman, PhD: The short-term cognitive benefits of preschool may fade, but long-term social benefits may sprout later in life.

Other studies support the idea that some social benefits persist even as cognitive gains disappear, says C. Cybele Raver, PhD, a psychologist and vice provost of academic, faculty and research affairs at New York University. "I think the field is starting to shift, offering confirmation of some of the points that Heckman has raised. Investments in early childhood reap rewards along the line, in ways that we're just now really understanding."

Not everyone agrees. "The Perry study is a thin reed on which to develop an all-encompassing theory of early intervention," says Grover J. "Russ" Whitehurst, PhD, a child psychologist with the Brookings Institution and former director of the Institute of Education Sciences at the U.S. Department of Education. When it comes to the long-term benefits of early education, he adds, "I think the evidence is mixed."

Mixed Messages

Though Abecedarian and Perry have been influential, they have limitations. Both projects were intensive and expensive, making them unlikely models for universal programs in an era of lean education budgets. They also began half a century ago and don't fully reflect our modern knowledge of developmental psychology and education.

Today, researchers are building on what is known about the benefits of early education. In a recent meta-analysis, Greg Duncan, PhD, at the University of California, Irvine, and Katherine Magnuson, PhD, at the University of Wisconsin-Madison, looked across 84 studies of preschool programs conducted from 1965 to 2007. They concluded that early education produced gains in children's language, reading and math skills, equal to about a third of a year of extra learning (*Journal of Economic Perspectives*, 2013).

Another review by Hirokazu Yoshikawa, PhD, of New York University, and colleagues also concluded that large-scale public preschools can have a substantial positive influence on children's learning, according to the 2013 report *Investing in our Future: The Evidence Base on Preschool Education,* from the Society for Research in Child Development. Among other examples, the researchers point to recent studies of urban pre-K

programs in Tulsa, Okla., and Boston, where children gained between half of a year and a full year in language, literacy and math skills. The gains seemed strongest among children from low-income families.

But other studies have raised concerns about the return on investment of such programs. Head Start, the federal program that promotes school readiness for low-income children under age 5, for example, has shown minimal academic benefits. In addition to early education services, the program provides health, nutrition and social services to families in need. A report released in December by the U.S. Department of Health and Human Services concluded that third-graders who attended the program as 3- and 4-year-olds showed no clear benefits in cognitive or social-emotional development compared with students who didn't attend Head Start.

"That doesn't suggest to me that the public investment is a slam-dunk by any means," says Whitehurst, who recently expressed similar reservations in congressional testimony to the House Committee on Education and the Workforce.

Some argue that the benefits of Head Start may show up later in life, as Heckman posited. Indeed, in their 2013 review, Yoshikawa and colleagues reported that some longer-term studies of Head Start have found more distant benefits, including more years of schooling, higher earnings and better health. Also, the program might benefit some kids more than others. Researchers at the University of California, Irvine, recently found that children whose mothers spent less time on "preacademic skills" — such as helping their kids recognize letters and count — got a bigger boost in math and literacy skills from Head Start compared to kids who spent more time on such skills at home (*Child Development,* 2014).

In any case, Willingham notes, Head Start doesn't necessarily belong in the same category with other preschool programs. "It traditionally has more modest goals: to give kids a safe place to go, and socialization with other kids," he says.

Certainly, social learning remains a valuable part of early education, Raver says. Researchers often discuss the cognitive and social-emotional benefits of early education as though they are two competing concepts, but the two domains are actually difficult to disentangle, she says. When a preschool supports cognitive development, children are more likely to feel engaged and build social relationships with their teachers and peers. Investing in their ability to regulate their emotions and attention, on the other hand, is likely to have cognitive and academic payoffs.

Raver and her colleagues demonstrated this with an intervention called the Chicago School Readiness Project in Head Start classrooms. The intervention aimed to improve children's emotional and behavioral regulation—and did—but also increased their vocabularies, letter recognition and math skills (*Child Development,* 2011). "With a moderate amount of investment, we saw a big gain in kids' behavioral and emotional health [and] in their academic achievement," Raver says.

Defining Quality

The mixed findings on early education may be frustrating for policymakers, but in many ways they're not surprising. After all, preschool education programs vary dramatically in all sorts of ways, from class size and length of the school day to teacher education and program curricula.

"Every policymaker says we want a high-quality program," says Robert Pianta, PhD, a psychologist and dean of the Curry School of Education at the University of Virginia. The big question is: What's high quality?

Policymakers tend to focus on structural features such as curriculum or teacher training, Pianta says. "Those become proxies for what kids are experiencing in classrooms. But those structural features don't really capture the features of programs that actually [affect] children's learning and development."

To move beyond those proxies, Pianta and his colleagues developed a system known as the Classroom Assessment Scoring System™ (CLASS) for evaluating teacher-student interactions. This system measures such classroom elements as how well a teacher tunes into behavioral cues (whether a child is losing interest in a classroom activity, say) as well as a teacher's conversational style (whether he or she asks for one-word answers or engages students in more complex dialogue, for example). "You can score those things in a fairly standard way," Pianta says.

He and his colleagues have compared their system with more typical structural indicators of quality, such as student-teacher ratios and teacher qualifications. They found that the quality of student-teacher interactions, as measured by CLASS, was a better predictor of how much kids learned (*Science*, 2013).

"When the qualities of interactions improve, we see very consistent benefits to the development of children's self-regulation skills and language behaviors, and to vocabulary and literacy skills when those are part of the curriculum," Pianta says. "Those benefits can last into kindergarten and, under some circumstances, beyond."

Of course, those high-quality interactions don't come naturally to every educator. "Teachers have to be good detectors of children's cues, and that's a very hard thing to do when you're in a classroom with 20 kids and all that information is flowing at you at once," Pianta says. Luckily, those cue-detection tactics can be taught.

Pianta and his colleagues have designed professional development programs to help teachers learn the skills that translate to better outcomes for kids. In a randomized study, they showed that teachers who took their 14-week course were more likely to use strategies that promoted kids' higher-order thinking. Those are the strategies that can have an effect on children's early literacy, language and cognitive development (*American Educational Research Journal*, 2012).

The CLASS system is just one example of the ways in which emerging science can shape preschool programs that actually benefit students. "There's clear room for continued improvement along the lines of bolstering quality and bolstering educational intensity," Pianta says. "I think the glass is absolutely half full, but there's a ways to go."

There's also progress to be made when it comes to understanding the impact of educational policy. For example, economic models may point to an optimal class size for high-quality pre-K. But psychology researchers can help explain which behaviors and interactions are affected when the student-teacher ratio grows or shrinks. "If you just make changes economically, it won't be a surprise to me if you don't have a big impact," Raver says.

Psychological research is certainly needed, agrees Stephanie Curenton, PhD, a developmental and community psychologist at Rutgers University and a fellow of the National Institute for Early Education Research. Yet this debate isn't just about dollar signs and student ID numbers. Before she became a psychologist, Curenton was a preschool teacher. And before that, she was a little girl enrolled in two years of Head Start.

"We look at these programs under the microscope and focus on averages. That's meaningful, and as a scientist I view the world that way a lot," she says. "But we also have to understand that there are real, living people affected by these programs. Sometimes that gets lost in the mix."

Further Reading

Society for Research in Child Development and Foundation for Child Development. (2013, October). Yoshikawa, H., Weiland, C., Brooks-Gunn, J., Burchinal, M.R., Espinosa, L., Gormley, W.,. . .Zaslow, M.J. *Investing in our future: The evidence base on preschool education.*

The Pew Center of the States. (2011, September). *Transforming public education: Pathway to a pre-K-12 future.* Retrieved from http://www.pewstates.org/uploadedFiles/PCS_Assets/2011/Pew_PreK_Transforming_Public_Education.pdf

U.S. Department of Health and Human Services. (2012, October). *Third grade follow-up to the Head Start Impact Study: Final report* (OPRE Report 2012-45). Retrieved from http://www.acf.hhs.gov/sites/default/files/opre/head_start_report.pdf.

Critical Thinking

1. Based on the article, how is universal pre-K education both a "political" and "scientific" question?

2. Using evidence from this article, what would you say to persuade someone who thought that pre-K education was a waste of time and money?

3. How can we judge if a preschool is "high quality"? What criteria, based on the article, may matter more than others?

Internet References

Education.com
http://www.education.com/reference/article/pre-k-what-exactly/

Foundation for Child Development
http://fcd-us.org/whats-new/long-term-effects-oklahomas-universal-prek-program

National Association for the Education of Young Children
https://www.naeyc.org/files/tyc/file/PreK-WhatExactlyIsIt.pdf

National Institute for Early Education Research
http://www.nieer.org/sites/nieer/files/Getting%20the%20Facts%20Right%20on%20Pre-K%20Fast%20Facts%20Summary.pdf

New York Times
http://www.nytimes.com/interactive/2013/02/13/education/State-Financed-Preschool-Access-In-the-US.html?_r=0

Washington Post.com
http://www.washingtonpost.com/blogs/wonkblog/wp/2015/02/02/why-conservatives-should-get-behind-obamas-push-for-universal-pre-k/

Weir, Kirsten. "The Preschool Puzzle," *Monitor on Psychology*, May 2014. Copyright © 2014 by American Psychological Association. Reprinted by permission.

Article

Prepared by: Chris J. Boyatzis, *Bucknell University*
Ellen N. Junn, *California State University, Dominguez Hills*

How Children Learn To Read

MARIA KONNIKOVA

Learning Outcomes

After reading this article, you will be able to:

- Explain how learning to read is crucially related to the development of white matter in the left temporoparietal region of the brain.

- Describe how reading development is an example of the interaction of both nature and nurture.

- Understand how there are different types of readers, including "stealth dyslexics."

Why is it easy for some people to learn to read, and difficult for others? It's a tough question with a long history. We know that it's not just about raw intelligence, nor is it wholly about repetition and dogged persistence. We also know that there are some conditions that, effort aside, can hold a child back. Socioeconomic status, for instance, has been reliably linked to reading achievement. And, regardless of background, children with lower general verbal ability and those who have difficulty with phonetic processing seem to struggle. But what underlies those differences? How do we learn to translate abstract symbols into meaningful sounds in the first place, and why are some children better at it than others?

This is the mystery that has animated the work of Fumiko Hoeft, a cognitive neuroscientist and psychiatrist currently at the University of California, San Francisco. "You know where the color of your eyes came from, your facial features, your hair, your height. Maybe even your personality—I'm stubborn like mom, sloppy like dad," Hoeft says. "But what we're trying to do is find out, by looking at brain networks and accounting for everything in the environment, is where your reading ability originates."

This fall, Hoeft and her colleagues at U.C.S.F. published the results of a three-year longitudinal study looking at the basic neuroscience of reading development. Between 2008 and 2009, Hoeft recruited a group of five- and six-year-old children. Some came from backgrounds predictive of reading difficulty. Others seemed to have no obvious risk factors. In addition to undergoing a brain scan, the children were tested for general cognitive ability, as well as a host of other factors, including how well they could follow instructions and how coherently they could express themselves. Each parent was also surveyed, and each child's home life, carefully analyzed: How did the child spend her time at home? Was she read to frequently? How much time did she spend watching television? Three years later, each child's brain was scanned again, and the children were tested on a number of reading and phonological tests.

When Hoeft took into account all of the explanatory factors that had been linked to reading difficulty in the past—genetic risk, environmental factors, pre-literate language ability, and over-all cognitive capacity—she found that only one thing consistently predicted how well a child would learn to read. That was the growth of white matter in one specific area of the brain, the left temporoparietal region. The amount of white matter that a child arrived with in kindergarten didn't make a difference. But the change in volume between kindergarten and third grade did.

What is white matter? You can think of it as a sort of neural highway in the brain—roads that connect the various parts of the cortex and the brain surface. Information, in the form of electrical signals, runs across the white matter, allowing for communication between the different parts of the brain: you see something, you give it meaning, you interpret that meaning. Hoeft saw an increase in the volume of pathways in the left temporoparietal, which is central in phonological processing, speech, and reading. Or, as Hoeft puts it, "it's where you do the tedious work of linking sounds and letters and how they correspond." Her results suggested that, if the increase in white matter doesn't occur at the critical time, children will have a hard time figuring out how to look at letters and then turn them into words that have meaning.

Hoeft's discovery builds on previous research that she conducted on dyslexia. In 2011, she found that, while no behavioral measure could predict which dyslexic children would improve their reading skills, greater neural activation in the right prefrontal cortex along with the distribution of white matter in the brain could, with seventy-two-per-cent accuracy, offer such a prediction. If she looked at over-all brain activation while the children performed an initial phonological task, the predictive power rose to more than ninety per cent. Over-all intelligence and I.Q. didn't matter; what was key was a very specific organizational pattern within your brain.

The group's new findings go a step further. They don't just show that white matter is important. They point to a crucial stage where the development of white matter is central to reading ability. And the white-matter development, Hoeft believes, is surely a function of both nature and nurture. "Our findings could be interpreted as meaning that there's still genetic influence," Hoeft says, noting that preexisting structural differences in the brain may indeed influence future white-matter development. But, she adds, "it's also likely that the dorsal white-matter development is representing the environment the kids are exposed to between kindergarten and third grade. The home environment, the school environment, the kind of reading instruction they're getting."

She likens it to the Dr. Seuss story of Horton and the egg. Horton sits on an egg that isn't his own, and, because of his dedication, the creature that eventually hatches looks half like his mother, and half like the elephant. In this particular case, Hoeft and her colleagues can't yet separate cause and effect: Were certain children predisposed to develop strong white-matter pathways that then helped them to learn to read, or was superior instruction and a rich environment prompting the building of those pathways?

Hoeft's goal isn't just to understand the neuroscience of how children read. Neuroscience is the tool to figure out a much broader question: How should early reading education work? In another study, which has just been submitted for publication, Hoeft and her colleagues try to turn their understanding of reading ability toward helping to identify the most effective teaching methods that could help develop it. Typically, children follow a very specific path toward reading. First, there is the fundamental phonological processing—the awareness of sounds themselves. This awareness builds into phonics, or the ability to decode a sound to match a letter. And those, finally, merge into full, automatic reading comprehension.

Some children, however, don't follow that path. In some cases, children who have problems with basic phonological awareness nonetheless master phonic decoding. There are also children who have problems with the decoding, yet their reading comprehension is high. "We want to use these surprising cases to understand what allows people to be resilient," Hoeft says.

She's studied, in particular, a concept known as stealth dyslexia: people who have all of the makings of dyslexia or other reading problems, but end up overcoming them and becoming superior readers. Hoeft may even be one of them: she suspects that she suffers from undiagnosed dyslexia. As a child in Japan, she had a difficulty with phonological processing very similar to that experienced by dyslexics—but, at the time, the diagnosis did not exist there. She struggled through without realizing until graduate school that a possible explanation for her problem existed in scientific literature. Studying stealth dyslexics, Hoeft posits, could be key to figuring out how to improve reading education more broadly. These stealth dyslexics have reading problems but are able to develop high comprehension all the same.

Hoeft's group, she told me, has found that stealth dyslexics display a unique dorsolateral prefrontal cortex. That's the part of the brain that is responsible, among other things, for executive function and self-control. In stealth dyslexics, it seems to be particularly well-developed. That may be partly genetic, but, Hoeft says, it may also point to a particular educational experience: "If it's superior executive function that is helping some kids develop despite genetic predisposition to the contrary, that is really good news, because that is something we do well—we know how to train executive function." There are multiple programs in place and multiple teaching methods, tested over the years, that help children develop self-regulation ability: for example, the KIPP schools that are using Walter Mischel's self-control research to teach children to delay gratification.

What Hoeft's studies demonstrate is that no matter a kid's starting point in kindergarten, reading development also depends to a great extent on the next three years—and that those three years can be used to teach something that Hoeft now knows to be tied to overcoming reading difficulty. "That might mean that, in the earliest stages, we need to pay attention to that executive function," she says. "We need to start not just giving flashcards, letters, and sounds the way we now do, but, especially if we know someone might be a problem reader, look at these other skills, at cognitive control and self-regulation." Being a better reader, in other words, may ultimately involve instruction around things other than reading.

Critical Thinking

1. How does this article provide evidence for the roles of nature and nurture in reading development? If growth in white matter in the brain is so crucial, why does environment still matter?

2. One of the fundamental questions in child psychology is whether there are "critical periods" in development. How does this article address that question? Is there a critical period for learning to read?

3. How does this article's information relate to information in other articles (e.g., "The Talking Cure")? How would you synthesize the information to create optimal reading programs and interventions for families and children?

Internet References

National Education Association, Reading & Read Across America
http://www.nea.org/home/19027.htm
http://www.nea.org/grants/886.htm

GetReadyToRead.org
http://www.getreadytoread.org/early-learning-childhood-basics/early-childhood/understanding-learning-and-thinking-in-preschoolers

National Reading Panel, National Institute of Child Health and Human Development
http://www.nichd.nih.gov/research/supported/Pages/nrp.aspx

National Reading Association
https://sites.google.com/site/nationalreadingassociation/

New Yorker
http://www.newyorker.com/science/maria-konnikova/how-children-learn-read

Konnikova, Maria. "How Children Learn to Read," *The New Yorker,* February 2015. Copyright © 2015 by Conde Nast Publications, Inc. Reprinted by permission.

Article

Prepared by: Chris J. Boyatzis, *Bucknell University*
Ellen N. Junn, *California State University, Dominguez Hills*

Is Your First Grader College Ready?

Laura Pappano

Learning Outcomes

After reading this article, you will be able to:

- Understand and describe recent efforts in elementary schools to prepare children for and to help them think about college.

- Describe and evaluate evidence that suggests such early preparation is helpful to children.

- Understand radically different perspectives on the appropriateness of exposing young children to thinking about college so early in life.

W hat is college? To Madison Comer, a confident 6-year-old, it is a very big place. "It's tall," she explained, outlining the head of Tuffy, the North Carolina State mascot, with a gray crayon. "It's like high school but it's higher."

Elizabeth Mangan, who plans to be a veterinarian because she loves her puppy, pointed out that she, too, would attend North Carolina State. "Me and Madison are going to the same college," she said.

And what is college? "It's someplace where you go to get your career."

Billy Nalls, meanwhile, was drawing curving horns and jagged teeth on Rameses the Ram on a paper pennant representing the University of North Carolina. "I'm drawing him as angry," he said. In college, Billy wants to learn to make a Transformer ("It's like a robot that comes from Cybertron"). And what happens at college? "You get smarter and smarter every day."

Matriculation is years away for the Class of 2030, but the first graders in Kelli Rigo's class at Johnsonville Elementary School in rural Harnett County, N.C., already have campuses picked out. Three have chosen West Point and one Harvard. In a writing assignment, the children will share their choice and what career they would pursue afterward. The future Harvard applicant wants to be a doctor. She can't wait to get to Cambridge because "my mom never lets me go anywhere." The mock applications they've filled out are stapled to the bulletin board.

"The age-old question is: 'What do you want to be when you grow up?' You always ask kids that," Ms. Rigo said. "We need to ask them, 'How will you get there?' Even if I am teaching preschool, the word 'college' has to be in there."

Forget meandering—the messaging now is about goals and focus. "It's sort of like, if you want your kids to be in the Olympics or to have the chance to be in the Olympics," said Wendy Segal, a tutor and college planner in Westchester County, N.Y., "you don't wait until your kid is 17 and say, 'My kid really loves ice skating.' You start when they are 5 or 6."

Credit President Obama and the Common Core Standards for putting the "college and career ready" mantra on the lips of K-12 educators across the country. Or blame a competitive culture that has turned wide-open years of childhood into a checklist of readiness skills. Whatever the reason, the fact remains that college prep has hit the playground set.

One has only to search Pinterest to see the trend. Dozens of elementary schoolteachers share cute activities that make the road to college as clear as ABC. One cut-and-paste work sheet has students using circles and squares to sequence the steps. There are four: mail your application, get accepted, graduate high school and "move in, go to class and study hard!" "College weeks" have become as much a staple of elementary school calendars as the winter band concert. And campus tours are now popular field trips.

Charter schools have long put the college message front and center. For at least a decade they have been taking low-income students to visit campuses, to provide incentive for hard work and offer concrete knowledge about the mysterious world of their wealthier peers. Now everyone wants to check out higher education options.

A four-year-old program in Santa Cruz County, Calif., takes 3,000 fourth graders on a single day in May to a local campus for tours, information sessions and a sampling of classes, including sociology and women's studies. Rice University, which has a teacher resource page ("Picture your students at Rice"), last year led 91 elementary and middle school tours and sent out 357 classroom packets with activities, literature and iron-on transfers for making T-shirts, nearly triple the number two years earlier.

The University of Maryland has been deluged with requests. After leading 8,000 children on guided tours in 2012–13, the program director for visitor services, Betty Spengler, said they had to limit slots. "We had so many requests, we were doing tours five days a week," she said. "It became impossible to sustain." She hopes a new teacher resource site unveiled last month will help those who can't get tour dates.

What do sixth graders do on a tour?

When a group of 65 children from Magnolia Elementary School, tucked into a neighborhood of modest homes on small, tidy lawns in Prince George's County, Md., spilled off school buses at the university's welcome center, the first stop was the model dorm room, behind glass.

If there's one thing about college that children struggle to grasp, it's sleeping at school—with strangers. The students, many clad in Magnolia Elementary hoodies, jostled to get a glimpse of the room with the perfectly made beds. They wanted to know: Can you pick the person you live with? Can you stay up as late as you want? "Your mom is not there to wake you up so you got to wake up by yourself so you can go to your classes," explained Belal Mobaidin, a cherubic 11-year-old who wants to be a brain surgeon.

The goal is to get students to picture themselves on campus. But not literally, warned Laura Browning, their teacher. "No posting! No selfies! No texting!" Ms. Browning sought order as they strolled by stately white-columned brick buildings. "Ladies and gentlemen, there are sidewalks. Please use them!"

For exuberant and chatty preteens (who did snap selfies), the tour hit what mattered: food, fun facts (the seventh floor of the library is so quiet that if you open chips everyone can hear) and the physically impressive. They gawked at the 54,000-seat football stadium and discovered that there is a Chick-fil-A in the basement of the student center. Enija Wright was surprised, but excited, to learn that candy is sold on campus.

The tour guides—Javier Scott, a peppy junior from Columbia, Md., and Carley Pouland, a senior from Fort Worth—briefly struck a serious note, urging students to chase their dreams. "College can help you do that," Mr. Scott said. "When you work hard, more opportunities will open up to you."

By lunchtime, having rubbed the mascot Testudo's nose for good luck (twice!) and piled their cafeteria trays with chicken fingers, fries and pizza slices, students were sold. David Oladimejij, 11, plans to attend. "At first I wanted to go to Harvard," he said. "In the news I heard that Harvard is the best college, but I think Maryland is the best."

It's a soft sell—Rice's classroom PowerPoint says that attending "*any*" college," not just Rice, is what matters. But Mikayla Donoho, a fifth grader who toured the campus with her class at Pine Forest Elementary School in Humble, Tex., is all in. What struck her? "We got to eat our lunch in this beautiful garden."

Reaching out to children years ahead of serious college consideration can seed brand awareness for the university. Or amp up an already anxiety-laced process.

"Children need to make mistakes and find themselves in dead ends and cul-de-sacs," said Joan Almon, a founder of the Alliance for Childhood who worries that the early focus cuts short self-exploration. "I'm concerned that we are putting so much pressure around college that by the time they get there they are already burned out."

Some agree. A number of colleges refuse to host tours for children in grades below high school, expressing sentiments similar to those on the Boston College website, which notes a "desire not to contribute to the college admissions frenzy."

In some quarters, that frenzy is well underway by middle school. The perception that it's harder to get into top colleges has parents starting earlier.

"It's created a little bit of a panic," said Megan Dorsey, a private counselor and founder of College Prep in Sugar Land, Tex. She points to a state law requiring public campuses to admit the top percentages of each high school class, making admission to the University of Texas, Austin, and Texas A&M particularly tough. "I see a lot of parents with junior high-age students who are really concerned," she said. "They want to know: Before high school, what should they be doing."

The impulse to line up achievements and to consider how a child's record will play on a college application is contagious, said Mary Meyer, whose sons are in fifth and eighth grades in the Lamar Consolidated Independent School District near Houston. "It is the game we are playing these days. It is too much, but I don't see it changing, so you have to join in or you will be left behind."

When her boys join the science club, volunteer at the food bank, even serve on the elementary school safety patrol, Ms. Meyer said, she can't help but view it as a steppingstone to college. "You have to have this résumé built or your kids will not even be looked at."

Barbara Poole is a seventh-grade English teacher at Rachel Carson Middle School in Fairfax County, Va., which is one of the nation's wealthiest suburbs and home to the perennially top-ranked Thomas Jefferson High School for Science and

Technology. She estimates that 60 percent of her students already know where they want to go to college.

Ms. Poole was among the first to pilot a middle-school version of Naviance, a college-prep subscription service that high schools offer their students. It's known for its scattergrams, which reveal the acceptance history of the school's students to specific colleges by test score and grade-point average. Ms. Poole said the software's résumé-building feature—it allows students to input extracurricular activities, awards, volunteer work and more—has made her students "more aware" of building that extracurricular record for college.

"We talk about endurance," she said. "If you are in band one year, but you don't do it eighth-grade year, it shows." Even as Ms. Poole is "reminding them that they are just kids," she also tells them, "It is competitive out there and what can you do and what are you doing other than going home and playing video games?" She nudges them. "You are 12 years old. Do you give back?"

The early planning trend shows in the Naviance numbers. Five years ago, the company began selling software that lets students as young as fifth grade explore career interests, majors and the colleges that offer them; 1,700 middle schools have signed on, representing nearly 1.1 million students. "We've seen an amazing rate of adoption," said Stephen M. Smith, a co-founder, adding that it is part of a larger shift toward making students mindful sooner about consequences of course selections.

"When they get to middle school, it is the first time they are asked which math class they want to take, which science, whether they want to take a foreign language," he said. Choices "can really change their trajectory as a student."

That trajectory, like an invisible dotted line leading to coveted colleges—or not—has applied fresh pressure on preteens to make smarter choices.

For example, the math you take in middle school determines if you reach calculus by 12th grade—a common expectation of elite colleges. That means finishing Algebra I in eighth grade. Even a foreign language pick in sixth grade has a college prep purpose, said Ms. Segal, the college planner, who warns that choosing French "because it sounds pretty" could have consequences later. "You have many, many more options if you take Spanish," because classes are taught often while French may be offered only once. "And what if it's at the same time as A.P. bio?"

This may sound overwrought, but Joan Nachman, the guidance counselor at Magnolia Elementary School, points out that colleges want Advanced Placement courses on transcripts but high school students can't just sign up. They must prepare with honors courses in middle school, which means strong work in elementary school. "You have to set the groundwork now," she said.

Magnolia draws from a middle-class African-American and Hispanic community where only about a quarter of adults have a college degree. Parents may not realize how choices now shape opportunities later, which is why last year the school added "Kids2College," a national college-awareness program, to the curriculum.

"We want to make certain children understand that they have options" and "the criteria for those options," Phyllis L. Gillens, the principal, said.

Research shows that the college advantage is growing only for students from educated, high-income families. Since 1970, the rate at which affluent students earn bachelor's degrees has nearly doubled (from 40 percent to 77 percent) while it has barely moved (from 6 percent to 9 percent) for low-income students, according to a report out this month from the Pell Institute for the Study of Opportunity in Higher Education and the Alliance for Higher Education and Democracy.

"The advantage has been widening based on family income," said Laura W. Perna, executive director of the alliance and a professor at the University of Pennsylvania. Families in upper-income brackets have lots of resources, she said, "and they are mobilizing those resources to maximize advantage."

Ms. Poole's seventh graders, for example, have parsed program options at the five high schools they can attend from their middle school. "They already know how they will achieve in high school to get to college," she said. "It's crazy. Not crazy. It's what they are doing."

When Ms. Rigo graduated from Morningside College in Sioux City, Iowa, in 2009, she became—and remains—the only person in her family, which includes seven siblings, to earn a college degree. It didn't come easily. It took eight years at three institutions in two states. "I was lost," said Ms. Rigo, who dropped out first semester, aghast to discover textbooks cost $600. "I didn't have anybody to talk to about that."

A well-organized mother of three who likes colorful charts and careful work (students must draw their college pennants in pencil before using crayon), Ms. Rigo has a calm teacher voice that grows sturdy when discussing the college project she has created for her first graders at Johnsonville. She wants students to know what she did not: the effort, cost and planning required to earn a degree. "They have to understand there are lots of steps, that you can't all of a sudden be a teacher."

In Harnett County, where prefab homes sit amid tall pines and undulating fields, just 18.5 percent of adults have a college degree. The best jobs are connected to the military, at Fort Bragg. Most piece together a living at fast-food restaurants—Bojangles', Wendy's, Taco Bell, KFC—and retail stores like Walmart. There are factory jobs at 3M and Coty Inc., the cosmetics company.

In Room 102, where Ms. Rigo retreated after guiding her first graders onto their buses, the phone rang. It was a parent upset at being expected to provide a binder for homework. The family couldn't afford it.

The college project, this year adopted by all five first-grade classes, has pleased some parents and puzzled others. One, Lora Collins, a Kansas State graduate, thought the college talk was useful. For many local families, she said, "it is just not in their mind, in their thought process, to think about going to college." A few have not been so receptive, complaining that students should be focusing on reading, writing, and math.

Another first-grade teacher, Jennifer Agnew, said she "had a couple of parents who were like, 'Their thoughts and feelings will change, why should we be talking about this now?'"

Young children simply cannot understand what college is, according to Marcy Guddemi, executive director of the Gesell Institute of Child Development. "You may as well be talking about Mars. It's totally meaningless."

As for older children, they can grasp college but developmentally struggle with making choices, she said, so early planning may not be fruitful—or fair.

"We are robbing children of childhood by talking about college and career so early in life," Dr. Guddemi said. "Kids being pressured to think college, to pick a college, that everything you do is for college, you miss the here and now." Also, she observed: "Not every child will go to college. That is just a fact." Equating degree-earning with success may set up some to feel like failures.

How you view the early start on college planning depends on where you sit.

Ms. Rigo became convinced of its importance after working as a teacher's assistant in the Chapel Hill public schools, where parents were professors, doctors, and lawyers. Census data show three-quarters of adults there have college degrees.

At Johnsonville Elementary, most of her students would be the first in their families to attend college.

"When I came here," she said, "I realized they were not getting the same message."

Critical Thinking

1. Are these attempts to get young children to think about college too extreme? What do you think about the remark by a critic in the article who said "we are robbing children of childhood by talking about college and career so early in life"? Are there potential advantages to helping kids see college in their future, especially for those from socioeconomic groups that would not typically see college as a realistic goal?

2. What other steps could be taken in addition to these efforts in schools to increase young children's aspirations about their future education and careers?

3. What are some reasons why families would support, or oppose, schools exposing their children so early to expectations about college?

Internet References

College Board
   http://media.collegeboard.com/digitalServices/pdf/advocacy/nosca/11b-4383_ES_Counselor_Guide_WEB_120213.pdf

Federal Student Aid, US Department of Education
   https://studentaid.ed.gov/sa/prepare-for-college/checklists/elementary-school

Forbes
   http://www.forbes.com/sites/jasonma/2012/04/01/why-to-start-preparing-for-college-in-sixth-grade/

New York Times
   http://www.nytimes.com/2015/02/08/education/edlife/is-your-first-grader-college-ready.html?_r=0

Pappano, Laura. "Is Your First Grader College Ready?." *The New York Times*, February 2015. Copyright © 2015 by New York Times. Reprinted by permission.

Article   Prepared by: Ellen Junn, *California State University, Dominguez Hills*

9 Ways to Support Your Child's Creativity

Margarita Tartakovsky

Learning Outcomes

After reading this article, you will be able to:

- Analyze why it is sometimes good for children to be "bored" and become acquainted with the power that comes in giving children "free time."

- Understand how subtle supports from parents can assist in fostering children's creativity.

- Identify multiple benefits in enhanced cognitive and social-emotional development by increasing children's opportunities for creativity.

- Learn simple methods for parents to use in supporting their children's creativity.

Kids are natural innovators with powerful imaginations. And creativity offers a bounty of intellectual, emotional, and even health benefits.

One study found that kids' imaginations helped them cope better with pain. Creativity also helps kids be more confident, develop social skills, and learn better. Below, three experts share how parents can encourage their kids' creativity.

1. **Designate a space for creating.** Carving out a space where your child can be creative is important, said Pam Allyn, executive director of Lit World and Lit Life and the author of many books, including *Your Child's Writing Life: How to Inspire Confidence, Creativity, and Skill at Every Age.*

   But this doesn't mean having a fancy playroom. It could be a tiny corner with a sack of LEGOs or a box of your old clothes for playing dress-up, she said. Allyn

has seen creativity flourish in the most cramped spaces, including the slums of Kenya. The key is for your child to feel like they have power over their space, she said.

2. **Keep it simple.** Just like you don't need to create an elaborate play area, you don't need the latest and greatest toys either. Child educational psychologist Charlotte Reznick, PhD, suggested keeping simple games and activities. For instance, she plays LEGOs with her child clients. But instead of following instructions, the kids let the wheels of their imagination spin and build what they want.

3. **Allow for "free time."** It's also important to give your child unstructured time, Allyn said. Spend a few hours at home without activities scheduled, so your child can just putter around and play, she said.

4. **Help your kids activate their senses.** Expose your kids to the world so they can use all of their senses, according to Reznick, who's also an associate clinical professor of psychology at UCLA and author of *The Power of Your Child's Imagination: How to Transform Stress and Anxiety into Joy and Success.*

   Again, this doesn't mean costly or complicated trips. Take them to the library, museum, and outdoors, she said. Ask them to imagine what traveling to faraway places, such as the African safari, might be like, Reznick said. What animals would they encounter? What would the safari look like? What would it smell like? What noises would the animals make?

5. **Discuss creativity.** Ask your kids when they come up with their best ideas or have their most creative moments, Allyn said. If it's in the car while getting to soccer practice, honor that by keeping a notebook, iPad, or even a tape recorder handy, she said.

6. **Cultivate creative critical thinking.** As your kids get older, ask them how they approach certain problems and how they might do things differently, Reznick said. Have your kids brainstorm their ideas on paper or use mind-mapping, she said.

7. **Avoid managing.** "Children have an amazing innate ability to be creative when they play freely on their own, and unfortunately, the act of overparenting dampens or even wipes out that innate ability," according to Mike Lanza of Playborhood.com and author of the upcoming book *Playborhood: Turn Your Neighborhood into a Place for Play.* So it's important to figure out how to facilitate your child's creativity without managing it, he said.

Lanza and his wife don't hover over their three boys as they play, and they also don't enroll them in many activities. Recently, Lanza's oldest son invented an intricate game of marbles with its own complex rules. (As Lanza said, he doesn't really understand it.) He's even adjusted the rules so that his younger brother can win once in a while and the game continues.

Kids learn a lot by playing on their own. Lanza cited Jean Piaget's *The Moral Judgment of the Child,* where he discusses "how children develop moral sensibilities and reasoning through playing marbles on their own."

He also mentioned Alison Gopnik's *The Philosophical Baby,* which describes how babies' brains work. Gopnik asserts that babies are born experimental scientists that take in scrolls of information by trying things on their own and tweaking as they go. Being more hands-off helps kids figure out how to problem-solve and create in their own unique ways.

8. **Help kids pursue their passions.** Pay attention to your child's interests and make these materials and activities available to them. Lanza's oldest son is especially interested in geology, so Lanza buys him books on the topic along with rock samples.

9. **Take the time for your own creativity.** Since kids learn from watching their parents, be creative, too, Reznick said. Join your child when they're drawing or building or coloring. One little girl wanted her parents to help her build an art jungle in the living room, she said. At first mom was hesitant. But this provided a great opportunity for the family to bond, and everyone had a fun time.

Critical Thinking

1. The article mentions that a key to creativity is allowing children to feel like they have power over their space. How do you think empowerment leads to creativity?

2. The ninth suggestion is that parent's take the time to foster their own creative sides. Should parents use the advice from this article to practice what they are preaching?

Create Central

www.mhhe.com/createcentral

Internet References

Brainy-Child.com
    http://www.brainy-child.com/article/child-creativity.shtml
Center for Childhood Creativity.org
    http://www.centerforchildhoodcreativity.org/research/
Psychology Today.com
    http://www.psychologytoday.com/blog/freedom-learn/201209/children-s-freedom-has-declined-so-has-their-creativity

---

MARGARITA TARTAKOVSKY, MS, is an Associate Editor at Psych Central and blogs regularly about eating and self-image issues on her own blog, Weightless.

http://psychcentral.com/blog/archives/2012/03/13/9-ways-to-support-your-childs-creativity/ Tartakovsky, Margarita. "9 Ways to Support Child's Creativity", March 12, 2012. PsychCentral, Copyright 2014 Psych Central.com. All rights reserved. Reprinted here with permission.

Article   Prepared by: Chris J. Boyatzis, *Bucknell University*

Social Awareness + Emotional Skills = Successful Kids

New funding and congressional support are poised to bring the best social and emotional learning research into more classrooms nationwide.

Tori DeAngelis

Learning Outcomes

After reading this article, you will be able to:

- Explain why social and emotional learning is an important quality for children to possess.

- Describe some school-based programs to enhance childrnen's social and emotional learning.

The sad truth is that most U.S. schools don't foster good mental health or strong connections with friends and nurturing adults. Data show that only 29 percent of sixth- through 12th-grade students report that their schools provide caring, encouraging environments. Another 30 percent of high school students say they engage in high-risk behaviors, such as substance use, sex, violence and even suicide attempts.

For decades, a dedicated group of prevention experts—many of them psychologists—has been trying to improve those statistics through an approach called social and emotional learning, or SEL. They believe that if schools teach youngsters to work well with others, regulate their emotions and constructively solve problems, students will be better equipped to deal with life's challenges, including academic ones.

"It's about creating an environment where a child can learn—because if a child isn't emotionally prepared to learn, he or she is not going to learn," says SEL researcher and program developer Marc Brackett, PhD, head of the Emotional Intelligence Unit at Yale University's Edward Zigler Center in Child Development and Social Policy.

Critics charge that SEL programs are too broad-based and that social and emotional learning shouldn't necessarily fall on teachers' shoulders. Instead, families should oversee their children's social, emotional and character development, they contend. Yet studies show the programs improve mental health and behavior, boost children's social competence, and create more positive school climates. Students who participated in SEL programs gained an average of 11 percentage points more on achievement tests than youngsters who didn't take part in the programs, according to a meta-analysis of 213 studies of SEL programs, in press at Child Development, by prevention experts Joseph A. Durlak, PhD, of Loyola University Chicago; Roger P. Weissberg, PhD, of the University of Illinois at Chicago; and colleagues.

"That's pretty remarkable given how difficult it is to alter achievement test scores," says Mark Greenberg, PhD, director of the Prevention Research Center at Pennsylvania State University and creator of one of the longest-running and most rigorously studied SEL programs, PATHS (Promoting Alternative Thinking Strategies).

Some studies also show major gains long after an SEL program has ended. In the Seattle Social Development Project— a longitudinal study of 808 elementary school children who received a comprehensive SEL intervention in the first through sixth grade starting in 1981—participants reported significantly lower lifetime rates of violence and heavy alcohol use at age 18 than no-intervention controls. In addition, intervention-group students were more likely to complete high school than controls—91 percent compared with 81 percent—and to have lower rates of major depression, post-traumatic stress disorder, anxiety and social phobia at ages 24 and 27. (See the *Archives of Pediatrics and Adolescent Medicine*, Vol. 153, No. 3; Vol. 156, No. 5; and Vol. 159, No. 1).

In a related vein, Greenberg and others are starting to show that the programs affect executive functioning, an ability some researchers think may be even more important than IQ.

"The ability to maintain attention, to shift your set and plan ahead—these are obviously important learning skills that our programs are significantly improving upon," Greenberg says.

Other researchers are starting to examine other untapped areas the programs may be affecting, including health, parenting and even the behavior of children whose parents underwent the original interventions. Researchers are also applying SEL programs abroad, with military families and with special-education populations.

The Tenets of Social and Emotional Learning

Researchers have been studying a version of SEL since the 1970s, but it was first popularized in "Emotional Intelligence," the 1995 best-seller by psychologist Daniel Goleman, PhD. He argued that emotional intelligence can be taught and that schools should teach it systematically.

While SEL programs vary somewhat in design and target different ages, they all work to develop core competencies: self-awareness, social awareness, self-management, relationship skills and responsible decision-making. Instead of focusing on a single negative behavior—such as drug use, sexual risk-taking or aggression, for instance—SEL researchers take a broad-brush approach to tackling these problems. They believe all of these behaviors share common roots: a lack of social and emotional competence, often exacerbated by factors such as family disruption, violent neighborhoods and genetic and biological dispositions. Schools and families can counter these risks, SEL proponents say, by facilitating students' emotional and social skills and providing environments that both nurture and challenge children.

A look at the PATHS program shows how these programs work. Like many SEL programs, it uses easy-to-understand, teacher-led lessons and activities that help students learn to recognize feelings in themselves and others, manage their thoughts and emotions more effectively and solve interpersonal problems. One activity, for instance, has youngsters construct posters resembling a three-color traffic signal. Each signal light represents a different aspect of constructive problem-solving: Red is "stop and calm down," yellow is "go slow and think," and green is "go ahead, try my plan." Children apply this guide to real-life problems, then evaluate how their solutions worked.

Active strategies like this are embedded in a comprehensive program that teachers share in 131 sequential lessons over a seven-year period, from kindergarten to sixth grade. Children don't just get didactic information but have many chances to practice these skills both in and out of the classroom, Greenberg explains.

"Comprehensive SEL programs create many opportunities for children to practice these skills in the challenging situations they face every day in the classroom and on the playground," he says. "They also build caring, safe school climates that involve everyone in the school."

An interesting synergy results when these programs are offered, Greenberg adds. When children are taught these skills, they learn how to foster their own well-being and become more resilient. That, in turn, builds a more positive classroom climate that better engages children in learning. And as they become more absorbed in learning, children are more likely to do better in school.

"Building emotional awareness, self-control and relationship skills are master skills," Greenberg says. "When we nurture them, children do better in all areas of their daily lives, including school."

The programs, however, are far from perfect, critics and proponents say. While a 2005 review shows that about 59 percent of schools use some kind of SEL programming, the quality varies widely, says Weissberg. In fact, the Collaborative for Academic, Social and Emotional Learning, or CASEL—a nonprofit organization founded by Goleman in 1994 dedicated to advancing the science and evidence base of SEL and promoting the quality of SEL programs—places only 22 of the nation's several hundred SEL programs (including Greenberg's and Hawkins') on its list of exemplary programs for being well-designed and evidence-based, among other criteria. Researchers also continue to debate whether universal or more targeted curricula are better, since SEL programs tend to have the greatest impact on troubled kids.

Meanwhile, educators are feeling an enormous pressure to have kids do well on standardized testing, even in tight economic times, says Weissberg. "So there are several barriers that make it a challenge to implement SEL programs with high quality and fidelity," he says.

SEL Goes National

That said, more money is pouring into the field, thanks to the positive research findings on social and emotional learning. The NoVo Foundation, a philanthropy headed by Peter and Jennifer Buffett (Peter is investor Warren Buffett's son), has offered $10 million in grants: $3.4 million in research funds and $6.3 million in development funds for CASEL.

Potentially more far-reaching is the Academic, Social, and Emotional Learning Act (H.R. 4223), announced at a CASEL forum in Washington, D.C., in December. The bill, introduced by Rep. Dale Kildee (D-Mich.) and co-sponsored by Rep. Tim Ryan (D-Ohio) and Rep. Judy Biggert (R-Ill.), would authorize the U.S. Department of Education to establish a national SEL training center and provide grants to support evidence-based SEL programs, as well as evaluate their success.

"I don't think I could have imagined that our field would have come this far," says Weissberg, CASEL's president.

In an effort to make the best SEL programming available nationwide, CASEL leaders plan to collaborate with evidence-based SEL providers, work with model school districts, share research to inform federal legislation and state policy and think realistically about how to implement these programs on a broad scale, says Weissberg. If the legislation passes, it should enhance these efforts, he adds.

The December CASEL forum underscored the field's growing clout and psychologists' central role in it, adds APA Chief Executive Officer Norman Anderson, PhD, who attended the meeting. There, psychologists and other SEL researchers and practitioners rubbed elbows with legislators, philanthropists, national media and even some Hollywood celebrities, including Goldie Hawn, who heads her own SEL-related organization.

"This group of experts is doing an outstanding job of moving the SEL model forward and making a real difference in the lives of our children," says Anderson. He is particularly pleased that research is starting to show a link between developing children's resilience and academic performance, he says.

"These efforts represent another bridge between the worlds of psychology and education," Anderson adds. "It's all very exciting."

Critical Thinking

1. Assume you have a close friend who is having problems with a child who is acting out consistently in class with teachers and peers. Describe how you would review, critique and present the data regarding SEL (Social and Emotional Leaning) programs to your friend.
2. Speculate as to whether SEL may differ in its effectiveness rates, depending on factors such as sex of participant, ethnicity, family history and demographics.

Create Central

www.mhhe.com/createcentral

Internet References

Collaborative for Academic, Social, and Emotional Learning (CASEL)
http://www.casel.org
Edutopia.org
http://www.edutopia.org/blog/sel-for-elementary-school-randy-taran
National School Climate Center
http://www.schoolclimate.org/guidelines/teachingandlearning.php

TORI DEANGELIS is a writer in Syracuse, N.Y.

From *Monitor on Psychology* by Tori DeAngelis, April, 2010, pp. 46–47. Copyright © 2010 by American Psychological Association. Reprinted by permission. No further distribution without permission from the American Psychological Association.

Prepared by: Chris J. Boyatzis, *Bucknell University*
Ellen N. Junn, *California State University, Dominguez Hills*

Article

What Homeschooling Actually Looks Like

Most parents don't plan to homeschool their kids. Many decide to try this method later on for a variety of reasons.

SARAH RIVERA

Learning Outcomes

After reading this article, you will be able to:

- Appreciate the personal reasons some families have for removing their children from public education and homeschooling them instead.

- Understand the difference between so-called "first choice" and "second choice" homeschoolers.

- Describe some differences in states' requirements for homeschooling.

Why Some Take the Plunge

"I *never* thought I would do it. I really enjoyed school," said Cyndi Miller, a mother who taught her daughter, Aurelia, at home from sixth to eighth grade. "I had a lot of respect for teachers. I'd worked as a substitute."

Because of a move, her daughter was going to have to change schools in sixth grade and asked her mom to teach her at home just for a year until junior high. The district they lived in had notoriously bad junior highs, so they stuck with homeschooling.

Cyndi was concerned about the social aspects of middle school, as well. "I envisioned her having a hard time peerwise. I dreaded that whole middle school experience for her." Aurelia was studious and shy, and while mature, she was still very much a child. People warned Cyndi that homeschooling would make her daughter socially awkward, particularly when she went on to public high school after being homeschooled for several years; but the opposite proved true.

"She developed a real sense of confidence. She really embraced herself." When Aurelia got to high school, she found a good group of friends. She was in honors programs and achieved a 4.0 GPA. Initially, Aurelia was intimidated by the size of the school, but she managed to get used to it.

Grades were hard for her, too. "She'd come home with a 95 percent and be disappointed," said the Cyndi.

Another family decided that they had to get out of the education rat race.

"Living in New York City, there is a huge pressure to get your kid into the right school, and it starts when you are pregnant. [There] is this insanity for both public and private school. We just felt like we weren't going to enjoy our children's childhood if we were worrying about their future all the time," said Leslie Burby, a mother of two who lives in New York City.

She and her husband also had learned from others' experiences at competitive schools. "We had friends who had eight-year-olds. They were having three-hour homework assignments in elementary school," said Leslie. "Homework in those days [ten years ago] was a good thing. Parents saw it as getting their kids ready for Harvard."

They also were concerned about how their son, Henry, now a homeschooled high school senior, would do in kindergarten. He had a huge vocabulary, but no interest in reading or learning to read. He was an "advanced thinker," but not a reader. As it was, they read to him *a lot*. He started reading when he was nine. "He was able to do it [at] his own pace." Henry scored a 770 on his verbal SAT and is applying to honors programs in college for next fall.

Another couple living in a highly regarded school district was told by classroom volunteers that their sons spent most of their school days reading because they finished their assignments so quickly. They took their boys out of school and started teaching them at a pace that challenged them. They relied heavily on online courses, such as those offered by Khan Academy, and also enrolled their kids in classes at the local community college.

First Choice vs. Second Choice Homeschoolers

The above cases involve parents who make the choice to homeschool because their kids are highly motivated and their schools don't meet their children's needs. These kinds of engaged parents are termed second choice homeschoolers, because their first choice was sending their kids to a school. First choice homeschoolers are parents who want to homeschool their kids from the get-go, for pedagogical or religious reasons.

"[Homeschooling] used to be an act of dissent," said Rachel Coleman, executive director of the Coalition for Responsible Home Education (CHRE). "It's now just seen as one more educational option." Coleman and other former homeschooled children founded CHRE to advocate for basic safeguards for the social and educational well-being of children.

As more families join the homeschool movement, it gets easier to find support. There are a great variety of online curricula. Many schools are allowing homeschooled kids to take individual classes at schools and join clubs as well as sports teams.

State Requirements

According to the National Home Education Research Institute, about 2.2 million students—three percent of all school-age children—are homeschooled. Homeschoolers are a fast-growing education sector. There is talk that the Common Core is also driving some parents out of the schools, as they seek to avoid what they view as a one-size-fits-all educational trend.

Most homeschooling parents aren't able to test their children to gauge how they are doing. One parent wanted to administer a state assessment to her daughter, but the school district wouldn't allow it because they said the tests were just for school students.

The requirements for homeschooling vary by state. Families can find out what requirements there are where they live through the Home School Legal Defense Association.

"You can literally do nothing," said Cyndi. She submitted her lesson plans and certification, all of which were returned to her. She was told that the only thing they needed was the signed form. Cyndi knew a mother who called her year of homeschooling her elementary-aged son "the year of G.I. Joe" because the child didn't want any schooling, even at home, and spent most of his time playing with his G.I. Joe toys. Another homeschooling family had a strong emphasis on gardening. *Only gardening.*

Coleman said these situations are not uncommon in homeschooling. One girl said that her parents hadn't taught her anything beyond fourth-grade content. Another boy reported that his mother tried to teach him algebra when he was 14 but gave up, and his math studies went no further. Beyond that, some parents use homeschooling to isolate and abuse children. While these are certainly the worst-case scenarios, they do underscore the fact that there is often little oversight for homeschooling families. While some parents teach their middle schoolers calculus, others may allow their children's math abilities to languish.

Finding Materials

For many homeschooling families, the homeschooling setting enables them to tailor their teaching to their children's needs.

Still, many new homeschooling parents have anxiety about providing clear and comprehensive instruction. "The one variable that people talk about is structure, especially their first year or two," said Brian Ray, president of the National Home Education Research Institute (NHERI) based in Salem, Oregon, which advocates for homeschooling.

Most start with a curriculum package at home and then start adding different bits as they go along and learn the ropes. The Burbys tried the online courses, but their kids missed human interaction.

Cyndi researched textbooks and found highly regarded, rigorous curricula. "We didn't get away from textbooks," she said.

Playing the Roles of Teacher and Parent

It's not easy for parents to assume the role of teacher.

"I have heard a lot of parents say, 'No way, I couldn't be patient enough [to homeschool],'" said Ray, a parent who opted to homeschool his kids. "It is going to change you as a parent. It is going to reveal some weaknesses in your character." He said he often finds parents who say that they—the parents—are having a blast studying history as they teach it. They find they have better relationships with their kids because they are also their teachers. There is no confusion about what a child is learning and what is going on at school.

"I put a lot of hours into reading ahead of her, making my own notes," [said] Cyndi, who works full-time.

Summers and weekends are no longer school-free for home-schooling families. They are often used as additional time for other lessons. Leslie met with other homeschooling mothers ("it's usually the moms") in her neighborhood for two hours each week to plan their homeschooling agendas. They developed intensive curricula around things such as the Silk Road and Greek and Roman history. They followed state guidelines with about six other families and spent at least one day a week together, during which they would give their kids a classroom experience.

"We didn't let them lie on the floor," she said. They worked out how they should speak in the group, whether raising hands or just waiting for a turn to speak. They would take field trips to museums and art classes, and they would avail their kids of educational programs that were funded through endowments.

Both of the mothers worked extensively with their children on writing.

"You are still their primary English teacher," said Leslie.

Cyndi said they worked on poetry, short stories, and essays. Her daughter learned very quickly that if she handed in something that wasn't up to par, her mother would make her re-do it. She said she didn't just give her a grade, never to address the assignment again. On the contrary, each assignment "was more how it works in the real world," she said. You don't get grades; you get suggestions for revisions. "She would do it again, and she would surpass my expectations."

The Burbys also had a younger son, Henry, who wanted to go to public high school. He got into a music-oriented school and was there for a year. Although he found it hard to get to school by 7:30 A.M. to get through the metal detectors, to have lunch at 10:30 A.M., and to receive instruction in the school's basement, he enjoyed negotiating New York City on his own and making a diverse group of friends.

He ultimately lasted just a year at the school and decided to go back to homeschooling. He seemed to have a different take on school than many of his peers; he thought that being at school was a privilege and learning was fun. Henry felt that his homeschooling group saw education in the same way he did and preferred taking classes with them. He also found many of his classmates disrespectful in their interactions with teachers. Even though he left the school, he still hangs out with his old high school friends. He's re-reading "Catch 22" because, as he tells it, he missed so much of it the first time around. "He's so excited by it. He wants to read it aloud to us," his mother said.

Sources

Coalition for Responsible Home Education. "The Case for Oversight." Retrieved from Coalition for Responsibile Home Education.

Coalition for Responsible Home Education. "How Have Scholars Divided Homeschoolers into Groups." Retrieved from Coalition for Responsible Home Education.

Home School Legal Defense Association "My State." Retrieved from Home School Legal Defense Association.

National Center for Educational Statistics. "Fast Facts: Homeschooling." Retrieved from National Center for Education Statistics.

Ray, Brian D. "Research Facts on Homeschooling." Jan. 1, 2014. National Home Education Research Institute. Retrieved from National Home Education Research Institute.

Critical Thinking

1. How does this article help you understand the varied reasons why parents would want to homeschool their children? Would you want to homeschool your child? What are some pros and cons for doing so?

2. How does this article help you appreciate the challenges parents face in their dual role of "teacher" and "parent"?

Internet References

Association for Supervision and Curriculum Development, ASCD
    http://www.ascd.org/publications/educational-leadership/sept94/vol52/num01/Why-Parents-Choose-Home-Schooling.aspx

EducationWeek.org
    http://www.edweek.org/ew/issues/home-schooling/

Homeschool.com
    http://www.homeschool.com/

NationalHomeEducationResearchInstitute.com
    http://www.nheri.org/research/research-facts-on-homeschooling.html

PublicSchools.org
    http://www.publicschools.org/homeschooling-pros-cons/

Rivera, Sarah. "What Homeschooling Actually Looks Like," *noodle.com,* January 2015. Copyright © 2015 by The Noodle Companies. Reprinted by permission.

Unit 2

UNIT

Prepared by: Chris J. Boyatzis, *Bucknell University*
Ellen N. Junn, *California State University, Dominguez Hills*

Social and Emotional Development

One of the truisms about our species is that we are social animals. From birth, each person's life is a constellation of relationships, from family at home to friends in the neighborhood, school, the community and beyond. This unit addresses how children's social and emotional development is influenced by important relationships with parents, peers, and teachers.

When John Donne in 1623 wrote, "No man is an island, entire of itself … any man's death diminishes me, because I am involved in mankind," he implied that all humans are connected to each other and that these connections make us who we are. Early in this century, sociologist C. H. Cooley highlighted the importance of relationships with the phrase "looking-glass self" to describe how people tend to see themselves as a function of how others perceive them. Personality theorist Alfred Adler, also writing in the early twentieth century, claimed that personal strength derived from the quality of one's connectedness to others: The stronger the relationships, the stronger the person. The notion that a person's self-concept arises from relations with others also has roots in developmental psychology. As Jean Piaget once wrote, "There is no such thing as isolated individuals; there

are only relations." The articles in this unit respect these traditions by emphasizing the theme that a child's emotional and social development occurs within the context of relationships.

A significant milestone of early childhood involves a child's ability to socialize, communicate, begin to understand ethics and morality, and play effectively with peers. Many studies now point to the importance of encouraging children to engage in contemplative behaviors. Other studies focus on understanding how culture and healthy peer interaction shapes children's socio-emotional well-being and how adults and teachers can serve as models for caring and pro-social behavior for children. Unfortunately, a variety of other factors may pose challenges for young children, such as growing up poor or minority, being shy or gay, being bullied, or coping with other environmental pressures. Children who face these challenges may suffer negative outcomes in later childhood and even adulthood.

The research and stories in this section offer teachers, parents, and others guidance and information of how they might safeguard their children and students and help in building a strong social-emotional understanding of themselves and others.

Article   Prepared by: Chris J. Boyatzis, *Bucknell University*

Raising a Moral Child

ADAM GRANT

Learning Outcomes

After reading this article, you will be able to:

- Describe the role of different kinds of praise in shaping children's kind and generous behaviors.

- Explain the effect of different kinds of praise on children of different ages.

- Develop a training program for parents or teachers to help them develop effective strategies to help children share.

What does it take to be a good parent? We know some of the tricks for teaching kids to become high achievers. For example, research suggests that when parents praise effort rather than ability, children develop a stronger work ethic and become more motivated.

Yet although some parents live vicariously through their children's accomplishments, success is not the No. 1 priority for most parents. We're much more concerned about our children becoming kind, compassionate and helpful. Surveys reveal that in the United States, parents from European, Asian, Hispanic and African ethnic groups all place far greater importance on caring than achievement. These patterns hold around the world: When people in 50 countries were asked to report their guiding principles in life, the value that mattered most was not achievement, but caring.

Despite the significance that it holds in our lives, teaching children to care about others is no simple task. In an Israeli study of nearly 600 families, parents who valued kindness and compassion frequently failed to raise children who shared those values.

Are some children simply good-natured—or not? For the past decade, I've been studying the surprising success of people who frequently help others without any strings attached. As the father of two daughters and a son, I've become increasingly curious about how these generous tendencies develop.

Genetic twin studies suggest that anywhere from a quarter to more than half of our propensity to be giving and caring is inherited. That leaves a lot of room for nurture, and the evidence on how parents raise kind and compassionate children flies in the face of what many of even the most well-intentioned parents do in praising good behavior, responding to bad behavior, and communicating their values.

By age 2, children experience some moral emotions—feelings triggered by right and wrong. To reinforce caring as the right behavior, research indicates, praise is more effective than rewards. Rewards run the risk of leading children to be kind only when a carrot is offered, whereas praise communicates that sharing is intrinsically worthwhile for its own sake. But what kind of praise should we give when our children show early signs of generosity?

Many parents believe it's important to compliment the behavior, not the child—that way, the child learns to repeat the behavior. Indeed, I know one couple who are careful to say, "That was such a helpful thing to do," instead of, "You're a helpful person."

But is that the right approach? In a clever experiment, the researchers Joan E. Grusec and Erica Redler set out to investigate what happens when we commend generous behavior versus generous character. After 7- and 8-year-olds won marbles and donated some to poor children, the experimenter remarked, "Gee, you shared quite a bit."

The researchers randomly assigned the children to receive different types of praise. For some of the children, they praised the action: "It was good that you gave some of your marbles to those poor children. Yes, that was a nice and helpful thing to do." For others, they praised the character behind the action: "I guess you're the kind of person who likes to help others whenever you can. Yes, you are a very nice and helpful person."

A couple of weeks later, when faced with more opportunities to give and share, the children were much more generous after their character had been praised than after their actions had been. Praising their character helped them internalize it as part of their identities. The children learned who they were from observing their own actions: I am a helpful person. This dovetails with new research led by the psychologist Christopher J. Bryan, who finds that for moral behaviors, nouns work better than verbs. To get 3- to 6-year-olds to help with a task, rather than inviting them "to help," it was 22 to 29 percent more effective to encourage them to "be a helper." Cheating was cut in half when instead of, "Please don't cheat," participants were told, "Please don't be a cheater." When our actions become a reflection of our character, we lean more heavily toward the moral and generous choices. Over time it can become part of us.

Praise appears to be particularly influential in the critical periods when children develop a stronger sense of identity. When the researchers Joan E. Grusec and Erica Redler praised the character of 5-year-olds, any benefits that may have emerged didn't have a lasting impact: They may have been too young to internalize moral character as part of a stable sense of self. And by the time children turned 10, the differences between praising character and praising actions vanished: Both were effective. Tying generosity to character appears to matter most around age 8, when children may be starting to crystallize notions of identity.

Praise in response to good behavior may be half the battle, but our responses to bad behavior have consequences, too. When children cause harm, they typically feel one of two moral emotions: shame or guilt. Despite the common belief that these emotions are interchangeable, research led by the psychologist June Price Tangney reveals that they have very different causes and consequences.

Shame is the feeling that I am a bad person, whereas guilt is the feeling that I have done a bad thing. Shame is a negative judgment about the core self, which is devastating: Shame makes children feel small and worthless, and they respond either by lashing out at the target or escaping the situation altogether. In contrast, guilt is a negative judgment about an action, which can be repaired by good behavior. When children feel guilt, they tend to experience remorse and regret, empathize with the person they have harmed, and aim to make it right.

In one study spearheaded by the psychologist Karen Caplovitz Barrett, parents rated their toddlers' tendencies to experience shame and guilt at home. The toddlers received a rag doll, and the leg fell off while they were playing with it alone. The shame-prone toddlers avoided the researcher and did not volunteer that they broke the doll. The guilt-prone toddlers were more likely to fix the doll, approach the experimenter, and explain what happened. The ashamed toddlers were avoiders; the guilty toddlers were amenders.

If we want our children to care about others, we need to teach them to feel guilt rather than shame when they misbehave. In a review of research on emotions and moral development, the psychologist Nancy Eisenberg suggests that shame emerges when parents express anger, withdraw their love, or try to assert their power through threats of punishment: Children may begin to believe that they are bad people. Fearing this effect, some parents fail to exercise discipline at all, which can hinder the development of strong moral standards.

The most effective response to bad behavior is to express disappointment. According to independent reviews by Professor Eisenberg and David R. Shaffer, parents raise caring children by expressing disappointment and explaining why the behavior was wrong, how it affected others, and how they can rectify the situation. This enables children to develop standards for judging their actions, feelings of empathy and responsibility for others, and a sense of moral identity, which are conducive to becoming a helpful person. The beauty of expressing disappointment is that it communicates disapproval of the bad behavior, coupled with high expectations and the potential for improvement: "You're a good person, even if you did a bad thing, and I know you can do better."

As powerful as it is to criticize bad behavior and praise good character, raising a generous child involves more than waiting for opportunities to react to the actions of our children. As parents, we want to be proactive in communicating our values to our children. Yet many of us do this the wrong way.

In a classic experiment, the psychologist J. Philippe Rushton gave 140 elementary- and middle-school-age children tokens for winning a game, which they could keep entirely or donate some to a child in poverty. They first watched a teacher figure play the game either selfishly or generously, and then preach to them the value of taking, giving, or neither. The adult's influence was significant: Actions spoke louder than words. When the adult behaved selfishly, children followed suit. The words didn't make much difference—children gave fewer tokens after observing the adult's selfish actions, regardless of whether the adult verbally advocated selfishness or generosity. When the adult acted generously, students gave the same amount whether generosity was preached or not—they donated 85 percent more than the norm in both cases. When the adult preached selfishness, even after the adult acted generously, the students still gave 49 percent more than the norm. Children learn generosity not by listening to what their role models say, but by observing what they do.

To test whether these role-modeling effects persisted over time, two months later, researchers observed the children playing the game again. Would the modeling or the preaching influence whether the children gave—and would they even remember it from two months earlier?

The most generous children were those who watched the teacher give but not say anything. Two months later, these children were 31 percent more generous than those who observed

than the controls. In ongoing work, Jamieson is replicating the experiment with remedial math students at a Midwestern community college: after they were told to think of stress as beneficial, their grades improved.

At first blush, you might assume that the statement about anxiety being beneficial simply calmed the students, reducing their stress and allowing them to focus. But that was not the case. Jamieson's team took saliva samples of the students, both the day before the practice test to set a base line and right after reading the lines about the new science—just moments before they started the first question. Jamieson had the saliva tested for biomarkers that show the level of activation of the body's sympathetic nervous system—our "fight or flight" response. The experimental group's stress levels were decidedly higher. The biological stress was real, but it had different physiological manifestations and had somehow been transformed into a positive force that drove performance.

If you went to an SAT testing site and could run physiological and neurological scans on the teenagers milling outside the door right before the exam, you would observe very different biomarkers from student to student. Those standing with shoulders hunched, or perhaps rubbing their hands, stamping their feet to get warm, might be approaching what Wendy Berry Mendes and colleagues call a "threat state." According to Mendes, an associate professor of psychology at the University of California, San Francisco, the hallmark of a threat state is vasoconstriction—a tightening of the smooth muscles that line every blood vessel in the body. Blood pressure rises; breathing gets shallow. Oxygenated blood levels drop, and energy supplies are reduced. Meanwhile, a rush of hormones amplifies activity in the brain's amygdala, making you more aware of risks and fearful of mistakes.

At that same test center, you might see students with shoulders back, chest open, putting weight on their toes. They may be in a "challenge state." Hormones activate the brain's reward centers and suppress the fear networks, so the person is excited to start in on the test. In this state, decision making becomes automatic. The blood vessels and lungs dilate. In a different study of stress, Jamieson found that the people told to feel positive about being anxious had their blood flow increase by an average of more than half a liter per minute, with more oxygen and energy coursing throughout the body and brain. Some had up to two liters per minute extra.

Jamieson is frustrated that our culture has such a negative view of stress: "When people say, 'I'm stressed out,' it means, 'I'm not doing well.' It doesn't mean, 'I'm excited—I have increased oxygenated blood going to my brain.'"

As the doors to the test center open, the line between challenge and threat is thin. Probably nothing induces a threat state more than feeling you can't make any mistakes.

Threat physiology can be activated with the sense of being judged, or anything that triggers the fear of disappointing others. As a student opens his test booklet, threat can flare when he sees a subject he has recently learned but hasn't mastered. Or when he sees a problem he has no idea how to solve.

Armando Rodriguez graduated last spring from Bright Star Secondary Charter Academy in Los Angeles, but he is waiting until next fall to start college. He is not taking a gap year to figure out what he wants to do with his life. He's recuperating from knee surgery for a bone condition, spending his days in physical therapy. And what does he miss about being out of school? Competing.

"It's an adrenaline rush—like no other thing." He misses being happy when he wins. He even misses losing. "At least it was a feeling you got," he said. "It made you want to be better, the next time." Without a competitive goal, he feels a little adrift. He finds himself mentally competing with other physical-therapy patients.

Rodriguez recorded a 3.86 G.P.A. his senior year of high school and was a defender for the school soccer team. The knee injury happened during a stint on the school's football team: his doctor had warned that it was too risky to play, but "I just had to try," he said. He used to constantly challenge his friends on quiz grades; it's how they made schoolwork fun.

But when he took the SAT last year, he experienced a different sensation. "My heart was racing," he said. "I had butterflies." Occasionally, he'd look up from his exam to see everyone else working on their own tests: they seemed to be concentrating so hard and answering questions faster than he was. "What if they're doing way better than me?" immediately led to the thought, "These people are smarter than me. All the good schools are going to want them, and not me." Within seconds, he arrived at the worst possible outcome: his hopes of a good college would be gone.

It might seem surprising that the same student can experience competition in such different ways. But this points to what researchers think is the difference between competition that challenges and competition that threatens.

Taking a standardized test is a competition in which the only thing anyone cares about is the final score. No one says, "I didn't do that well, but it was still worth doing, because I learned so much math from all the months of studying." Nobody has ever come out of an SAT test saying, "Well, I won't get into the college I wanted, but that's O.K. because I made a lot of new friends at the Kaplan center." Standardized tests lack the side benefits of competing that normally buffer children's anxiety. When you sign your child up for the swim team, he may really want to finish first, but there are many other reasons to be in the pool, even if he finishes last.

High-stakes academic testing isn't going away. Nor should competition among students. In fact, several scholars have concluded that what students need is more academic competition but modeled on the kinds children enjoy.

David and Christi Bergin, professors of educational and developmental psychology at the University of Missouri, have begun a pilot study of junior high school students participating in math competitions. They have observed that, within a few weeks, students were tackling more complex problems than they would even at the end of a year-long class. Some were even doing college-level math. That was true even for students who didn't like math before joining the team and were forced into it by their parents. Knowing they were going up against other teams in front of an audience, the children took ownership over the material. They became excited about discovering ever more advanced concepts, having realized each new fact was another weapon in their intellectual arsenal.

In-class spelling bees. Science fairs. Chess teams. "The performance is highly motivating," David Bergin says. Even if a child knows her science project won't win the science fair, she still gets that moment to perform. That moment can be stressful and invigorating and scary, but if the child handles it well, it feels like a victory.

"Children benefit from competition they have prepared for intensely, especially when viewed as an opportunity to gain recognition for their efforts and improve for the next time," says Rena Subotnik, a psychologist at the American Psychological Association. Subotnik notes that scholastic competitions can raise the social status of academic work as well as that of the contestants. Competitions like these are certainly not without stress, but the pressure comes in predictable ebbs and flows, broken up by moments of fun and excitement.

Maybe the best thing about academic competitions is that they benefit both Warriors and Worriers equally. The Warriors get the thrilling intensity their minds are suited for, where they can shine. The Worriers get the gradual stress inoculation they need, so that one day they can do more than just tolerate stress—they can embrace it. And through the cycle of preparation, performance and recovery, what they learn becomes ingrained.

It may be difficult to believe, as Jamieson advises, that stress can benefit your performance. We can read it, and we can talk about it, but it's the sort of thing that needs to be practiced, perhaps for years, before it can become a deeply held conviction.

It turns out that Armando Rodriguez was accepted at five colleges. He rallied that day on the SAT. It wasn't his best score—he did better the second time around—but it was not as bad as he feared. Rodriguez had never heard of Jeremy Jamieson. He had never read, or ever been told, that intense stress could be harnessed to perform his best. But he understood it and drew strength from it. In the middle of his downward spiral of panic, he realized something: "I'm in a competition. This is a competition. I've got to beat them."

Critical Thinking

1. How has this article's explanation of how biology helps explain why some kids may handle stress well while others don't changed how you view children or your fellow students? Do you have either a more objective or a more emphathic view of students who can't handle pressure?

2. Based on the article, what strategies could you teach to children—or your fellow students—to cope better with stress in their daily lives or when anticipating stressful events like tests and deadlines?

3. Are you a Warrior or a Worrier? How might you benefit from trying to adapt some qualities of the other type?

Create Central

www.mhhe.com/createcentral

Internet References

Kids Health: Helping Kids Cope with Stress
http://kidshealth.org/parent/emotions/feelings/stress_coping.html

Learning Dynamics: Psychological, Educational, Social Services
http://learningdynamicsinc.org/child-adolescent-counseling

Psychology Foundation of Canada
http://psychologyfoundation.org/index.php/programs/kids-have-stress-too

WebMD
http://www.webmd.com/anxiety-panic/features/school-stress-anxiety-children

Po Bronson and **Ashley Merryman** are the authors of *Top Dog: The Science of Winning and Losing.*

Bronson, Po and Merryman, Ashley. "Why Can Some Kids Handle Pressure While Others Fall Apart?" Reprinted by permission of Curtis Brown, Ltd., February 6, 2013.

Article   Prepared by: Chris J. Boyatzis, *Bucknell University*

The Moral Life of Babies

PAUL BLOOM

Learning Outcomes

After reading this article, you will be able to:

- Describe the methods and findings from the studies to test morality in young children.

- Evaluate the conclusion that young children have a moral sense.

- Explain how traits can be passed from one generation to the next.

Not long ago, a team of researchers watched a 1-year-old boy take justice into his own hands. The boy had just seen a puppet show in which one puppet played with a ball while interacting with two other puppets. The center puppet would slide the ball to the puppet on the right, who would pass it back. And the center puppet would slide the ball to the puppet on the left . . . who would run away with it. Then the two puppets on the ends were brought down from the stage and set before the toddler. Each was placed next to a pile of treats. At this point, the toddler was asked to take a treat away from one puppet. Like most children in this situation, the boy took it from the pile of the "naughty" one. But this punishment wasn't enough—he then leaned over and smacked the puppet in the head.

This incident occurred in one of several psychology studies that I have been involved with at the Infant Cognition Center at Yale University in collaboration with my colleague (and wife), Karen Wynn, who runs the lab, and a graduate student, Kiley Hamlin, who is the lead author of the studies. We are one of a handful of research teams around the world exploring the moral life of babies.

Like many scientists and humanists, I have long been fascinated by the capacities and inclinations of babies and children. The mental life of young humans not only is an interesting topic in its own right, it also raises—and can help answer—fundamental questions of philosophy and psychology, including how biological evolution and cultural experience conspire to shape human nature. In graduate school, I studied early language development and later moved on to fairly traditional topics in cognitive development, like how we come to understand the minds of other people—what they know, want and experience.

But the current work I'm involved in, on baby morality, might seem like a perverse and misguided next step. Why would anyone even entertain the thought of babies as moral beings? From Sigmund Freud to Jean Piaget to Lawrence Kohlberg, psychologists have long argued that we begin life as amoral animals. One important task of society, particularly of parents, is to turn babies into civilized beings—social creatures who can experience empathy, guilt and shame; who can override selfish impulses in the name of higher principles; and who will respond with outrage to unfairness and injustice. Many parents and educators would endorse a view of infants and toddlers close to that of a recent Onion headline: "New Study Reveals Most Children Unrepentant Sociopaths." If children enter the world already equipped with moral notions, why is it that we have to work so hard to humanize them?

A growing body of evidence, though, suggests that humans do have a rudimentary moral sense from the very start of life. With the help of well-designed experiments, you can see glimmers of moral thought, moral judgment and moral feeling even in the first year of life. Some sense of good and evil seems to be bred in the bone. Which is not to say that parents are wrong to concern themselves with moral development or that their interactions with their children are a waste of time. Socialization is critically important. But this is not because babies and young children lack a sense of right and wrong; it's because the sense of right and wrong that they naturally possess diverges in important ways from what we adults would want it to be.

Smart Babies

Babies seem spastic in their actions, undisciplined in their attention. In 1762, Jean-Jacques Rousseau called the baby "a perfect idiot," and in 1890, William James famously described a baby's mental life as "one great blooming, buzzing confusion." A sympathetic parent might see the spark of consciousness in a baby's large eyes and eagerly accept the popular claim that babies are wonderful learners, but it is hard to avoid the impression that they begin as ignorant as bread loaves. Many developmental psychologists will tell you that the ignorance of human babies extends well into childhood. For many years, the conventional view was that young humans take a surprisingly long time to learn basic facts about the physical world (like that objects continue to exist once they are out of sight) and basic facts about people (like that they have beliefs and desires and goals)—let alone how long it takes them to learn about morality.

I am admittedly biased, but I think one of the great discoveries in modern psychology is that this view of babies is mistaken.

A reason this view has persisted is that, for many years, scientists weren't sure how to go about studying the mental life of babies. It's a challenge to study the cognitive abilities of any creature that lacks language, but human babies present an additional difficulty, because, even compared to rats or birds, they are behaviorally limited: they can't run mazes or peck at levers. In the 1980s, however, psychologists interested in exploring how much babies know began making use of one of the few behaviors that young babies can control: the movement of their eyes. The eyes are a window to the baby's soul. As adults do, when babies see something that they find interesting or surprising, they tend to look at it longer than they would at something they find uninteresting or expected. And when given a choice between two things to look at, babies usually opt to look at the more pleasing thing. You can use "looking time," then, as a rough but reliable proxy for what captures babies' attention: what babies are surprised by or what babies like.

The studies in the 1980s that made use of this methodology were able to discover surprising things about what babies know about the nature and workings of physical objects—a baby's "naïve physics." Psychologists—most notably Elizabeth Spelke and Renée Baillargeon—conducted studies that essentially involved showing babies magic tricks, events that seemed to violate some law of the universe: you remove the supports from beneath a block and it floats in midair, unsupported; an object disappears and then reappears in another location; a box is placed behind a screen, the screen falls backward into empty space. Like adults, babies tend to linger on such scenes—they look longer at them than at scenes that are identical in all regards except that they don't violate physical laws. This suggests that babies have expectations about how objects should behave. A vast body of research now suggests that—contrary to what was taught for decades to legions of psychology undergraduates—babies think of objects largely as adults do, as connected masses that move as units, that are solid and subject to gravity and that move in continuous paths through space and time.

Other studies, starting with a 1992 paper by my wife, Karen, have found that babies can do rudimentary math with objects. The demonstration is simple. Show a baby an empty stage. Raise a screen to obscure part of the stage. In view of the baby, put a Mickey Mouse doll behind the screen. Then put another Mickey Mouse doll behind the screen. Now drop the screen. Adults expect two dolls—and so do 5-month-olds: if the screen drops to reveal one or three dolls, the babies look longer, in surprise, than they do if the screen drops to reveal two.

A second wave of studies used looking-time methods to explore what babies know about the minds of others—a baby's "naïve psychology." Psychologists had known for a while that even the youngest of babies treat people different from inanimate objects. Babies like to look at faces; they mimic them, they smile at them. They expect engagement: if a moving object becomes still, they merely lose interest; if a person's face becomes still, however, they become distressed.

But the new studies found that babies have an actual understanding of mental life: they have some grasp of how people think and why they act as they do. The studies showed that, though babies expect inanimate objects to move as the result of push-pull interactions, they expect people to move rationally in accordance with their beliefs and desires: babies show surprise when someone takes a roundabout path to something he wants. They expect someone who reaches for an object to reach for the same object later, even if its location has changed. And well before their 2nd birthdays, babies are sharp enough to know that other people can have false beliefs. The psychologists Kristine Onishi and Renée Baillargeon have found that 15-month-olds expect that if a person sees an object in one box, and then the object is moved to another box when the person isn't looking, the person will later reach into the box where he first saw the object, not the box where it actually is. That is, toddlers have a mental model not merely of the world but of the world as understood by someone else.

These discoveries inevitably raise a question: If babies have such a rich understanding of objects and people so early in life, why do they seem so ignorant and helpless? Why don't they put their knowledge to more active use? One possible answer is that these capacities are the psychological equivalent of physical traits like testicles or ovaries, which are formed in infancy and then sit around, useless, for years and years. Another possibility is that babies do, in fact, use their knowledge from Day 1, not for action but for learning. One lesson from the study of artificial intelligence (and from cognitive science more generally) is that an empty head learns nothing: a system that is capable of rapidly absorbing information needs to have some prewired understanding of what to pay attention to and what generalizations to make. Babies might start off smart, then, because it enables them to get smarter.

Nice Babies

Psychologists like myself who are interested in the cognitive capacities of babies and toddlers are now turning our attention to whether babies have a "naïve morality." But there is reason to proceed with caution. Morality, after all, is a different sort of affair than physics or psychology. The truths of physics and psychology are universal: objects obey the same physical laws everywhere; and people everywhere have minds, goals, desires and beliefs. But the existence of a universal moral code is a highly controversial claim; there is considerable evidence for wide variation from society to society.

In the journal *Science,* a couple of months ago, the psychologist Joseph Henrich and several of his colleagues reported a cross-cultural study of 15 diverse populations and found that people's propensities to behave kindly to strangers and to punish unfairness are strongest in large-scale communities with market economies, where such norms are essential to the smooth functioning of trade. Henrich and his colleagues concluded that much of the morality that humans possess is a consequence of the culture in which they are raised, not their innate capacities.

At the same time, though, people everywhere have *some* sense of right and wrong. You won't find a society where people don't have some notion of fairness, don't put some value on loyalty and kindness, don't distinguish between acts of cruelty and innocent mistakes, don't categorize people as nasty or nice. These universals make evolutionary sense. Since natural selection works, at least in part, at a genetic level, there is a logic to being instinctively kind to our kin, whose survival and well-being promote the spread of our genes. More than that, it is often beneficial for humans to work together with other humans, which means that it would have been adaptive to evaluate the niceness and nastiness of other individuals. All this is reason to consider the innateness of at least basic moral concepts.

In addition, scientists know that certain compassionate feelings and impulses emerge early and apparently universally in human development. These are not moral concepts, exactly, but they seem closely related. One example is feeling pain at the pain of others. In his book "The Expression of the Emotions in Man and Animals," Charles Darwin, a keen observer of human nature, tells the story of how his first son, William, was fooled by his nurse into expressing sympathy at a very young age: "When a few days over 6 months old, his nurse pretended to cry, and I saw that his face instantly assumed a melancholy expression, with the corners of his mouth strongly depressed."

There seems to be something evolutionarily ancient to this empathetic response. If you want to cause a rat distress, you can expose it to the screams of other rats. Human babies, notably, cry more to the cries of other babies than to tape recordings of their *own* crying, suggesting that they are responding to their awareness of someone else's pain, not merely to a certain pitch of sound. Babies also seem to want to assuage the pain of others: once they have enough physical competence (starting at about 1 year old), they soothe others in distress by stroking and touching or by handing over a bottle or toy. There are individual differences, to be sure, in the intensity of response: some babies are great soothers; others don't care as much. But the basic impulse seems common to all. (Some other primates behave similarly: the primatologist Frans de Waal reports that chimpanzees "will approach a victim of attack, put an arm around her and gently pat her back or groom her." Monkeys, on the other hand, tend to shun victims of aggression.)

Some recent studies have explored the existence of behavior in toddlers that is "altruistic" in an even stronger sense—like when they give up their time and energy to help a stranger accomplish a difficult task. The psychologists Felix Warneken and Michael Tomasello have put toddlers in situations in which an adult is struggling to get something done, like opening a cabinet door with his hands full or trying to get to an object out of reach. The toddlers tend to spontaneously help, even without any prompting, encouragement or reward.

Is any of the above behavior recognizable as moral conduct? Not obviously so. Moral ideas seem to involve much more than mere compassion. Morality, for instance, is closely related to notions of praise and blame: we want to reward what we see as good and punish what we see as bad. Morality is also closely connected to the ideal of impartiality—if it's immoral for you to do something to me, then, all else being equal, it is immoral for me to do the same thing to you. In addition, moral principles are different from other types of rules or laws: they cannot, for instance, be overruled solely by virtue of authority. (Even a 4-year-old knows not only that unprovoked hitting is wrong but also that it would continue to be wrong even if a teacher said that it was O.K.) And we tend to associate morality with the possibility of free and rational choice; people *choose* to do good or evil. To hold someone responsible for an act means that we believe that he could have chosen to act otherwise.

Babies and toddlers might not know or exhibit any of these moral subtleties. Their sympathetic reactions and motivations—including their desire to alleviate the pain of others—may not be much different in kind from purely nonmoral reactions and motivations like growing hungry or wanting to void a full bladder. Even if that is true, though, it is hard to conceive of a moral system that didn't have, as a starting point, these empathetic capacities. As David Hume argued, mere rationality can't be the foundation of morality, since our most basic desires are neither rational nor irrational. "Tis not contrary to reason," he wrote, "to prefer the destruction of the whole world to the scratching of my finger." To have a genuinely moral system, in other words, some things first have to matter, and what we see in babies is the development of *mattering*.

Moral-Baby Experiments

So what do babies really understand about morality? Our first experiments exploring this question were done in collaboration with a postdoctoral researcher named Valerie Kuhlmeier (who is now an associate professor of psychology at Queen's University in Ontario). Building on previous work by the psychologists David and Ann Premack, we began by investigating what babies think about two particular kinds of action: helping and hindering.

Our experiments involved having children watch animated movies of geometrical characters with faces. In one, a red ball would try to go up a hill. On some attempts, a yellow square got behind the ball and gently nudged it upward; in others, a green triangle got in front of it and pushed it down. We were interested in babies' expectations about the ball's attitudes—what would the baby expect the ball to make of the character who helped it and the one who hindered it? To find out, we then showed the babies additional movies in which the ball either approached the square or the triangle. When the ball approached the triangle (the hinderer), both 9- and 12-month-olds looked longer than they did when the ball approached the square (the helper). This was consistent with the interpretation that the former action surprised them; they expected the ball to approach the helper. A later study, using somewhat different stimuli, replicated the finding with 10-month-olds, but found that 6-month-olds seem to have no expectations at all. (This effect is robust only when the animated characters have faces; when they are simple faceless figures, it is apparently harder for babies to interpret what they are seeing as a social interaction.)

This experiment was designed to explore babies' expectations about social interactions, not their moral capacities per se. But if you look at the movies, it's clear that, at least to adult eyes, there is some latent moral content to the situation: the triangle is kind of a jerk; the square is a sweetheart. So we set out to investigate whether babies make the same judgments about the characters that adults do. Forget about how babies expect the ball to act toward the other characters; what do babies themselves think about the square and the triangle? Do they prefer the good guy and dislike the bad guy?

Here we began our more focused investigations into baby morality. For these studies, parents took their babies to the Infant Cognition Center, which is within one of the Yale psychology buildings. (The center is just a couple of blocks away from where Stanley Milgram did his famous experiments on obedience in the early 1960s, tricking New Haven residents into believing that they had severely harmed or even killed strangers with electrical shocks.) The parents were told about what was going to happen and filled out consent forms, which described the study, the risks to the baby (minimal) and the benefits to the baby (minimal, though it is a nice-enough experience). Parents often asked, reasonably enough, if they would learn how their baby does, and the answer was no. This sort of study provides no clinical or educational feedback about individual babies; the findings make sense only when computed as a group.

For the experiment proper, a parent will carry his or her baby into a small testing room. A typical experiment takes about 15 minutes. Usually, the parent sits on a chair, with the baby on his or her lap, though for some studies, the baby is strapped into a high chair with the parent standing behind. At this point, some of the babies are either sleeping or too fussy to continue; there will then be a short break for the baby to wake up or calm down, but on average this kind of study ends up losing about a quarter of the subjects. Just as critics describe much of experimental psychology as the study of the American college undergraduate who wants to make some extra money or needs to fulfill an Intro Psych requirement, there's some truth to the claim that this developmental work is a science of the interested and alert baby.

In one of our first studies of moral evaluation, we decided not to use two-dimensional animated movies but rather a three-dimensional display in which real geometrical objects, manipulated like puppets, acted out the helping/hindering situations: a yellow square would help the circle up the hill; a red triangle would push it down. After showing the babies the scene, the experimenter placed the helper and the hinderer on a tray and brought them to the child. In this instance, we opted to record not the babies' looking time but rather which character they reached for, on the theory that what a baby reaches for is a reliable indicator of what a baby wants. In the end, we found that 6- and 10-month-old infants overwhelmingly preferred the helpful individual to the hindering individual. This wasn't a subtle statistical trend; just about all the babies reached for the good guy.

(Experimental minutiae: What if babies simply like the color red or prefer squares or something like that? To control for this, half the babies got the yellow square as the helper; half got it as the hinderer. What about problems of unconscious cueing and unconscious bias? To avoid this, at the moment when the two characters were offered on the tray, the parent had his or her eyes closed, and the experimenter holding out the characters and recording the responses hadn't seen the puppet show, so he or she didn't know who was the good guy and who the bad guy.)

One question that arose with these experiments was how to understand the babies' preference: did they act as they did because they were attracted to the helpful individual or because they were repelled by the hinderer or was it both? We explored this question in a further series of studies that introduced a neutral character, one that neither helps nor hinders. We found that, given a choice, infants prefer a helpful character to a neutral one and prefer a neutral character to one who hinders. This finding indicates that both inclinations are at work—babies are drawn to the nice guy and repelled by the mean guy. Again, these results were not subtle; babies almost always showed this pattern of response.

Does our research show that babies believe that the helpful character is *good* and the hindering character is *bad?* Not necessarily. All that we can safely infer from what the babies reached for is that babies prefer the good guy and show an aversion to the bad guy. But what's exciting here is that these preferences are based on how one individual treated another, on whether one individual was helping another individual achieve its goals or hindering it. This is preference of a very special sort; babies were responding to behaviors that adults would describe as nice or mean. When we showed these scenes to much older kids—18-month-olds—and asked them, "Who was nice? Who was good?" and "Who was mean? Who was bad?" they responded as adults would, identifying the helper as nice and the hinderer as mean.

To increase our confidence that the babies we studied were really responding to niceness and naughtiness, Karen Wynn and Kiley Hamlin, in a separate series of studies, created different sets of one-act morality plays to show the babies. In one, an individual struggled to open a box; the lid would be partly opened but then fall back down. Then, on alternating trials, one puppet would grab the lid and open it all the way, and another puppet would jump on the box and slam it shut. In another study (the one I mentioned at the beginning of this article), a puppet would play with a ball. The puppet would roll the ball to another puppet, who would roll it back, and the first puppet would roll the ball to a different puppet who would run away with it. In both studies, 5-month-olds preferred the good guy—the one who helped to open the box; the one who rolled the ball back—to the bad guy. This all suggests that the babies we studied have a general appreciation of good and bad behavior, one that spans a range of actions.

A further question that arises is whether babies possess more subtle moral capacities than preferring good and avoiding bad. Part and parcel of adult morality, for instance, is the idea that good acts should meet with a positive response and bad acts with a negative response—justice demands the good be rewarded and the bad punished. For our next studies, we turned our attention back to the older babies and toddlers and

tried to explore whether the preferences that we were finding had anything to do with moral judgment in this mature sense. In collaboration with Neha Mahajan, a psychology graduate student at Yale, Hamlin, Wynn and I exposed 21-month-olds to the good guy/bad guy situations described above, and we gave them the opportunity to reward or punish either by giving a treat to, or taking a treat from, one of the characters. We found that when asked to give, they tended to choose the positive character; when asked to take, they tended to choose the negative one.

Dispensing justice like this is a more elaborate conceptual operation than merely preferring good to bad, but there are still-more-elaborate moral calculations that adults, at least, can easily make. For example: Which individual would you prefer—someone who rewarded good guys and punished bad guys or someone who punished good guys and rewarded bad guys? The same amount of rewarding and punishing is going on in both cases, but by adult lights, one individual is acting justly and the other isn't. Can babies see this, too?

To find out, we tested 8-month-olds by first showing them a character who acted as a helper (for instance, helping a puppet trying to open a box) and then presenting a scene in which this helper was the target of a good action by one puppet and a bad action by another puppet. Then we got the babies to choose between these two puppets. That is, they had to choose between a puppet who rewarded a good guy versus a puppet who punished a good guy. Likewise, we showed them a character who acted as a hinderer (for example, keeping a puppet from opening a box) and then had them choose between a puppet who rewarded the bad guy versus one who punished the bad guy.

The results were striking. When the target of the action was itself a good guy, babies preferred the puppet who was nice to it. This alone wasn't very surprising, given that the other studies found an overall preference among babies for those who act nicely. What was more interesting was what happened when they watched the bad guy being rewarded or punished. Here they chose the punisher. Despite their overall preference for good actors over bad, then, babies are drawn to bad actors when those actors are punishing bad behavior.

All of this research, taken together, supports a general picture of baby morality. It's even possible, as a thought experiment, to ask what it would be like to see the world in the moral terms that a baby does. Babies probably have no conscious access to moral notions, no idea why certain acts are good or bad. They respond on a gut level. Indeed, if you watch the older babies during the experiments, they don't act like impassive judges—they tend to smile and clap during good events and frown, shake their heads and look sad during the naughty events (remember the toddler who smacked the bad puppet).

The babies' experiences might be cognitively empty but emotionally intense, replete with strong feelings and strong desires. But this shouldn't strike you as an altogether alien experience: while we adults possess the additional critical capacity of being able to consciously reason about morality, we're not otherwise that different from babies—our moral feelings are often instinctive. In fact, one discovery of contemporary research in social psychology and social neuroscience is the powerful emotional underpinning of what we once thought of as cool, untroubled, mature moral deliberation.

Is This the Morality We're Looking For?

What do these findings about babies' moral notions tell us about adult morality? Some scholars think that the very existence of an innate moral sense has profound implications. In 1869, Alfred Russel Wallace, who along with Darwin discovered natural selection, wrote that certain human capacities—including "the higher moral faculties"—are richer than what you could expect from a product of biological evolution. He concluded that some sort of godly force must intervene to create these capacities. (Darwin was horrified at this suggestion, writing to Wallace, "I hope you have not murdered too completely your own and my child.")

A few years ago, in his book "What's So Great About Christianity," the social and cultural critic Dinesh D'Souza revived this argument. He conceded that evolution can explain our niceness in instances like kindness to kin, where the niceness has a clear genetic payoff, but he drew the line at "high altruism," acts of entirely disinterested kindness. For D'Souza, "there is no Darwinian rationale" for why you would give up your seat for an old lady on a bus, an act of nice-guyness that does nothing for your genes. And what about those who donate blood to strangers or sacrifice their lives for a worthy cause? D'Souza reasoned that these stirrings of conscience are best explained not by evolution or psychology but by "the voice of God within our souls."

The evolutionary psychologist has a quick response to this: To say that a biological trait evolves for a purpose doesn't mean that it always functions, in the here and now, for that purpose. Sexual arousal, for instance, presumably evolved because of its connection to making babies; but of course we can get aroused in all sorts of situations in which baby-making just isn't an option—for instance, while looking at pornography. Similarly, our impulse to help others has likely evolved because of the reproductive benefit that it gives us in certain contexts—and it's not a problem for this argument that some acts of niceness that people perform don't provide this sort of

benefit. (And for what it's worth, giving up a bus seat for an old lady, although the motives might be psychologically pure, turns out to be a coldbloodedly smart move from a Darwinian standpoint, an easy way to show off yourself as an attractively good person.)

The general argument that critics like Wallace and D'Souza put forward, however, still needs to be taken seriously. The morality of contemporary humans really does outstrip what evolution could possibly have endowed us with; moral actions are often of a sort that have no plausible relation to our reproductive success and don't appear to be accidental byproducts of evolved adaptations. Many of us care about strangers in faraway lands, sometimes to the extent that we give up resources that could be used for our friends and family; many of us care about the fates of nonhuman animals, so much so that we deprive ourselves of pleasures like rib-eye steak and veal scaloppine. We possess abstract moral notions of equality and freedom for all; we see racism and sexism as evil; we reject slavery and genocide; we try to love our enemies. Of course, our actions typically fall short, often far short, of our moral principles, but these principles do shape, in a substantial way, the world that we live in. It makes sense then to marvel at the extent of our moral insight and to reject the notion that it can be explained in the language of natural selection. If this higher morality or higher altruism were found in babies, the case for divine creation would get just a bit stronger.

But it is not present in babies. In fact, our initial moral sense appears to be biased toward our own kind. There's plenty of research showing that babies have within-group preferences: 3-month-olds prefer the faces of the race that is most familiar to them to those of other races; 11-month-olds prefer individuals who share their own taste in food and expect these individuals to be nicer than those with different tastes; 12-month-olds prefer to learn from someone who speaks their own language over someone who speaks a foreign language. And studies with young children have found that once they are segregated into different groups—even under the most arbitrary of schemes, like wearing different colored T-shirts—they eagerly favor their own groups in their attitudes and their actions.

The notion at the core of any mature morality is that of impartiality. If you are asked to justify your actions, and you say, "Because I wanted to," this is just an expression of selfish desire. But explanations like "It was my turn" or "It's my fair share" are potentially moral, because they imply that anyone else in the same situation could have done the same. This is the sort of argument that could be convincing to a neutral observer and is at the foundation of standards of justice and law. The philosopher Peter Singer has pointed out that this notion of impartiality can be found in religious and philosophical systems of morality, from the golden rule in Christianity to the teachings of Confucius to the political philosopher John Rawls's land-mark theory of justice. This is an insight that emerges within communities of intelligent, deliberating and negotiating beings, and it can override our parochial impulses.

The aspect of morality that we truly marvel at—its general-ity and universality—is the product of culture, not of biology. There is no need to posit divine intervention. A fully devel-oped morality is the product of cultural development, of the accumulation of rational insight and hard-earned innovations. The morality we start off with is primitive, not merely in the obvious sense that it's incomplete but in the deeper sense that when individuals and societies aspire toward an enlightened in which all beings capable of reason and suffering are on an equal footing, where all people are equal—they are fighting with what children have from the get-go. The biologist Richard Dawkins was right, then, when he said at the start of his book *The Selfish Gene,* "Be warned that if you wish, as I do, to build a society in which individuals cooperate generously and unself-ishly toward a common good, you can expect little help from biological nature." Or as a character in the Kingsley Amis novel *One Fat Englishman* puts it, "It was no wonder that people were so horrible when they started life as children."

Morality, then, is a synthesis of the biological and the cultural, of the unlearned, the discovered and the invented. Babies pos-sess certain moral foundations—the capacity and willingness to judge the actions of others, some sense of justice, gut responses to altruism and nastiness. Regardless of how smart we are, if we didn't start with this basic apparatus, we would be nothing more than amoral agents, ruthlessly driven to pursue our self-interest.

But our capacities as babies are sharply limited. It is the insights of rational individuals that make a truly universal and unselfish morality something that our species can aspire to.

Critical Thinking

1. Given the information in this article, would you conclude that babies have a moral life? What qualifications or reserva-tions would you have?

2. In what ways could the various findings cited in this article be used to argue that morality is determined by "nature"? In what ways could they support the "naurture" argument?

Create Central

www.mhhe.com/createcentral

Internet References

EarlyChildhoodNews.com
> http://www.earlychildhoodnews.com/earlychildhood/article_view.aspx?ArticleID=118

International Centre for Educators' Styles
> http://www.icels-educators-for-learning.ca/index.php?option=com_content&view=article&id=48&Itemid=62

PsychologyToday.com
> http://www.psychologytoday.com/blog/child-myths/200911/learning-right-wrong-how-does-morality-develop

PAUL BLOOM is a professor of psychology at Yale. His new book, *How Pleasure Works,* will be published next month.

From *The New York Times Magazine*, May 3, 2010. Copyright © 2010 by Paul Bloom. Reprinted by permission of PARS International.

Article   Prepared by: Chris J. Boyatzis, *Bucknell University*
Ellen N. Junn, *California State University, Dominguez Hills*

Building Resilience among Black Boys

Psychologists are helping black boys capitalize on their strengths, in part by giving them strategies to recognize and respond to racism.

Tori DeAngelis

Learning Outcomes

After reading this article, you will be able to:

- Describe the research showing African American boys face more stressors such as negative stereotyping, racial profiling, and discrimination. Summarize the impact these stressors have for African American boys and young men.

- Discuss the interventions and strategies that some psychologists are suggesting to counteract these stressors for young African American boys.

- Imagine that you are a future teacher or professional working with young African American boys and youth. Based on the research in the article, what specific interventions would use and why?

The shooting death of Michael Brown in August was the latest in what's become an all-too-common story. Brown, 18, an unarmed black teenager, was stopped by white police and shot to death in his hometown of Ferguson, Missouri. The tragedy echoes similar confrontations in which the response appeared to far outweigh the initial incident, including the shooting deaths of black teens Trayvon Martin and Jordan Davis in 2012, and in a particularly bleak historical example, the gruesome 1955 murder of 14-year-old Emmett Till, whose alleged crime was flirting with a white woman.

Brown's death stirred up intense public reaction, including demonstrations, looting and a full-scale national response from African-American leaders and the press.

In particular, the event underscored the uphill battle that black boys in this country face from negative stereotyping, racial profiling and discrimination—a battle that too often results in violence and even death.

"African-American boys have a lot of potential stressors, even relative to African-American girls," says Virginia Commonwealth University psychology professor Faye Z. Belgrave, PhD, co-author with Josh Brevard of the forthcoming book, *African-American Boys,* a summary of research on this population. "Especially as they get older and move into adolescence, they face racism and discrimination that other racial and ethnic groups simply don't face to the same extent."

Now, efforts are under way to turn this negative situation around and to give black boys better chances of success. On the national level, President Obama's "My Brother's Keeper" initiative, launched in February, is directly tackling both the bad publicity these boys can receive and the structural, societal and economic realities they face in this country. The program, initially funded by foundations and philanthropists at approximately $200 million, was expanded in July with an additional $104 million in commitments from school districts, foundations, agencies and corporations.

Psychologists are undertaking their own positive efforts, examining ways that parents, schools, community institutions and society can more fully recognize and foster the natural strengths of these young people. In particular they're looking at how factors like teaching styles, classroom interventions and parental monitoring can be used to steer these boys onto healthy, successful paths.

In addition, psychologists are working with the boys themselves to help them recognize racism and to develop their positive cultural and racial identity to combat it, a strategy known as "racial socialization".

"Our work is based on an African proverb that the lion's story will never be known as long as the hunter is the one to tell it," says Howard Stevenson, PhD, a University of Pennsylvania social psychologist who trains educators to help black boys respond to heated situations using creativity and humor. "Part of our job is to help the boys tell their story and not follow someone else's script about them."

A Complex Challenge

Research suggests that people often see black boys through negative lenses—and that boys can suffer the consequences.

In a study in the February issue of the *Journal of Personality and Social Psychology,* University of California, Los Angeles social psychologists Phillip Atiba Goff, PhD, and Matthew Jackson, PhD, found that white female undergraduates judged all children as equally innocent up to age 9 but saw black children as significantly less so starting at age 10.

In a second study reported in the same article, police officers who viewed black boys in more dehumanized ways than they did white boys were more likely than other officers to use force against them in custody.

A confounding issue is that a subset of African-American boys—20 percent to 30 percent—do start to act out behaviorally and to perform worse academically than other children in school. That downward trajectory continues into adulthood, research finds.

"Part of the puzzle is trying to figure out what happens along the way that creates such disparate outcomes for them," says Oscar Barbarin III, PhD, a Tulane University professor of psychology who organized and co-leads a multi-university initiative, the Boys of Color Collaborative, which is gathering and analyzing data on these boys' development.

One factor is that these boys may come from homes that don't provide them the same school-preparation perks that their peers may get. So by the time they start school, they are already behind other children in language skills, says Barbarin, who edited and wrote several articles in a special 2013 issue of the *American Journal of Orthopsychiatry* on boys of color.

What's more, if teachers and other students expect these boys to do poorly in school, it can become a self-fulfilling prophecy, adds Barbarin, who also provides training, consulting and research for Head Start, the federal program that promotes school readiness in low-income children.

Other data show that black youth, and black boys in particular, are far more likely to be suspended or expelled from school than their white peers. In surveying 72,000 schools in 7,000 school districts in 2012, the U.S. Department of Education found that black students were three-and-a-half times more likely to be expelled or suspended than white kids, with black boys twice as likely to be suspended as black girls. While it's not completely clear why such large disparities exist, researchers cite unintended bias, unequal access to highly effective teachers and differences in school leadership styles as possible reasons.

"That's not to say in some cases boys aren't doing things that require some correction and redirection," says Barbarin, "but often, the punishment is more severe than it needs to be."

Schools as Solutions

Psychologists' research points to specific factors that can help change black boys' trajectories for the better.

Some are related to the school environment. In particular, a teaching style that Barbarin calls "warm demanding"—being emotionally responsive while maintaining high expectations—is a promising way to counter the tendency of some teachers to emotionally distance themselves from youngsters they fear will act out behaviorally. A more interactive style "really has to do with affirming that there's something [good] about the child," he says.

Classroom structure may also be a factor. In a study reported in the *American Journal of Orthopsychiatry* special issue, Barbarin found a significant drop in teacher ratings of black boys' social competence between pre-K and kindergarten. A possible reason, he and others surmise, may be schools' abrupt shift from a developmental, early childhood model that allows for activity and play, to a more rigid academic one.

Meanwhile, some schools are adopting innovative interventions to foster prosocial outcomes for kids who act out. One called restorative justice is a growing movement in educational, criminal justice and other settings. It reframes discipline in terms of helping the perpetrator make amends and reconcile with the community, rather than punishing him or her. The framework includes following a set of specific practices, such as having the victim and perpetrator talk directly about how the perpetrator's actions may have caused harm and giving the perpetrator a task to repair the damage. Once the young person has finished the assignment, the group welcomes him or her back.

Research suggests the approach works. After a year of a restorative-justice intervention at Cole Middle School in Oakland, California, suspension rates fell by 89 percent, while a restorative school discipline program launched in 2011 at Richmond High School in Richmond, California, cut suspension rates in half a year later, according to FixSchoolDiscipline.org, an online resource that's a project of Public Counsel, a pro-bono law firm dedicated to education rights in California.

Moms and Dads as Solutions

Parents can also play a powerful role in their kids' academic and behavioral development. One way for them to intervene, research shows, is to monitor their children's activities with peers and after school, says Belgrave.

"If you know where your boys are, who they're with, what they're doing, you'll be ahead of the game," she says.

In one study, researchers found that black teens who refused drugs or didn't use drugs at all were more likely than those who used drugs to have parents who expressed negative attitudes toward drug use and to monitor their behaviors (*Journal of Black Psychology,* 2012).

Another study underscores the importance of parent-child communication in black youngsters' emotional well-being. In a 2012 study in the *Journal of Child and Family Studies,* researchers found that African-American teens were more likely to be depressed when their parents didn't grasp the extent of their emotional and behavioral problems. That included teens who reported having many problems, whose parents perceived they had only a few, and the reverse—teens who reported having few problems when their parents thought they had a lot.

"If something is going on with the kid, [these kinds of parents] don't know how to intervene because they don't know that anything's wrong," says study author Alfiee M. Breland-Noble, PhD, who directs The African-American Knowledge Optimized for Mindfully Healthy Adolescents Project at Georgetown University.

Parents may be absent for many reasons, she adds, including being too consumed with their own problems, not recognizing mental health problems in themselves, being preoccupied with work, and being worn out from dealing with racism and discrimination.

Communities as Solutions

When Breland-Noble first began studying mental health awareness in black churches, she observed many ways that black boys were absorbing good influences. Many had good role models, were respected and valued by their communities, and assumed leadership roles, such as performing solos in a choir concert or helping to run church services.

"It helps children of color to see people they look up to, who also look like them," she says.

In an April article in *Applied Developmental Science,* a team led by Joanna L. Williams, PhD, of the University of Virginia, examined how measures of positive ethnic identity and positive youth development could be used to inform community or other programs. In a sample of 254 low-income black and Latino urban male teens, the team found that the teens who scored higher in positive youth development were more likely than peers with lower scores to be engaged in prosocial activities, such as clubs or school government, and less likely to be involved in criminal activities. Those with a positive sense of ethnic identity also had lower levels of depression, the team found.

These findings suggest that adding culturally relevant factors into community programs can make these programs, and the kids who engage in them, stronger, the authors say.

Researchers also are exploring how religious leaders, coaches and even barbers can influence young black men's lives for the better. One such study is called SHAPE-UP: Barbers Building Better Brothers, a project funded by the National Institute of Child Health and Human Development that Stevenson is co-leading with University of Pennsylvania colleagues Loretta Jemmott, PhD, John Jemmott, PhD, and Christopher Coleman, PhD. Through the intervention, Stevenson will examine whether the free-wheeling, debate-style discussions that take place in black barber shops could be used as springboards to educate young black men about a range of hot-button topics such as sexually transmitted diseases, the risks of retaliating violently, and the benefits of learning effective negotiation skills instead.

"Barbers see themselves as invisible heroes," says Stevenson. "They do an amazing job of keeping young men and boys out of trouble."

Critical Thinking

1. Evaluate and critique the research solutions offered by the psychologists in working with schools, parents and the community. Of these three areas for intervention, which one is the most powerful in your opinion? Explain why.

2. Imagine that you are the parent of a young African American boy. How does this article make you feel? What specific measures would you engage in to better support your child?

3. While this article focused on African American boys, how might these finding apply to African American girls or children of other races or disabilities? Compare and contrast for other groups.

Internet References

American Institute for Research
http://www.air.org/sites/default/files/downloads/report/Effective%20Strategies%20for%20Mentoring%20African%20American%20Boys.pdf

Journal of African American Males in Education
http://journalofafricanamericanmales.com/wp-content/uploads/downloads/2010/03/African-American-Male-Discipline-Patterns1.pdf

National Association for the Advancement of Colored People, NAACP
http://naacp.3cdn.net/e5524b7d7cf40a3578_2rm6bn7vr.pdf

National Black Child Development Institute
http://www.nbcdi.org/sites/default/files/resource-files/Being%20Black%20Is%20Not%20a%20Risk%20Factor_0.pdf

Science Direct
http://www.sciencedirect.com/science/article/pii/S0022440512000428

DeAngelis, Tori. "Building Resilience Among Black Boys," *Monitor on Psychology,* October 2014. Copyright © 2014 by American Psychological Association. Reprinted by permission.

Article   Prepared by: Ellen N. Junn, *California State University, Dominguez Hills*

Is Your Child Gay?

If your son likes sissy stuff or your daughter shuns feminine frocks, he or she is more likely to buck the heterosexual norm. But predicting sexual preference is still an inexact science.

JESSE BERING

Learning Outcomes

After reading this article, you will be able to:

- Understand how forms of play may act indicators of sexual orientation.

- Comprehend the difference between assessing sexual orientation with prospective and retrospective models.

W e all know the stereotypes: an unusually light, delicate, effeminate air in a little boy's step, an interest in dolls, makeup, princesses and dresses, and a strong distaste for rough play with other boys. In little girls, there is the outwardly boyish stance, perhaps a penchant for tools, a square-jawed readiness for physical tussles with boys, and an aversion to all the perfumed, delicate trappings of femininity.

These behavioral patterns are feared, loathed and often spoken of directly as harbingers of adult homosexuality. It is only relatively recently, however, that developmental scientists have conducted controlled studies to identify the earliest and most reliable signs of adult homosexuality. In looking carefully at the childhoods of gay adults, researchers are finding an intriguing set of behavioral indicators that homosexuals seem to have in common. Curiously enough, the age-old homophobic fears of many parents reflect some genuine predictive currency.

J. Michael Bailey and Kenneth J. Zucker, both psychologists, published a seminal paper on childhood markers of homosexuality in 1995. Bailey and Zucker examined sex-typed behavior—that long, now scientifically canonical list of innate sex differences in the behaviors of young males versus young females. In innumerable studies, scientists have documented that these sex differences are largely impervious to learning.

They are also found in every culture examined. Of course, there are exceptions to the rule; it is only when comparing the aggregate data that sex differences leap into the stratosphere of statistical significance.

The most salient differences are in the domain of play. Boys engage in what developmental psychologists refer to as "rough-and-tumble play." Girls prefer the company of dolls to a knee in the ribs. Toy interests are another key sex difference, with boys gravitating toward toy machine guns and monster trucks and girls orienting toward baby dolls and hyperfeminized figurines. Young children of both sexes enjoy pretend play, but the roles within the fantasy context are gender-segregated by age two. Girls enact the role of, say, cooing mothers, ballerinas or fairy princesses and boys prefer to be soldiers and superheroes. Not surprisingly, therefore, boys naturally select other boys for playmates and girls would much rather play with other girls.

So on the basis of some earlier, shakier research, along with a good dose of common sense, Bailey and Zucker hypothesized that homosexuals would show an inverted pattern of sex-typed childhood behaviors—little boys preferring girls as playmates and becoming infatuated with their mother's makeup kit; little girls strangely enamored of field hockey or professional wrestling—that sort of thing. Empirically, the authors explain, there are two ways to investigate this hypothesis, with either a prospective or retrospective study. Using the prospective method, young children displaying sex-atypical patterns are followed into adolescence and early adulthood so that their sexual orientation can be assessed at maturity.

This method is not terribly practical for several reasons. Given that a small proportion of the population is homosexual, prospective studies require a large number of children. This approach also takes a long time, around 16 years. Finally, not a lot of parents are likely to volunteer their children. Right or wrong, this is a sensitive topic, and usually it is only children who present significant sex-atypical behaviors who are brought into clinics and whose cases are made available to researchers.

Rough-and-Tumble Girls

For example, in a 2008 study, psychologist Kelley Drummond and her colleagues interviewed 25 adult women who were referred by their parents for assessment at a mental health clinic when they were between three and 12 years old. At the time, all these girls had several diagnostic indicators of gender identity disorder. They might have strongly preferred male playmates, insisted on wearing boys' clothing, favored rough-and-tumble play, stated that they would eventually grow a penis or refused to urinate in a sitting position. Although only 12 percent of these women grew up to be gender dysphoric (the uncomfortable sense that your biological sex does not match your gender), the odds of these women reporting a bisexual or homosexual orientation were up to 23 times higher than would occur in a general sample of young women. Not all tomboys become lesbians, of course, but these data suggest that lesbians often have a history of cross-sex-typed behaviors.

And the same holds for gay men. Bailey and Zucker, who conducted a retrospective study in which adults answered questions about their past, revealed that 89 percent of randomly sampled gay men recalled cross-sex-typed childhood behaviors exceeding the heterosexual median.

Critics have argued that participants' memories may be distorted to fit with societal expectations and stereotypes. But in a clever study published in 2008 in *Developmental Psychology*, evidence from childhood home videos validated this retrospective method. People blindly coded child targets on the latter's sex-typical behaviors, as shown on the screen. The authors found that "those targets who, as adults, identified themselves as homosexual were judged to be gender nonconforming as children."

Numerous studies have since replicated this general pattern, revealing a strong link between childhood deviations from gender role norms and adult sexual orientation. There is also evidence of a "dosage effect": the more gender-nonconforming characteristics there are in childhood, the more likely it is that a homosexual or bisexual orientation will be present in adulthood.

Not all little boys who like to wear dresses grow up to be gay, nor do all little girls who despise dresses become lesbians. Many will be straight, and some, let's not forget, will be transsexuals. I was rather androgynous, showing a mosaic pattern of sex-typical and atypical behaviors. In spite of my parents' preferred theory that I was simply a young Casanova, Zucker and

Bailey's findings may account for that old Polaroid snapshot in which 11 of the 13 other children at my seventh birthday party are little girls. But I wasn't an overly effeminate child, was never bullied as a "sissy" and, by the time I was 10, was indistinguishably as annoying, uncouth and wired as my close male peers.

On the Monkey Bars

In fact, by age 13, I was deeply socialized into masculine norms. I took to middle school wrestling as a rather scrawny 80-pound eighth grader, and in so doing, ironically became all too conscious of my homosexual orientation.

Cross-cultural data show that prehomosexual boys are more attracted to solitary sports such as swimming, cycling and tennis than they are to rougher contact sports such as football and soccer; they are also less likely to be childhood bullies. In any event, I distinctly recall being with the girls on the monkey bars during recess in second grade while the boys were in the field playing football and looking over at them, thinking to myself how that was rather strange. I wondered why anyone would want to act that way.

Researchers readily concede that there are quite likely multiple—and no doubt extremely complicated—developmental routes to adult homosexuality. Heritable, biological factors interact with environmental experiences to produce sexual orientation. Because the data often reveal very early emerging traits in prehomosexuals, children who show pronounced sex-atypical behaviors may have more of a genetic loading to their homosexuality, whereas gay adults who were sex-typical as children might trace their homosexuality more directly to particular childhood experiences.

Then we arrive at the most important question of all. Why do parents worry so much about whether their child may or may not be gay? All else being equal, I suspect we would be hard-pressed to find parents who would actually prefer their offspring to be homosexual. Evolutionarily, parental homophobia is a no-brainer: gay sons and lesbian daughters are not likely to reproduce (unless they get creative).

But bear this in mind, parents, there are other ways for your child to contribute to your overall genetic success than humdrum sexual reproduction. I don't know how much money or residual fame is trickling down to, say, k. d. lang, Elton John and Rachel Maddow's close relatives, but I can only imagine that these straight kin are far better off in terms of their own reproductive opportunities than they would be without a homosexual dangling so magnificently on their family trees. So cultivate your little prehomosexual's native talents, and your ultimate genetic payoff could, strangely enough, be even larger with one very special gay child than it would be if 10 mediocre straight offspring leaped from your loins.

If researchers eventually perfect the forecasting of adult sexual orientation in children, would parents want to know? I can say as a once prehomosexual pipsqueak that some preparation on the part of others would have made it easier on me, rather than constantly fearing rejection or worrying about some careless slipup leading to my "exposure." It would have at least avoided all those awkward, incessant questions during my teenage years about why I wasn't dating a nice pretty girl (or questions from the nice pretty girl about why I was dating her and rejecting her advances).

And another thing: it must be pretty hard to look into your prehomosexual toddler's limpid eyes, brush away the cookie crumbs from her cheek and toss her out on the streets for being gay.

Critical Thinking

1. According to the author, how can you tell if a young child is gay?
2. Suppose you are a parent and you observe your child exhibiting sex-atypical behavior. How do you react to your child, and why?

3. Does the article's author have a personal bias? Do his personal anecdotes influence your interpretation of the findings or understanding of children's sexuality?
4. What role might environmental experiences play in the development of sexual orientation?
5. Do the research findings in this article suggest a strong genetic link to homosexuality? Why or why not?

Create Central

www.mhhe.com/createcentral

Internet References

Advocates for Youth.org
　http://www.advocatesforyouth.org/pu
Parenting.com
　http://www.parenting.com/article/could-your-child-be-gay
PFLAG.org
　http://community.pflag.org/Page.aspx?pid=194&srcid=-2

From *Scientific American Mind*, July 2012, pp. 74–83. Copyright © 2012 by Scientific American, a division of Nature America, Inc. All rights reserved. Reprinted by permission.

Article   Prepared by: Chris J. Boyatzis, *Bucknell University*

To Help a Shy Child, Listen

Perri Klass

Learning Outcomes

After reading this article, you will be able to:

- Explain the role of temperament in how children react to the world and handle new situations.
- Describe effective strategies that teachers and parents could use to help shy children adapt and cope with new surroundings.

Toward the end of the summer, I was seeing a middle-school girl for a physical. The notes from a clinic visit last spring said she was a good student but didn't talk enough in class. So I asked her: Is this still a problem for you?

I'm shy, she said. I'm just shy.

Should I have turned to her mother and suggested—a counselor? An academic evaluation? Should I have probed further? How do you feel in school, do you have some friends, is anybody bullying you?

Or should I have said: Lots of people are shy. It's one of the healthy, normal styles of being human.

All of these responses, together, would have been correct. A child who is being bullied or bothered may be anxious about drawing attention to herself; a child who doesn't ever talk in class may be holding back because some learning problem is getting in the way, making her self-conscious. So you do need to listen—especially to a child who talks less rather than more—and find ways to ask questions. Are you happy, anxious, afraid?

But shyness is also part of the great and glorious range of the human normal. Two years ago, Kathleen Merikangas, a senior investigator at the National Institute of Mental Health, and her colleagues published a study of 10,000 older children, ranging from 13 to 18 years old. "We found that about half of kids in America describe themselves as shy," she told me.

Common though it may be, our schools—and our broader culture—do not always celebrate the reserved and retiring.

"Children who are shy, who don't raise their hand, who don't talk in class, are really penalized in this society," Dr. Merikangas said.

I have heard it said that temperament was invented by the first parent to have a second child—that's when parents realize that children come wired with many of the determinants of disposition and personality. What worked with Baby 1 doesn't necessarily work with Baby 2. The analysis of temperament has been a topic of discussion in pediatrics and psychology for decades.

"Temperament is the largely inborn set of behaviors that are the style with which a person functions, not to be confused with their motivation or their developmental status and abilities," said Dr. William B. Carey, a clinical professor of pediatrics at the Children's Hospital of Philadelphia and the author of *Understanding Your Child's Temperament.*

Shyness reflects a child's place on the temperamental continuum, the part of it that involves dealing with new and unfamiliar circumstances. And starting a new school year may be hard on those who find new situations more difficult and more full of anxiety. What most children need is time to settle in, support from parents and teachers, and sometimes help making connections and participating in class.

If a child is not more comfortable after a month or so, parents should look at whether more help is needed, said Anne Marie Albano, director of the Columbia University Clinic for Anxiety and Related Disorders. Treatment usually involves cognitive behavioral strategies to help the child cope with anxiety.

All ranges of temperament have their uncomfortable, or even pathological, outer zones. Just as there are children whose rambunctious eagerness to participate makes trouble for them in school or signals the presence of other problems, there are children whose silence is a shout for help.

I'm struck by the parallels between the ways we discuss shyness and the ways we discuss impulsivity and hyperactivity. In both cases, there is concern about the risk of "pathologizing" children who are well within the range of normal and worry that we are too likely to medicate outliers. By this thinking, children who would once have been considered shy and quiet too often get antidepressants, just as children who would once have been considered lively and rambunctious too often get A.D.H.D. medications.

But the most important question is whether children are in distress. Dr. Merikangas's study distinguished between the common trait of shyness and the psychiatric diagnosis of social phobia. Over all, about 5 percent of the adolescents in the study were severely restricted by social anxiety; they included some who described themselves as shy and some who did not. The authors questioned whether the debate about the "medicalization" of shyness might be obscuring the detection of the distinct signs of social phobia.

For parents who simply want to help a shy child cope with, for example, a brand new classroom full of brand new people, consider rehearsing, scripting encounters and interactions. "The best thing they can do is do a role play and behavioral rehearsal ahead of time," said Steven Kurtz, a senior clinician at the Child Mind Institute in Manhattan. Parents should "plan on rewarding the bravery."

But don't take over. "The danger point is rescuing too soon, too often, too much, so the kids don't develop coping mechanisms," said Dr. Kurtz.

Cognitive behavioral therapy relies on "successive approximations," in which children slowly close in on the behaviors they are hoping to achieve. In that spirit, a parent might arrange to meet another parent on the way to school, so a shy child can walk with another and bond. A teacher might look for the right partner to pair up with a shy child for cooperative activities in the classroom.

"Probably the worst thing to do is to say, 'Don't be shy. Don't be quiet,'" Dr. Merikangas told me. This is not about trying to change the child's temperament. It's about respecting and honoring temperament and variation and helping children navigate the world with their own instruments.

Critical Thinking

1. What would you do to help a shy child adjust to a new classroom? What are some suggestions you could give parents and teachers to help shy children adapt?

2. Do you think shyness is valued and desired in American culture? Why might we want or encourage children to be outgoing?

Create Central

www.mhhe.com/createcentral

Internet References

Ask Dr. Sears
http://www.askdrsears.com/topics/parenting/child-rearing-and-development/8-ways-help-shy-child

Better Health Channel
http://www.betterhealth.vic.gov.au/bhcv2/bhcarticles.nsf/pages/Shyness_and_children

Healthy Children.org
http://www.healthychildren.org/English/ages-stages/gradeschool/Pages/Shyness-in-Children.aspx

ShakeYourShyness.com
http://www.shakeyourshyness.com/parentingshychildren.htm

WebMD.org
http://www.webmd.com/parenting/features/parent-shy-child

Klass, Peri, "To Help a Shy Child Listen" in *The New York Times*, September 16, 2013. Copyright © 2013 by The New York Times Company. All rights reserved. Used by permission via PARS International and protected by the Copyright Laws of the United States. The printing, copying, redistribution or retransmission of this Content without express written permission is prohibited.

Prepared by: Chris J. Boyatzis, *Bucknell University*
Ellen N. Junn, *California State University, Dominguez Hills*

Article

An All-out Anti-bullying Focus

A psychologist-run center at the University at Buffalo is dedicated to helping educators and parents understand the lifelong consequences of bullying—and how they can prevent it.

AMY NOVOTNEY

Learning Outcomes

After reading this article, you will be able to:

• Describe some of the intensive, long-term anti-bullying programs now implemented in schools.

• Define bullying, and distinguish it from other, more common forms of children being mean or unkind to each other.

• Understand the connections between research on bullying and intervention practices.

Forget zero tolerance policies or one-day awareness events. A series of studies points to limited evidence that they actually curb bullying behaviors among children and teens.

Instead, schools and communities really need to implement intensive, long-lasting programs that are regularly assessed and monitored—and also train parents, says Amanda Nickerson, PhD, a professor of counseling, school and educational psychology at the University at Buffalo, State University of New York. A 2011 meta-analysis conducted by Maria Ttofi, PhD, found that school-based interventions that met the above criteria helped decrease bullying by 20 percent to 23 percent, and victimization by nearly 20 percent, on average (*Journal of Experimental Criminology*).

Since 2011, Nickerson has directed the Alberti Center for Bullying Abuse Prevention, which seeks to reduce bullying by developing effective tools to change the language, attitudes and behaviors of educators, parents, students and society.

The center—the only one of its kind nationwide—was established in 2010 thanks to a gift from University at Buffalo Graduate School of Education alumna psychologist Jean M. Alberti, PhD, who was disturbed that many educators viewed bullying as "normal, kids-will-be-kids behavior."

"If an adult exhibited these bullying behaviors to a child, we'd call it child abuse," Alberti says. "Why do we allow children to do it to other children? We teach children to be kind and compassionate rather than self-centered, and we teach them to wait their turn rather than allowing them to push their way to be first all their lives. We need to teach them in this same way to not bully each other."

Since its launch, the center has conducted research; developed presentations, fact sheets and anti-bullying toolkits for students, parents and educators; and hosted conferences and colloquia for researchers, educators and community agency professionals. While the center does not offer a specific degree, its 10 faculty affiliates—who represent diverse fields of psychology, including school, counseling, clinical, educational and developmental—conduct research and teach courses relevant to aggression, human behavior in multiple contexts and intervention in schools.

Most important, its work has focused on staying true to the science around bullying abuse prevention, says Dorothy Espelage, PhD, educational psychologist at the University of Illinois, Urbana-Champaign, and a member of the center's advisory council.

"This is the first center on bullying that has concentrated on outreach while also serving as a gatekeeper for good science and weeding out non-evidence-based work," she says. "That's important because as the area of bullying has gained interest, we've been moving away from the science with the pressure for quick fixes."

Unit 3

UNIT

Prepared by: Chris J. Boyatzis, *Bucknell University*
Ellen N. Junn, *California State University, Dominguez Hills*

Parenting and Family Issues

Few people today realize that the potential freedom to choose parenthood—deciding whether to become a parent, deciding when to have children, or deciding how many children to have—is a development due to the advent of reliable methods of contraception and other recent sociocultural changes. Moreover, unlike any other significant adult job to which we may aspire, few, if any, of us will receive any formal training or information about the lifelong responsibility of parenting. For most of us, our behavior is generally based on our own conscious and subconscious recollections of how we were parented as well as on our observations of the parenting practices of others around us. In fact, our society often behaves as if the mere act of producing a baby automatically confers upon the parents an innate parenting ability, and furthermore, that a family's parenting practices should remain private and not be subjected to scrutiny or criticism by outsiders.

Given this climate, it is not surprising that misconceptions about many parenting practices persist. Only within the last 60 years or so have researchers turned their lenses on the scientific study of the family. Social, historical, cultural, and economic forces also have dramatically changed the face of the American family today. In fact, the vast majority of parents today never take courses or learn of the research on parenting. This unit helps present some of the research on the many complex factors related to successful parenting.

One of the most fundamental achievements of infancy is for the baby to develop a strong attachment to a parent or primary adult caregiver whether that be with a mother or a father. With the growing numbers of parents in two-parent working households, coping with the demands of full-time employment and childcare, researchers are now studying the impact that childcare has on the short and long term consequences of work and childcare on family dynamics.

Moreover, many first marriages in the United States today will end in divorce. Researchers today are studying the effects of divorce and making recommendations that might improve children's adjustment to divorce.

"Spare the rod or spoil the child" is an oft-heard retort used to justify spanking children for misbehaving. Even today, a majority of parents in the United States admit to relying on spanking as a form of disciplirelying on spanking as a form of discipline for their children, and many do not view spanking as inappropriate. Researchers are beginning to accumulate evidence of the negative consequences and effects of spanking for children and advocating the use of other more effective forms of discipline.

Finally, the powerful role that siblings, families, morality, and other influences such as media also play on child growth and development represent other fast-growing and fruitful areas of research and intervention.

Article   Prepared by: Chris J. Boyatzis, *Bucknell University*

Why Fathers Really Matter

JUDITH SHULEVITZ

Learning Outcomes

After reading this article, you will be able to:

- Comprehend how a man's health can have an impact on his future child.

- Evaluate the role that genetics plays in the health of children.

Motherhood begins as a tempestuously physical experience but quickly becomes a political one. Once a woman's pregnancy goes public, the storm moves outside. Don't pile on the pounds! Your child will be obese. Don't eat too little, or your baby will be born too small. For heaven's sake, don't drink alcohol. Oh, please: you can sip some wine now and again. And no matter how many contradictory things the experts say, don't panic. Stress hormones wreak havoc on a baby's budding nervous system.

All this advice rains down on expectant mothers for the obvious reason that mothers carry babies and create the environments in which they grow. What if it turned out, though, that expectant fathers molded babies, too, and not just by way of genes?

Biology is making it clearer by the day that a man's health and well-being have a measurable impact on his future children's health and happiness. This is not because a strong, resilient man has a greater likelihood of being a fabulous dad—or not only for that reason—or because he's probably got good genes. Whether a man's genes are good or bad (and whatever "good" and "bad" mean in this context), his children's bodies and minds will reflect lifestyle choices he has made over the years, even if he made those choices long before he ever imagined himself strapping on a Baby Bjorn.

Doctors have been telling men for years that smoking, drinking, and recreational drugs can lower the quality of their sperm. What doctors should probably add is that the health of unborn children can be affected by what and how much men eat; the toxins they absorb; the traumas they endure; their poverty or powerlessness; and their age at the time of conception. In other words, what a man needs to know is that his life experience leaves biological traces on his children. Even more astonishingly, those children may pass those traces along to their children.

Before I began reading up on fathers and their influence on future generations, I had a high-school-biology-level understanding of how a man passes his traits on to his child. His sperm and the mother's egg smash into each other, his sperm tosses in one set of chromosomes, the egg tosses in another, and a child's genetic future is set for life. Physical features: check. Character: check. Cognitive style: check. But the pathways of inheritance, I've learned, are subtler and more varied than that. Genes matter, and culture matters, and how fathers behave matters, too.

Lately scientists have become obsessed with a means of inheritance that isn't genetic but isn't nongenetic either. It's epigenetic. "Epi," in Greek, means "above" or "beyond." Think of epigenetics as the way our bodies modify their genetic makeup. Epigenetics describes how genes are turned on or off, in part through compounds that hitch on top of DNA—or else jump off it—determining whether it makes the proteins that tell our bodies what to do.

In the past decade or so, the study of epigenetics has become so popular it's practically a fad. Psychologists and sociologists particularly like it because gene expression or suppression is to some degree dictated by the environment and plays at least as large a role as genes do in the development of a person's temperament, body shape, and predisposition to disease. I've become obsessed with epigenetics because it strikes me as both game-changing and terrifying. Our genes can be switched on or off by three environmental factors, among other things: what we ingest (food, drink, air, toxins); what we experience (stress, trauma); and how long we live.

Epigenetics means that our physical and mental tendencies were not set in stone during the Pleistocene age, as evolutionary psychology sometimes seems to claim. Rather, they're shaped by the life we lead and the world we live in right now. Epigenetics proves that we are the products of history, public as well as private, in parts of us that are so intimately ours that few people ever imagined that history could reach them. (One person who did imagine it is the French 18th-century naturalist Jean-Baptiste Lamarck, who believed that acquired traits could be inherited. Twentieth-century Darwinian genetics dismissed Lamarckism as laughable, but because of epigenetics, Lamarckism is staging a comeback.)

The best-known example of the power of nutrition to affect the genes of fathers and sons comes from a corner of northern Sweden called Overkalix. Until the 20th century, Overkalix was cut off from the rest of the world, unreachable by road, train, or even, in wintertime, boat, because the frozen Baltic Sea could not be crossed. Thus, when there were bad harvests in Overkalix, the children starved, and when there were good harvests, they stuffed themselves.

More than a decade ago, three Swedish researchers dug up records from Overkalix going back to 1799 in order to correlate its children's health data with records of regional harvests and other documents showing when food was and wasn't available. What the researchers learned was extremely odd. They found that when boys ate badly during the years right before puberty, between the ages of 9 and 12, their sons, as adults, had lower than normal rates of heart disease. When boys ate all too well during that period, their grandsons had higher rates of diabetes.

When the study appeared in 2002, a British geneticist published an essay speculating that how much a boy ate in pre-puberty could permanently reprogram the epigenetic switches that would govern the manufacture of sperm a few years later. And then, in a process so intricate that no one agrees yet how it happens but probably has something to do with the germline (the reproductive cells that are handed down to children, and to children's children), those reprogrammed switches are transferred to his sons and his sons' sons.

A decade later, animal studies confirm that a male mammal's nutritional past has a surprisingly strong effect on his offspring. Male rats that are starved before they're mated produce offspring with less blood sugar and altered levels of corticosterone (which protects against stress) and insulin-like growth factor 1 (which helps babies develop).

Southeast Asian men who chew betel nuts, a snack that contains a chemical affecting metabolic functioning, are more likely to have children with weight problems and heart disease.

Animal studies have shown that the effects of betel nut consumption by a male may extend to his grandchildren.

Environmental toxins leave even more florid traces on grandchildren and great-grandchildren. Vinclozin, a fungicide that used to be sprayed all over America (it's less common now), is what's known as an endocrine disrupter; it blocks the production of testosterone. Male rats whose mothers receive a fat dose of vinclozin late in their pregnancy are highly likely to be born with defective testicles and reduced fertility. These problems seem to reappear in up to four generations of male rats after the mother is poisoned.

That food and poison change us is not all that surprising, even if it is surprising how far down the change goes. What is unexpected are the psychological dimensions of epigenetics. To learn more about these, I visited the Mount Sinai Medical Center laboratory of Dr. Eric Nestler, a psychiatrist who did a discomfiting study on male mice and what he calls "social defeat." His researchers put small normal field mice in cages with big, nasty retired breeders, and let the big mice attack the smaller mice for about five minutes a day. If a mean mouse and a little mouse were pried apart by means of a screen, the torturer would claw at the screen, trying to get at his victim. All this subjected the field mouse to "a horrendous level of stress," Dr. Nestler told me. This process was repeated for 10 days, with a different tormentor placed in each cage every day. By the time the torture stopped, about two-thirds of the field mice exhibited permanent and quantifiable symptoms of the mouse equivalents of depression, anxiety, and post-traumatic stress disorder. The researchers then bred these unhappy mice with normal females. When their pups grew up, they tended to overreact to social stress, becoming so anxious and depressed that they wouldn't even drink sugar water. They avoided other mice as much as they could.

Dr. Nestler is not sure exactly how the mouse fathers' trauma communicates itself to their offspring. It may be via sperm, or it may be through some more complicated dance of nature and nurture that involves not only sperm but also other factors. When instead of letting the "defeated" mice mate, Dr. Nestler's researchers killed them, harvested their sperm, and impregnated the female mice through artificial means, the offspring were largely normal. Perhaps the sperm was harvested at the wrong stage in the process, says Dr. Nestler. Or maybe the female mouse picked up some signal when she had sex with the dysfunctional male mouse, some telltale pheromone or squeak, that made her body withhold nutrition and care from his pups. Females have been known to not invest in the spawn of non-optimal males, an outcome that makes perfect evolutionary sense—why waste resources on a loser?

When it comes to the epigenetics of aging, however, there is little question that the chemical insults and social setbacks of everyday life distill themselves in sperm. A woman is born with all the eggs she'll ever carry. By the time a man turns 40, on the other hand, his gonad cells will have divided 610 times to make spermatozoa. By the time he's in his 50s, that number goes up to 840. Each time those cells copy themselves, mistakes may appear in the DNA chain. Some researchers now think that a percentage of those mistakes reflects not just random mutations but experience-based epigenetic markings that insinuate themselves from sperm to fetus and influence brain development. Another theory holds that aging gonad cells are more error-prone because the parts of the DNA that should have spotted and repaired any mistakes have been epigenetically tamped down. In any case, we now know that the children of older fathers show more signs of schizophrenia, autism, and bipolar disorder than children of younger ones.

In a meta-analysis of a population study of more than a million people published last year, Christina Hultman of the Karolinska Institute of Sweden concluded that children of men older than 50 were 2.2 times as likely to have autism as children of 29-year-olds, even after the study had factored out mothers' ages and known risk factors for autism. By the time the men passed 55, the risk doubled to 4.4 times that of 29-year-olds. Can the aging of the parent population explain the apparent spike in autism cases? A study published last month in *Nature* that used whole-genome sequencing on 78 Icelandic families made the strongest case to date that as fathers age, mutations in their sperm spike dramatically. Some of the mutations found by the researchers in Reykjavik have been linked to autism and schizophrenia in children.

In his Washington Heights laboratory at the New York State Psychiatric Institute, Jay Gingrich, a professor of psychobiology, compares the pups of young male mice (3 months old or so) to those of old male mice (12 to 14 months old). The differences between the pups, he told me, weren't "earth-shattering"—they weighed about the same and there weren't big gaps in their early development. But discrepancies appeared when the mice grew up. The adult offspring of the older fathers had less adventuresome personalities; they also reacted to loud noises in unusual ways that paralleled reactions evinced by schizophrenics who heard similar sounds.

Still, Dr. Gingrich said, "the differences were subtle" until he decided to pool the data on their behavior and graph it on a bell curve. A "vast majority" of the children of the older mice were "completely normal," he said, which meant their score fell under the upside-down parabola of the curve. The real differences came at the tails or skinny ends of the bell curve. There was about a sixfold increase in likelihood that one of the "abnormal outliers," mice with cognitive or behavioral handicaps, "would come from an older father." Conversely, the super-high-performing mice were about six times more likely to come

from a younger father. "I'm an inherently skeptical person," Dr. Gingrich told me, but he was impressed by these results.

One unanswered question about autism and schizophrenia is how they crop up in generation after generation; after all, wildly dysfunctional individuals don't usually flourish romantically. "I think we're going to have to consider that advanced paternal age, with its epigenetic effects, may be a way of explaining the mysteries of schizophrenia and autism, insofar as the rates of these disorders have maintained themselves—and autism may be going up," Dr. Gingrich said. "From a cruel Darwinian perspective, it's not clear how much success these folks have at procreating, or how else these genes maintain themselves in the population."

When you're an older mother, you get used to the sidelong glances of sonogram technicians, the extra battery of medical tests, the fear that your baby has Down syndrome, the real or imagined hints from younger mothers that you're having children so late because you care more about professional advancement than family. But as the research on paternal inheritance piles up, the needle of doubt may swing at least partway to fathers. "We're living through a paradigm shift," said Dolores Malaspina, a professor of psychiatry at New York University who has done pioneering work on older fathers and schizophrenia. Older mothers no longer need to shoulder all the blame: "It's the aging man who damages the offspring."

Aging, though, is only one of the vicissitudes of life that assault a man's reproductive vitality. Think of epigenetics as having ushered in a new age of sexual equality, in which both sexes have to worry about threats to which women once felt uniquely exposed. Dr. Malaspina remembers that before she went to medical school, she worked in a chemical plant making radioactive drugs. The women who worked there came under constant, invasive scrutiny, lest the toxic workplace contaminate their eggs. But maybe, Dr. Malaspina points out, the plant managers should have spared some concern for the men, whose germlines were just as susceptible to poisoning as the women's, and maybe even more so. The well-being of the children used to be the sole responsibility of their mothers. Now fathers have to be held accountable, too. Having twice endured the self-scrutiny and second-guessing that goes along with being pregnant, I wish them luck.

Critical Thinking

1. What biological and genetic processes in fathers may affect their offspring?

2. How might these effects be passed on over multiple generations?

3. Why should we be concerned about how fathers' age and health may affect their reproductive health?

Create Central

www.mhhe.com/createcentral

Internet References

Child Welfare.gov

https://www.childwelfare.gov/pubs/usermanuals/fatherhood/chaptertwo.cfm

Parents.com

http://www.parents.com/parenting/better-parenting/style/the-role-of
-fathers-with-daughters-and-sons

Zero to Three.org

http://www.zerotothree.org/about-us/funded-projects/parenting-resources/
podcast/daddy-papi-papa-or-baba.html

JUDITH SHULEVITZ is the science editor for *The New Republic.*

From *The New York Times*, September 9, 2012. Copyright © 2012 by The New York Times Company. All rights reserved. Used by permission via PARS International and protected by the Copyright Laws of the United States. The printing, copying, redistribution or retransmission of this Content without express written permission is prohibited.

This last one Sandseter describes as "the most important for the children." She told me, "When they are left alone and can take full responsibility for their actions, and the consequences of their decisions, it's a thrilling experience."

To gauge the effects of losing these experiences, Sandseter turns to evolutionary psychology. Children are born with the instinct to take risks in play, because historically, learning to negotiate risk has been crucial to survival; in another era, they would have had to learn to run from some danger, defend themselves from others, be independent. Even today, growing up is a process of managing fears and learning to arrive at sound decisions. By engaging in risky play, children are effectively subjecting themselves to a form of exposure therapy, in which they force themselves to do the thing they're afraid of in order to overcome their fear. But if they never go through that process, the fear can turn into a phobia. Paradoxically, Sandseter writes, "our fear of children being harmed," mostly in minor ways, "may result in more fearful children and increased levels of psychopathology." She cites a study showing that children who injured themselves falling from heights when they were between 5 and 9 years old are less likely to be afraid of heights at age 18. "Risky play with great heights will provide a desensitizing or habituating experience," she writes.

We might accept a few more phobias in our children in exchange for fewer injuries. But the final irony is that our close attention to safety has not in fact made a tremendous difference in the number of accidents children have. According to the National Electronic Injury Surveillance System, which monitors hospital visits, the frequency of emergency-room visits related to playground equipment, including home equipment, in 1980 was 156,000, or one visit per 1,452 Americans. In 2012, it was 271,475, or one per 1,156 Americans. The number of deaths hasn't changed much either. From 2001 through 2008, the Consumer Product Safety Commission reported 100 deaths associated with playground equipment—an average of 13 a year, or 10 fewer than were reported in 1980. Head injuries, runaway motorcycles, a fatal fall onto a rock—most of the horrors Sweeney and Frost described all those years ago turn out to be freakishly rare, unexpected tragedies that no amount of safety-proofing can prevent.

Even rubber surfacing doesn't seem to have made much of a difference in the real world. David Ball, a professor of risk management at Middlesex University, analyzed U.K. injury statistics and found that as in the U.S., there was no clear trend over time. "The advent of all these special surfaces for playgrounds has contributed very little, if anything at all, to the safety of children," he told me. Ball has found some evidence that long-bone injuries, which are far more common than head injuries, are actually increasing. The best theory for that is "risk compensation"—kids don't worry as much about falling on rubber, so they're not as careful, and end up hurting themselves more often. The problem, says Ball, is that "we have come to think of accidents as preventable and not a natural part of life."

The category of risky play on Sandseter's list that likely makes this current generation of parents most nervous is the one involving children getting lost, or straying from adult supervision. "Children love to walk off alone and go exploring away from the eyes of adults," she writes. They "experience a feeling of risk and danger of getting lost" when "given the opportunity to 'cruise' on their own exploring unknown areas; still, they have an urge to do it." Here again Sandseter cites evidence showing that the number of separation experiences before age 9 correlates negatively with separation-anxiety symptoms at age 18, "suggesting an 'inoculation' effect."

But parents these days have little tolerance for children's wandering on their own, for reasons that, much like the growing fear of playground injuries, have their roots in the 1970s. In 1979, nine months after Frank Nelson fell off that slide in Chicago, 6-year-old Etan Patz left his parents' downtown New York apartment to walk by himself to the school-bus stop. Etan had been begging his mother to let him walk by himself; many of his friends did, and that morning was the first time she let him. But, as just about anyone who grew up in New York in that era knows, he never came home. (In 2012, a New Jersey man was arrested for Etan's murder.) I was nearly 10 at the time, and I remember watching the nightly news and seeing his school picture, with a smile almost as wide as Mick Jagger's. I also remember that, sometime during those weeks of endless coverage of the search for Etan, the parents in my neighborhood for the first time organized a walk pool to take us to the bus stop.

The Etan Patz case launched the era of the ubiquitous missing child, as Paula Fass chronicles in *Kidnapped: Child Abduction in America*. Children's faces began to appear on milk cartons, and Ronald Reagan chose the date of Etan's disappearance as National Missing Children's Day. Although no one knew what had happened to Etan, a theory developed that he had been sexually abused; soon *The New York Times* quoted a psychologist who said that the Patz case heralded an "epidemic of sexual abuse of children." In a short period, writes Fass, Americans came to think child molestations were very prevalent. Over time, the fear drove a new parenting absolute: children were never to talk to strangers.

But abduction cases like Etan Patz's were incredibly uncommon a generation ago, and remain so today. David Finkelhor is the director of the Crimes Against Children Research Center and the most reliable authority on sexual-abuse and abduction statistics for children. In his research, Finkelhor singles out a category of crime called the "stereotypical abduction," by which he means the kind of abduction that's likely to make the news, during which the victim disappears overnight, or is taken more than 50 miles away, or is killed. Finkelhor says these cases remain exceedingly rare and do not appear to have increased since at least the mid-'1980s, and he guesses the '1970s, although he was not keeping track then. Overall, crimes against children have been declining, in keeping with the general crime drop since the '1990s. A child from a happy, intact family who walks to the bus stop and never comes home is still a singular tragedy, not a national epidemic.

One kind of crime that *has* increased, says Finkelhor, is family abduction (which is lumped together with stereotypical abduction in FBI crime reports, accounting for the seemingly alarming numbers sometimes reported in the media). The explosion in divorce in the '1970s meant many more custody wars and many more children being smuggled away by one or the other of their parents. If a mother is afraid that her child might be abducted, her ironclad rule should not be *Don't talk to strangers.* It should be *Don't talk to your father.*

The gap between what people fear (abduction by a stranger) and what's actually happening (family turmoil and custody battles) is revealing. What has changed since the 1970s is the nature of the American family, and the broader sense of community. For a variety of reasons—divorce, more single-parent families, more mothers working—both families and neighborhoods have lost some of their cohesion. It is perhaps natural that trust in general has eroded, and that parents have sought to control more closely what they can—most of all, their children.

As we parents began to see public spaces—playgrounds, streets, public ball fields, the distance between school and home—as dangerous, other, smaller daily decisions fell into place. Ask any of my parenting peers to chronicle a typical week in their child's life and they will likely mention school, homework, after-school classes, organized playdates, sports teams coached by a fellow parent, and very little free, unsupervised time. Failure to supervise has become, in fact, synonymous with failure to parent. The result is a "continuous and ultimately dramatic decline in children's opportunities to play and explore in their own chosen ways," writes Peter Gray, a psychologist at Boston College and the author of *Free to Learn.* No more pickup games, idle walks home from school, or cops and robbers in the garage all afternoon. The child culture from my Queens days, with its own traditions and codas, its particular pleasures and distresses, is virtually extinct.

In 1972, the British-born geography student Roger Hart settled on an unusual project for his dissertation. He moved to a rural New England town and, for two years, tracked the movements of 86 children in the local elementary school, to create what he called a "geography of children," including actual maps that would show where and how far the children typically roamed away from home. Usually research on children is conducted by interviewing parents, but Hart decided he would go straight to the source. The principal of the school lent him a room, which became known as "Roger's room," and he slowly got to know the children. Hart asked them questions about where they went each day and how they felt about those places, but mostly he just wandered around with them. Even now, as a father and a settled academic, Hart has a dreamy, puckish air. Children were comfortable with him and loved to share their moments of pride, their secrets. Often they took him to places adults had never seen before—playhouses or forts the kids had made just for themselves.

Hart's methodology was novel, but he didn't think he was recording anything radical. Many of his observations must have seemed mundane at the time. For example: "I was struck by the large amount of time children spend modifying the landscape in order to make places for themselves and for their play." But reading his dissertation today feels like coming upon a lost civilization, a child culture with its own ways of playing and thinking and feeling that seems utterly foreign now. The children spent immense amounts of time on their own, creating imaginary landscapes their parents sometimes knew nothing about. The parents played no role in their coming together—"it is through cycling around that the older boys chance to fall into games with each other," Hart observed. The forts they built were not praised and cooed over by their parents, because their parents almost never saw them.

Through his maps, Hart discovered broad patterns: between second and third grade, for instance, the children's "free range"—the distance they were allowed to travel away from home without checking in first—tended to expand significantly, because they were permitted to ride bikes alone to a friend's house or to a ball field. By fifth grade, the boys especially gained a "dramatic new freedom" and could go pretty much wherever they wanted without checking in at all. (The girls were more restricted because they often helped their mothers with chores or errands, or stayed behind to look after younger siblings.) To the children, each little addition to their free range—being allowed to cross a paved road, or go to the center of town—was a sign of growing up. The kids took special pride, Hart noted, in "knowing how to get places," and in finding shortcuts that adults wouldn't normally use.

Hart's research became the basis for a BBC documentary, which he recently showed me in his office at the City University of New York. One long scene takes place across a river where the kids would go to build what they called "river houses," structures made from branches and odds and ends they'd snuck out from home. In one scene, Joanne and her sister Sylvia show the filmmakers the "house" they made, mostly from orange and brown sheets slung over branches. The furniture has been built with love and wit—the TV, for example, is a crate on a rock with a magazine glamour shot taped onto the front. The phone is a stone with a curled piece of wire coming out from under it.

The girls should be self-conscious because they are being filmed, but they are utterly at home, flipping their hair, sitting close to each other on crates, and drawing up plans for how to renovate. Nearby, their 4-year-old brother is cutting down a small tree with a hatchet for a new addition. The girls and their siblings have logged hundreds of hours here over the years; their mother has never been here, not once, they say, because she doesn't like to get her toes wet.

In another scene, Andrew and Jenny, a brother and sister who are 6 and 4, respectively, explore a patch of woods to find the best ferns to make a bed with. Jenny walks around in her knee-high white socks, her braids swinging, looking for the biggest fronds. Her big brother tries to arrange them just so. The sun is shining through the dense trees and the camera stays on the children for a long time. When they are satisfied with their bed, they lie down next to each other. "Don't take any of my ferns," Jenny scolds, and Andrew sticks his tongue out. At this point, I could hear in my head the parent intervening: "Come on, kids, share. There's plenty to go around." But no parents are there; the kids have been out of their sight for several hours now. I teared up while watching the film, and it was only a few days later that I understood why. In all my years as a parent, I have never come upon children who are so inwardly focused, so in tune with each other, so utterly absorbed by the world they've created, and I think that's because in all my years as a parent, I've mostly met children who take it for granted that they are always being *watched.*

In 2004, Hart returned to the same town to do a follow-up study. His aim was to reconnect with any kids he had written about who still lived within 100 miles of the town and see how they were raising their own children, and also to track some of the kids who now lived in the town. But from the first day he arrived, he knew he would never be able to do the research in the same way. Hart started at the house of a boy he'd known, now a father, and asked whether he could talk to his son outside. The mother said they could go in the backyard, but she followed them, always staying about 200 yards behind them. Hart didn't get the sense that the parents were suspicious of him, more that they'd "gotten used to the idea of always being close to their children, and didn't like them going off." He realized that this time around, he could get to the children only through the adults; even the kids didn't seem that interested in talking to him alone; they got plenty of adult attention already. "They were so used to having their lives organized by their parents," he told me. Meanwhile, the new principal at the school said he didn't want Hart doing any research there, because it was not directly related to the curriculum.

At one point Hart tracked down Sylvia, one of the girls he'd filmed at the river house. "Roger Hart! Oh my God, my childhood existed," she screamed into the phone. "It's just that I'm always telling people what we used to do, and they don't believe me!" Sylvia was now a suburban mom of two kids (ages 5 and 4), and she and her husband had moved into a new house 30 miles away. When Hart went to visit Sylvia, he filmed the exchange. Standing outside in her backyard, Sylvia tells him she bought this house because she wanted to give her own children the kinds of childhood experiences she'd had, and when she saw the little wooded area out back, her "heart leapt." But "there's no way they'd be out in the woods," she adds. "My hometown is now so diverse, with people coming in and out and lots of transients." Hart reminds her how she used to spend most of her time across the river, playing. "There's no river here," she tells him, then whispers, "and I'm really glad about that." There will soon be a fence around the yard—she mentions the fence several times—"so they'll be contained," and she'll always be able to see her kids from the kitchen window. As Sylvia is being interviewed, her son makes some half-hearted attempts to cut the hedges with a pair of scissors, but he doesn't really seem to know how to do it, and he never strays more than a few inches from his father.

When Hart shows Jenny and Andrew the film of themselves playing in the ferns, they are both deeply moved, because they'd never seen a film of themselves as children, and because for them, too, the memories had receded into hazy unreality. They are both parents and are still living in that New England town. Of all the people Hart caught up with, they seem to have tried the hardest to create some of the same recreational opportunities for their own children that they'd had. Jenny bought a house, with a barn, near a large patch of woods; she doesn't let her sons watch TV or play video games all that much, instead encouraging them to go to the barn and play in the hay, or tend the garden. She says she wouldn't really mind if they strayed into the woods, but "they don't want to go out of sight." Anyway, they get their exercise from the various sports teams they play on. Jenny gets some of her girlish self back when she talks about how she and the boys pile up rocks in the backyard to build a ski jump or use sticks to make a fort. But Jenny initiates these activities; the boys usually don't discover them on their own.

Among this new set of kids, the free range is fairly limited. They don't roam all that far from home, and they don't seem to want to. Hart talked with a law-enforcement officer in the area, who said that there weren't all that many transients and that over the years, crime has stayed pretty steady—steadily low. "There's a fear" among the parents, Hart told me, "an exaggeration of the dangers, a loss of trust that isn't totally clearly explainable." Hart hasn't yet published his findings from his more recent research, and he told me he's wary of running into his own nostalgia for the Rousseauean children of his memories. For example, he said he has to be honest about the things that have improved in the new version of childhood. In the old days, when children were left on their own, child power hierarchies formed fairly quickly, and some children always remained on the bottom, or were excluded entirely. Also, fathers were largely absent; now children are much closer to their dads—closer to both their parents than kids were back then. I would add that the 1970s was the decade of the divorce boom, and many children felt neglected by their parents; perhaps today's close supervision is part of a vow not to repeat that mistake. And yet despite all this, Hart can't help but wonder what disappeared with "the erosion of child culture," in which children were "inventing their own activities and building up a kind of community of their own that they knew much more about than their parents."

One common concern of parents these days is that children grow up too fast. But sometimes it seems as if children don't get the space to grow up at all; they just become adept at mimicking the habits of adulthood. As Hart's research shows, children used to gradually take on responsibilities, year by year. They crossed the road, went to the store; eventually some of them got small neighborhood jobs. Their pride was wrapped up in competence and independence, which grew as they tried and mastered activities they hadn't known how to do the previous year. But these days, middle-class children, at least, skip these milestones. They spend a lot of time in the company of adults, so they can talk and think like them, but they never build up the confidence to be truly independent and self-reliant.

Lately parents have come to think along the class lines defined by the University of Pennsylvania sociologist Annette Lareau. Middle-class parents see their children as projects: they engage in what she calls "concerted cultivation," an active pursuit of their child's enrichment. Working-class and poor parents, meanwhile, speak fewer words to their children, watch their progress less closely, and promote what Lareau calls the "accomplishment of natural growth," perhaps leaving the children less prepared to lead middle-class lives as adults. Many people interpret her findings as proof that middle-class parenting styles, in their totality, are superior. But this may be an overly simplistic and self-serving conclusion; perhaps each form of child-rearing has something to recommend it to the other.

When Claire Griffiths, the Land's manager, applies for grants to fund her innovative play spaces, she often lists the concrete advantages of enticing children outside: combatting obesity, developing motor skills. She also talks about the same issue Lady Allen talked about all those years ago—encouraging children to take risks so they build their confidence. But the more nebulous benefits of a freer child culture are harder to explain in a grant application, even though experiments bear them out. For example, beginning in 2011, Swanson Primary School in New Zealand submitted itself to a university experiment and agreed to suspend all playground rules, allowing the kids to run, climb trees, slide down a muddy hill, jump off swings, and play in a "loose-parts pit" that was like a mini adventure playground. The teachers feared chaos, but in fact what they got was less naughtiness and bullying—because the kids were too busy and engaged to want to cause trouble, the principal said.

In an essay called "The Play Deficit," Peter Gray, the Boston College psychologist, chronicles the fallout from the loss of the old childhood culture, and it's a familiar list of the usual ills attributed to Millennials: depression, narcissism, and a decline in empathy. In the past decade, the percentage of college-age kids taking psychiatric medication has spiked, according to a 2012 study by the American College Counseling Association. Practicing psychologists have written about the unique identity crisis this generation faces—a fear of growing up and, in the words of Brooke Donatone, a New York–based therapist, an inability "to think for themselves."

In his essay, Gray highlights the work of Kyung-Hee Kim, an educational psychologist at the College of William and Mary and the author of the 2011 paper "The Creativity Crisis." Kim has analyzed results from the Torrance Tests of Creative Thinking and found that American children's scores have declined steadily across the past decade or more. The data show that children have become:

> less emotionally expressive, less energetic, less talkative and verbally expressive, less humorous, less imaginative, less unconventional, less lively and passionate, less perceptive, less apt to connect seemingly irrelevant things, less synthesizing, and less likely to see things from a different angle.

The largest drop, Kim noted, has been in the measure of "elaboration," or the ability to take an idea and expand on it in a novel way.

The stereotypes about Millennials have alarmed researchers and parents enough that they've started pushing back against the culture of parental control. Many recent parenting books have called for a retreat, among them *Duct Tape Parenting, Baby Knows Best,* and the upcoming *The Kids Will Be Fine.* In her excellent new book, *All Joy and No Fun,* Jennifer Senior takes the route that parents are making themselves miserable by believing they always have to maximize their children's happiness and success.

In the U.K., the safety paranoia is easing up. The British equivalent of the Consumer Product Safety Commission recently released a statement saying it "wants to make sure that mistaken health and safety concerns do not create sterile play environments that lack challenge and so prevent children from expanding their learning and stretching their abilities." When I was in the U.K., Tim Gill, the author of *No Fear,* took me to a newly built London playground that reminded me of the old days, with long, fast slides down a rocky hill, high drops from a climbing rock, and few fenced-in areas. Meanwhile, the Welsh government has explicitly adopted a strategy to encourage active independent play, rather than book learning, among young children, paving the way for a handful of adventure playgrounds like the Land and other play initiatives.

Whether Americans will pick up on the British vibe is hard to say, although some hopeful signs are appearing. There is rising American interest in European-style "forest kindergartens," where kids receive little formal instruction and have more freedom to explore in nature. And in Washington, D.C., not far from where I live, we finally have our first exciting playground since the "forgotten playground" was leveled. Located at a private school called Beauvoir, it has a zip line and climbing structures that kids of all ages perceive as treacherous. I recently met someone who worked on the playground and asked him why the school board wasn't put off by safety concerns, especially since it keeps the park open to the public on weekends. He said the board was concerned about safety but also wanted an exciting playground; the safety guidelines are, after all these years, still just guidelines.

But the real cultural shift has to come from parents. There is a big difference between avoiding major hazards and making every decision with the primary goal of optimizing child safety (or enrichment, or happiness). We can no more create the perfect environment for our children than we can create perfect children. To believe otherwise is a delusion, and a harmful one; remind yourself of that every time the panic rises.

As the sun set over the Land, I noticed out of the corner of my eye a gray bin, like the kind you'd keep your recycling in, about to be pushed down the slope that led to the creek. A kid's head poked out of the top, and I realized it was my son's. Even by my relatively laissez-faire parenting standards, the situation seemed dicey. The light was fading, the slope was very steep, and Christian, the kid who was doing the pushing, was only 7. Also, the creek was frigid, and I had no change of clothes for Gideon.

I hadn't seen much of my son that day. Kids, unparented, take on pack habits, so as the youngest and newest player, he'd been taken care of by the veterans of the Land. I inched close enough to hear the exchange.

"You might fall in the creek," said Christian.
"I know," said Gideon.

Christian had already taught Gideon how to climb up to the highest slide and manage the rope swing. At this point, he'd earned some trust. "I'll push you gently, okay?" "Ready, steady, go!," Gideon said in response. Down he went, and landed in the creek. In my experience, Gideon is very finicky about water. He hates to have even a drop land on his sleeve while he's brushing his teeth. I hadn't rented a car on this trip, and the woman who'd been driving us around had left for a while. I started scheming how to get him new clothes. Could I knock on one of the neighbors' doors? Ask Christian to get his father? Or, failing that, persuade Gideon to sit a while with the big boys by the fire?

"I'm wet," Gideon said to Christian, and then they raced over to claim some hammers to build a new fort.

Critical Thinking

1. Think back to when you were a child. Where were you allowed to play and how often did you need to be supervised or watched? Contrast that to what parents expect of their children's free play time after school and on weekends. Discuss some of the factors that have contributed to this trend for more control over children's play spaces and free time.

2. Evaluate the pros and cons of reduced creative, closely supervised play environments for children.

3. Imagine you are a parent of a preschooler or young child. Given the information and research in this article, would you permit your child free, unsupervised access to play areas outside of your home? Explain and justify your answer in light of the findings in the article.

Internet References

Early Childhood News.com
http://www.earlychildhoodnews.com/earlychildhood/article_view.aspx?ArticleID=249

Early Childhood Research and Practice, ERCP
http://ecrp.uiuc.edu/v4n1/bergen.html

International Chiropractic Pediatric Association, ICPA
http://icpa4kids.org/Wellness-Articles/child-playgrounds.html

National Association for the Education of Young Children, NAEYC
http://www.naeyc.org/play

National Program for Playground Safety, NPPS
http://playgroundsafety.org/safe/age-appropriate-design

Rosin, Hanna. "The Overprotected Kid," *The Atlantic,* April 2014. Copyright © 2014 The Atlantic Media Co., as first published in The Atlantic Magazine. All rights reserved. Distributed by Tribune Content Agency, LLC. Reprinted by permission.

Article

Prepared by: Chris J. Boyatzis, *Bucknell University*
Ellen N. Junn, *California State University, Dominguez Hills*

Psychological Biases Play a Part in Vaccination Decisions

Tania Lombrozo

Learning Outcomes

After reading this article, you will be able to:

- Describe the controversy and reasons surrounding parents' fears of vaccinating their child.

- Evaluate and assess the research supporting the pros and cons for childhood vaccinations.

- Reflect upon your own psychological biases either for or against childhood vaccinations. Based on this article, explain how and why your biases have changed or not.

W ith the recent outbreak of measles originating from Disneyland, there's been no shortage of speculation, accusation and recrimination concerning why some people won't vaccinate their children. There's also been some—but only some—more historically and psychologically informed discussion.

Some people's motivation for skipping vaccines likely comes from persistent misinformation and, in particular, the unfounded belief that there's a link between vaccines and autism. And, as Adam Frank pointed out in a post last week, vaccinations also play into a larger cultural conversation about science and its place in society.

What's received less attention is how vaccination plays into subtle psychological biases that can contribute to parents' unwillingness to "intervene" on their kids. The particular bias I have in mind is sometimes called "omission bias," and it has to do with the difference between bringing about some outcome by *acting* versus by *failing to act*. For example, *lying* about whether one is married (an action) seems worse than failing to correct an invalid assumption (an omission), even if the outcome—in terms of what the other person believes about one's marital status—is the same in each case.

With vaccination, choosing to vaccinate is an action—it involves a deliberate intervention on your child. In contrast, having a child fall prey to an illness that could have been prevented results from an omission, the failure to vaccinate.

The action/omission distinction is subtle, and it might seem irrelevant here: Surely, the relevant question to ask, in choosing to vaccinate, is whether the risk of the vaccine (typically very, very low) is higher or lower than the risk of the disease (typically much higher). It's not surprising that people with different beliefs about the risks might make decisions differently and, in fact, at least one study has found that parents who objected to vaccinating their children (in this case, with the DPT vaccine) were more likely than others to think that vaccinating was more dangerous than not vaccinating.

But people also vary in the extent to which they exhibit omission bias, and this bias may influence parents' decisions above and beyond the straight calculation of relative risk.

To illustrate, consider a vignette used in the same study. Participants were asked to imagine the following vaccination decision: There's been a flu epidemic in your state, and the kind of flu in question can be fatal to children under 3. In fact, out of 10,000 children under 3 who are not vaccinated, 10 will die from the flu. A vaccine is available, and while it completely eliminates the chance of contracting the flu, it leads to fatal side effects in 5 out of 10,000 children under 3. Would you vaccinate your child under 3?

Based on a straight calculation of risk, parents should have said they would vaccinate: A risk of 5 in 10,000 is lower than a risk of 10 in 10,000. But that's not what the researchers found. Parents who objected to the DPT vaccine for their children showed a stronger omission bias than those who did not object to the vaccine, in the sense that the mean "tolerable risk" was higher for this group: They would only vaccinate when the risk from the hypothetical flu vaccine corresponded to an average of 2.4 deaths per 10,000 (versus 10 per 10,000 deaths from the flu), whereas those who had vaccinated or intended to vaccinate their kids with the DPT vaccine accepted a mean tolerable risk corresponding to 5.4 deaths per 10,000 (versus 10 per 10,000 deaths from the flu). Both groups, on average, needed a higher risk from the disease than from the vaccine to favor vaccination, but the gap was much greater for nonvaccinators.

Why might this be?

One factor could be some people's preference for what they perceive to be "natural." For instance, those parents who objected to the DPT vaccine were more likely than vaccinating parents to endorse the claim, "I do not want to interfere with nature by giving the DPT vaccine." Another study found that university employees who didn't take advantage of a free flu vaccine were more likely than those who did to exhibit a "naturalness bias," as reflected in their preference for a medication extracted from an herb rather than a chemically identical one that was synthesized in a laboratory.

Another factor seems to be people's feelings of causal responsibility for actions versus omissions. For example, one study that had participants decide whether to opt for a hypothetical flu vaccine for their child found that those who exhibited omission bias explained that they would feel more responsible for a death caused by their decision to vaccinate than for a death caused by the decision not to vaccinate.

A final and related factor may be anticipated regret. If some parents feel they would be more causally responsible for the negative consequences of a decision to vaccinate (as opposed to a decision to abstain), they may also anticipate that they would experience greater regret were the vaccine to lead to negative outcomes. And that, in turn, could make them hesitant to pursue a course with this risk: The fear of anticipated regret could push them away from vaccination.

In fact, other studies suggest that it is anticipated regret *per se*—and not omission bias—that drives attitudes toward vaccination, and that greater anticipated regret can go either way. That is, some parents worry more about the regret they would feel if vaccination led to a negative outcome, but others worry more about the regret they would feel if their *failure to vaccinate* led to a negative outcome.

Studying these issues is difficult, in part, because what we construe as an "act" versus an "omission" could itself depend to some extent on the personal and social context of our decisions.

In an environment in which vaccination is the norm—and in which *withholding* vaccination requires applying for a rare exemption—that application for exemption could be construed as the act and not the omission. There's also evidence that how a behavior is construed—as *doing* harm versus merely *allowing* harm—depends on whether the behavior itself is regarded as morally good (doing one's duty for herd immunity, say) versus morally bad (free-riding on others' immunization, or putting one's child at unnecessary risk).

There's more than one lesson to draw from this body of research, but let me end with some bad news and some good news.

The bad news is that educating people about the relative risks of vaccination versus the diseases they prevent is almost certainly insufficient to change attitudes toward vaccination. There's a lot more in play here, including a host of psychological biases that don't always lead to optimal decision-making.

The good news is that relatively simple measures—such as communicating pro-vaccination community norms and focusing on exemptions from vaccination (rather than vaccination itself) as the deliberative *act* could potentially have some positive effects.

Critical Thinking

1. Recent research finds no significant correlation between childhood vaccinations and increases in conditions such as autism. Explain why there appears to be public and parental fear of vaccinating children?

2. Design an education program that might address parental fear of childhood vaccinations.

3. Examine the research on childhood vaccinations worldwide and evaluate the consequences for childhood diseases. How does this global data add to the debate in America?

Internet References

Autism Science Foundation
   http://www.autismsciencefoundation.org/autismandvaccines.html
Centers for Disease Control and Prevention, CDC
   http://www.cdc.gov/vaccinesafety/concerns/autism/
Mayo Clinic
   http://www.mayoclinic.org/healthy-lifestyle/infant-and-toddler-health/in-depth/vaccines/art-20048334
National Center for Biotechnology Information, NCBI, NIH
   http://www.ncbi.nlm.nih.gov/pmc/articles/PMC3096324/
   http://www.ncbi.nlm.nih.gov/pubmed/23444591
Princeton University Study
   http://www.princeton.edu/main/news/archive/S43/10/03O18/index.xml?section=topstories

Lombrozo, Tania. "Psychological Biases Play A Part In Vaccination Decisions," *NPR.com*, February 2015. Copyright © 2015 by Tania Lombrozo. Reprinted by permission.

Prepared by: Chris J. Boyatzis, *Bucknell University*
Ellen N. Junn, *California State University, Dominguez Hills*

Article

New Ways to Protect Kids

A conference co-sponsored by APA and the American Bar Association calls for paradigm shifts in preventing and treating child abuse.

Rebecca A. Clay

Learning Outcomes

After reading this article, you will be able to:

- Describe findings on the pervasiveness of child maltreatment.

- Explain why parenting interventions and training programs (such as the Triple P) may help build children's resilience.

P sychologist James Garbarino, PhD, once interviewed a murderer so violent, six correctional officers were needed to control him when he appeared in court. The offender had killed two inmates while in prison. But when Garbarino asked the man to reveal something about himself that would surprise others, he confessed that he cried himself to sleep every night.

"I always try to impress upon a jury that they're not looking at a big, scary man, but really the untreated, traumatized child who inhabits that big, scary man," said Garbarino, a psychology professor at Loyola University Chicago.

Garbarino's story was one of many that challenged conventional thinking about violence at a conference cosponsored by APA and the American Bar Association in May. The event, with the theme "Confronting Family and Community Violence: The Intersection of Law and Psychology," brought psychologists, attorneys, judges and others together to discuss new ways to prevent child abuse, respond to troubled children and prevent family violence in the first place.

Understanding Child Maltreatment

Family violence is rampant in our society, said George W. Holden, PhD, a psychology professor at Southern Methodist University in Dallas.

An estimated 676,000 children each year suffer from child maltreatment, which typically takes the form of physical, psychological or sexual abuse or neglect. But those confirmed cases are "a woeful underestimate of the problem," said Holden.

For one, many cases are still not reported. And that number doesn't include the 10 percent of children who research suggests are exposed to intimate partner violence at home. For a quarter to half of them, such an environment can cause signs of post-traumatic stress disorder. Other reactions include attachment problems and disruptions in eating and sleeping routines in toddlers and anxiety, depression and aggression among older children, Holden said.

What's more, many children face multiple challenges simultaneously. "One of the major new insights in the last 15 years is the concept of polyvictimization—that is, children being multiply victimized," Holden said, adding that the Adverse Childhood Experiences (ACE) study of 17,000 adults was the first major research to reveal the extent of polyvictimization. Almost two-thirds of participants reported at least one adverse experience, while more than one in five had three or more such experiences. The more adverse experiences a child has, the more problems those experiences are likely to cause, Holden said.

The problems may also continue on into adulthood. The ACE study and other research have found that adverse child experiences are linked to diabetes, cardiovascular disease and even cancer in adulthood, Holden said. Part of the reason may be that maltreatment in the first three years of life—and the resulting release of stress hormones—can affect brain development and compromise the immune system, research has found. Meanwhile, children's social and emotional health can suffer from an insecure attachment style and negative ideas about themselves and others that can affect later relationships.

The good news: Many children are resilient. In fact, studies find that about one-third of children exposed to violence experience no negative consequences. "The key finding is that resiliency is not a personality trait but rather is better characterized as a mindset," Holden said, explaining that resilient children view their vulnerabilities as areas for development instead of personality flaws. What's needed, he said, are interventions to help all children develop this kind of mindset.

Promoting Positive Parenting

Finding ways to promote resiliency among parents is also key, said Mary E. Haskett, PhD, a psychology professor at North Carolina State University.

Most child maltreatment prevention efforts focus on families who are already struggling with parenting challenges. And child abuse prevention messages have typically emphasized that abusive parents are toxic to kids and defective in some way. "The message has been that there are these people out there, essentially with horns, called abusive parents," Haskett said. "They are different from the rest of us."

But that isn't accurate or helpful to families, said Haskett. Instead, the field should widen prevention efforts to target all families, she said.

"If everyone in a community is being supported around challenges related to parenting because we basically all experience those challenges, there's less stigma around asking for help," she said. "We're not saying, 'I'm a bad parent,' we're saying, 'I need some help with a current challenge I'm experiencing.'"

Triple P, the Positive Parenting Program, is one such program. The evidence-based program offers five levels of intervention, starting with universal prevention messages delivered via the media that emphasize that parenting can be challenging for everyone. One message, for example, emphasizes that potty training is something any parent might struggle with. Subsequent levels of intervention offer support to parents having minor to moderate struggles, with the most intensive intervention reserved for high-risk parents. "Parents get what they need and only what they need," said Haskett.

Results from the ACE study—which found positive effects for children with nurturing parents as well as negative outcomes for those with a history of maltreatment—support this shift to a public health approach to preventing child maltreatment, said Haskett.

The shift is already happening, thanks to the health implications revealed by the ACE study. The Public Health Leadership Initiative at the U.S. Centers for Disease Control and Prevention (CDC), for instance, encourages public health and other agencies to take responsibility for preventing child maltreatment instead of expecting child welfare agencies to take on the sole responsibility.

"The CDC said, 'We're not going to focus on child abuse prevention per se,'" said Haskett. "Instead, they said, 'We're going to talk about supporting safe, stable, nurturing relationships.'" While the shift is subtle, she says, it communicates a more positive message of universal prevention.

Protecting Versus Controlling Children

It's especially important to change the way parents and society at large discipline children, said Robert D. Macy, PhD, founder and president of the International Trauma Center in Boston and a founding member of the National Child Traumatic Stress Network. Children, Macy argued, are being punished for normal development and their experience of trauma.

"This requires a revolution—from society controlling the child to society protecting the child," he said.

For hundreds of years, society called for strong discipline of children and even termination of parental rights for parents not using corporal punishment to control their children's behavior. The same philosophy of trying to control children looms today. These days, such efforts tend to target racial and ethnic minority youth, said Macy, pointing to the disproportionate minority racial and ethnic representation in the juvenile justice system.

"Kids are being punished for their development," said Macy.

Because of the way the brain develops, he said, adolescents have trouble controlling their impulsivity, making good decisions and anticipating consequences. APA recognized these and other developmental factors in an amicus brief in the 2012 Supreme Court case prohibiting life without parole for juvenile homicide offenders. The brief explained that juveniles have diminished culpability because of their developmental differences from adults.

Even more important is addressing the trauma that underlies many young people's violent acts, said Macy. The research is clear that trauma has a negative influence on brain development, said Macy. And new epigenetic evidence suggests that traumatic environments can actually change genes across generations.

While the traditional American approach has blamed problems on individuals' lack of motivation or discipline, Macy said that approach hasn't worked. Instead, he called for trauma-informed care. Rather than trying to suppress violence in young people who have been maltreated, the field should treat their trauma, he said.

"Traumatic childhood events are documented in the histories in as much as 98.6 percent of juvenile delinquents," Macy said. "We have to stop asking, 'What's wrong with you?' and ask this question: 'What happened to you?'"

Rejecting Labels

It's also important to have a trauma-informed view of adult offenders, many of whom have suffered maltreatment as children, said Garbarino.

"What's the most effective way to produce a sociopath?" he asked. "It's some combination of traumatizing them in childhood, then putting them in a socially toxic environment."

The clinical and law enforcement worlds often fail to recognize trauma's role in violence, Garbarino said. Instead, the tendency is to label the consequences of childhood maltreatment—acting out, being aggressive and violating the rights of others—as conduct disorder, antisocial personality disorder or sociopathy. "The more you accept these diagnostic labels, particularly for children, the more you're on the road to depersonalization and dehumanization of the other," he said. But the very traits caused by abuse, including hypersensitivity to threats and the sense of aggression as a legitimate response to threats, make it easier to see these individuals as perpetrators rather than victims.

"Dissociative symptoms make it hard for a person to be seen as a trauma victim, especially if they've committed a violent act, because they're remorseless and emotionally numb," said Garbarino. "The more you can make people see the traumatized child within, the more you can open the floodgates of compassion."

Critical Thinking

1. Why would parenting training programs help reduce child abuse and maltreatment? What could be some obstacles to implementing such training programs in communities, such as parent beliefs or attitudes or socioeconomic status?

2. An interesting fact about child development is that while it is true that the vast majority of juvenile delinquents had traumatic childhoods, it is not the case that all children who have traumatic childhoods grow up to be juvenile delinquents or criminals. Why is that? How does parenting or other community influences affect how kids turn out?

Internet References

American Academy of Pediatrics
http://www2.aap.org/sections/childabuseneglect/
Centers for Disease Control and Prevention, CDC.gov
http://www.cdc.gov/violenceprevention/childmaltreatment/
ChildWelfare.gov
https://www.childwelfare.gov/pubpdfs/whatiscan.pdf
https://www.childwelfare.gov/topics/can/?hasBeenRedirected=1
Health and Human Services.gov, Administration for Children and Families
http://www.acf.hhs.gov/programs/cb/focus-areas/child-abuse-neglect
National Institute of Health.gov
http://www.nlm.nih.gov/medlineplus/childabuse.html
WebMD.com
http://www.webmd.com/parenting/tc/child-maltreatment-topic-overview

Clay, Rebecca A.. "New Ways to Protect Kids," *Monitor on Psychology,* July/August 2014. Copyright © 2014 by American Psychological Association. Reprinted by permission.

Article   Prepared by: Ellen N. Junn, *California State University, Dominguez Hills*

The Case Against Spanking
Physical Discipline Is Slowly Declining as Some Studies Reveal Lasting Harms for Children

BRENDAN L. SMITH

Learning Outcomes

After reading this article, you will be able to:

- Consider the environment that children grow up in and how that environment can lead to more or less spanking.

- Develop a program that could be used in working with parents to educate them on alternative techniques of working with their children.

- Understand how cultural relativism influences the prevalence of spanking in the family scene.

A growing body of research has shown that spanking and other forms of physical discipline can pose serious risks to children, but many parents aren't hearing the message. "It's a very controversial area even though the research is extremely telling and very clear and consistent about the negative effects on children," says Sandra Graham-Bermann, PhD, a psychology professor and principal investigator for the Child Violence and Trauma Laboratory at the University of Michigan. "People get frustrated and hit their kids. Maybe they don't see there are other options."

Many studies have shown that physical punishment—including spanking, hitting and other means of causing pain—can lead to increased aggression, antisocial behavior, physical injury and mental health problems for children. Americans' acceptance of physical punishment has declined since the 1960s, yet surveys show that two-thirds of Americans still approve of parents spanking their kids.

But spanking doesn't work, says Alan Kazdin, PhD, a Yale University psychology professor and director of the Yale Parenting Center and Child Conduct Clinic. "You cannot punish

out these behaviors that you do not want," says Kazdin, who served as APA president in 2008. "There is no need for corporal punishment based on the research. We are not giving up an effective technique. We are saying this is a horrible thing that does not work."

Evidence of Harm

On the international front, physical discipline is increasingly being viewed as a violation of children's human rights. The United Nations Committee on the Rights of the Child issued a directive in 2006 calling physical punishment "legalized violence against children" that should be eliminated in all settings through "legislative, administrative, social and educational measures." The treaty that established the committee has been supported by 192 countries, with only the United States and Somalia failing to ratify it.

Around the world, 30 countries have banned physical punishment of children in all settings, including the home. The legal bans typically have been used as public education tools, rather than attempts to criminalize behavior by parents who spank their children, says Elizabeth Gershoff, PhD, a leading researcher on physical punishment at the University of Texas at Austin.

"Physical punishment doesn't work to get kids to comply, so parents think they have to keep escalating it. That is why it is so dangerous," she says.

After reviewing decades of research, Gershoff wrote the Report on Physical Punishment in the United States: *What Research Tells Us About Its Effects on Children*, published in 2008 in conjunction with Phoenix Children's Hospital. The report recommends that parents and caregivers make every effort to avoid physical punishment and calls for the banning of physical discipline in all U.S. schools. The report has been endorsed by dozens of organizations, including the American Academy of Pediatrics, American Medical Association and Psychologists for Social Responsibility.

After three years of work on the APA Task Force on Physical Punishment of Children, Gershoff and Graham-Bermann wrote a report in 2008 summarizing the task force's recommendations. That report recommends that "parents and caregivers reduce and potentially eliminate their use of any physical punishment as a disciplinary method." The report calls on psychologists and other professionals to "indicate to parents that physical punishment is not an appropriate, or even a consistently effective, method of discipline."

"We have the opportunity here to take a strong stand in favor of protecting children," says Graham-Bermann, who chaired the task force.

APA's Committee on Children, Youth and Families (CYF) and the Board for the Advancement of Psychology in the Public Interest unanimously approved a proposed resolution last year based on the task force recommendations. It states that APA supports "parents' use of non-physical methods of disciplining children" and opposes "the use of severe or injurious physical punishment of any child." APA also should support additional research and a public education campaign on "the effectiveness and outcomes associated with corporal punishment and non-physical methods of discipline," the proposed resolution states. After obtaining feedback from other APA boards and committees in the spring of 2012, APA's Council of Representatives will consider adopting the resolution as APA policy.

Preston Britner, PhD, a child developmental psychologist and professor at the University of Connecticut, helped draft the proposed resolution as co-chair of CYF. "It addresses the concerns about physical punishment and a growing body of research on alternatives to physical punishment, along with the idea that psychology and psychologists have much to contribute to the development of those alternative strategies," he says.

More than three decades have passed since APA approved a resolution in 1975 opposing corporal punishment in schools and other institutions, but it didn't address physical discipline in the home. That resolution stated that corporal punishment can "instill hostility, rage and a sense of powerlessness without reducing the undesirable behavior."

Research Findings

Physical punishment can work momentarily to stop problematic behavior because children are afraid of being hit, but it doesn't work in the long term and can make children more aggressive, Graham-Bermann says.

A study published last year in *Child Abuse and Neglect* revealed an intergenerational cycle of violence in homes where physical punishment was used. Researchers interviewed parents and children aged 3 to 7 from more than 100 families. Children who were physically punished were more likely to endorse hitting as a means of resolving their conflicts with peers and siblings. Parents who had experienced frequent physical punishment during their childhood were more likely to believe it was acceptable, and they frequently spanked their children. Their children, in turn, often believed spanking was an appropriate disciplinary method.

The negative effects of physical punishment may not become apparent for some time, Gershoff says. "A child doesn't get spanked and then run out and rob a store," she says. "There are indirect changes in how the child thinks about things and feels about things."

As in many areas of science, some researchers disagree about the validity of the studies on physical punishment. Robert Larzelere, PhD, an Oklahoma State University professor who studies parental discipline, was a member of the APA task force who issued his own minority report because he disagreed with the scientific basis of the task force recommendations. While he agrees that parents should reduce their use of physical punishment, he says most of the cited studies are correlational and don't show a causal link between physical punishment and long-term negative effects for children.

"The studies do not discriminate well between non-abusive and overly severe types of corporal punishment," Larzelere says. "You get worse outcomes from corporal punishment than from alternative disciplinary techniques only when it is used more severely or as the primary discipline tactic."

In a meta-analysis of 26 studies, Larzelere and a colleague found that an approach they described as "conditional spanking" led to greater reductions in child defiance or anti-social behavior than 10 of 13 alternative discipline techniques, including reasoning, removal of privileges and time out (*Clinical Child and Family Psychology Review*, 2005). Larzelere defines conditional spanking as a disciplinary technique for 2- to 6-year-old children in which parents use two open-handed swats on the buttocks only after the child has defied milder discipline such as time out.

Gershoff says all of the studies on physical punishment have some shortcomings. "Unfortunately, all research on parent discipline is going to be correlational because we can't randomly assign kids to parents for an experiment. But I don't think we have to disregard all research that has been done," she says. "I can just about count on one hand the studies that have found anything positive about physical punishment and hundreds that have been negative."

about the future, they reckoned that child-care costs would eat up most of his after-tax salary, so he decided to extend his leave indefinitely. When Somerfeld informed the school that he would not be returning, at least not anytime soon, his principal went on the PA system and announced, "Mr. Somerfeld will be leaving us next year to become a modern man!"

Critical Thinking

1. Why might "daddy time" after a child's birth promote fathers' greater involvement with childcare?

2. What are some obstacles, from personal to professional to cultural, that could impede fathers' willingness to take advantage of paternity leave?

3. Regardless of your gender, if you have children now or in the future, what do you envision regarding "daddy time" in your family? How might it influence you personally?

Create Central

www.mhhe.com/createcentral

Internet References

Baby Center.com
http://www.babycenter.com/0_paternity-leave-what-are-the-options-for-dads_8258.bc

Human Impact Partners
http://workfamilyca.org/resources/HIPFactSheet_2011.pdf

The Future of Children.org
http://futureofchildren.org/publications/journals/article/index.xml?journalid=44&articleid=191&sectionid=1254

http://futureofchildren.org/publications/journals/article/index.xml?journalid=76&articleid=557&sectionid=3855

Mundy, Liza, "Daddy Track: The Case for Paternity Leave," The Atlantic, December 22, 2013. © 2013 The Atlantic Media Co., as first published in The Atlantic Magazine. All rights reserved. Distributed by Tribune Content Agency, LLC

Article   Prepared by: Chris J. Boyatzis, *Bucknell University*

Why Parents Need to Let Their Children Fail

A new study explores what happens to students who aren't allowed to suffer through setbacks.

JESSICA LAHEY

Learning Outcomes

After reading this article, you will be able to:

- Discuss the implications of parental overprotectiveness and how the child is affected by it.

- Understand why it is so important for children to receive autonomy in their learning experience.

Thirteen years ago, when I was a relatively new teacher, stumbling around my classroom on wobbly legs, I had to call a student's mother to inform her that I would be initiating disciplinary proceedings against her daughter for plagiarism, and that furthermore, her daughter would receive a zero for the plagiarized paper.

"You can't do that. She didn't do anything wrong," the mother informed me, enraged.

"But she did. I was able to find entire paragraphs lifted off of web sites," I stammered.

"No, I mean *she* didn't do it. I did. *I* wrote her paper."

I don't remember what I said in response, but I'm fairly confident I had to take a moment to digest what I had just heard. And what would I do, anyway? Suspend the mother? Keep her in for lunch detention and make her write "I will not write my daughter's papers using articles plagiarized from the Internet" one hundred times on the board? In all fairness, the mother submitted a defense: her daughter had been stressed out, and she did not want her to get sick or overwhelmed.

In the end, my student received a zero and I made sure she re-wrote the paper. Herself. Sure, I didn't have the authority to discipline the student's mother, but I have done so many times in my dreams.

While I am not sure what the mother gained from the experience, the daughter gained an understanding of consequences, and I gained a war story. I don't even bother with the old reliables anymore: the mother who "helps" a bit too much with the child's math homework, the father who builds the student's science project. Please. Don't waste my time.

The stories teachers exchange these days reveal a whole new level of overprotectiveness: parents who raise their children in a state of helplessness and powerlessness, children destined to an anxious adulthood, lacking the emotional resources they will need to cope with inevitable setback and failure.

I believed my accumulated compendium of teacher war stories were pretty good—until I read a study out of Queensland University of Technology, by Judith Locke, et al., a self-described "examination by parenting professionals of the concept of overparenting."

Overparenting is characterized in the study as parents' "misguided attempt to improve their child's current and future personal and academic success." In an attempt to understand such behaviors, the authors surveyed psychologists, guidance counselors, and teachers. The authors asked these professionals if they had witnessed examples of overparenting, and left space for descriptions of said examples. While the relatively small sample size and questionable method of subjective self-reporting cast a shadow on the study's statistical significance, the examples cited in the report provide enough ammunition for a year of dinner parties.

Some of the examples are the usual fare: a child isn't allowed to go to camp or learn to drive, a parent cuts up a 10-year-old's food or brings separate plates to parties for a 16-year-old because he's a picky eater. Yawn. These barely rank a "Tsk, tsk" among my colleagues. And while I pity those kids, I'm not that worried. They will go out on their own someday and recover from their overprotective childhoods.

What worry me most are the examples of overparenting that have the potential to ruin a child's confidence and undermine an education in independence. According to the authors, parents guilty of this kind of overparenting "take their child's perception as truth, regardless of the facts," and are "quick to believe their child over the adult and deny the possibility that their child was at fault or would even do something of that nature."

This is what we teachers see most often: what the authors term "high responsiveness and low demandingness" parents. These parents are highly responsive to the perceived needs and issues of their children, and don't give their children the chance to solve their own problems. These parents "rush to school at the whim of a phone call from their child to deliver items such as forgotten lunches, forgotten assignments, forgotten uniforms" and "demand better grades on the final semester reports or threaten withdrawal from school." One study participant described the problem this way:

> I have worked with quite a number of parents who are so overprotective of their children that the children do not learn to take responsibility (and the natural consequences) of their actions. The children may develop a sense of entitlement and the parents then find it difficult to work with the school in a trusting, cooperative and solution focused manner, which would benefit both child and school.

These are the parents who worry me the most—parents who won't let their child learn. You see, teachers don't just teach reading, writing, and arithmetic. We teach responsibility, organization, manners, restraint, and foresight. These skills may not get assessed on standardized testing, but as children plot their journey into adulthood, they are, by far, the most important life skills I teach.

I'm not suggesting that parents place blind trust in their children's teachers; I would never do such a thing myself. But children make mistakes, and when they do, it's vital that parents remember that the educational benefits of consequences

are a gift, not a dereliction of duty. Year after year, my "best" students—the ones who are happiest and successful in their lives—are the students who were allowed to fail, held responsible for missteps, and challenged to be the best people they could be in the face of their mistakes.

I'm done fantasizing about ways to make that mom from 13 years ago see the light. That ship has sailed, and I did the best I could for her daughter. Every year, I reassure some parent, "This setback will be the best thing that ever happened to your child," and I've long since accepted that most parents won't believe me. That's fine. I'm patient. The lessons I teach in middle school don't typically pay off for years, and I don't expect thank-you cards.

I have learned to enjoy and find satisfaction in these day-to-day lessons and in the time I get to spend with children in need of an education. But I fantasize about the day I will be trusted to teach my students how to roll with the punches, find their way through the gauntlet of adolescence, and stand firm in the face of the challenges—challenges that have the power to transform today's children into resourceful, competent, and confident adults.

Critical Thinking

1. As a teacher, how would you work with a child whose parents were overly intrusive on his or her learning experience?

2. What are the benefits of allowing children to learn on their own? Is there benefit of having parental involvement?

Create Central

www.mhhe.com/createcentral

Internet References

Frank Porter Graham Child Development Institute
   http://fpg.unc.edu/emphasis-area/physical-and-social-health
Mental Help.net
   http://www.mentalhelp.net/poc/view_doc.php?id=1326&type=book &cn=28
The Effects of Intrusive Parenting: The Long Term Effects of Denying Children Their Independence
   http://voices.yahoo.com/the-effects-intrusive-parenting-6659550.html

Lahey, Jessica, "Why Parents Need to Let Their Children Fail," January 29, 2013. © 2013 The Atlantic Media Co., as first published in The Atlantic Magazine. All rights reserved. Distributed by Tribune Content Agency, LLC

Unit 4

UNIT

Prepared by: Chris J. Boyatzis, *Bucknell University*
Ellen N. Junn, *California State University, Dominguez Hills*

Cultural and Societal Influences

Social scientists and developmental psychologists have come to realize that children are influenced by a multitude of complex social and larger societal forces. In this unit we present articles to illuminate how children and adolescents are influenced by broad factors such as economics, culture, politics, the media, and technology. These influences also affect the family, which is a major context of child development, and many children are now faced with more complex family challenges than ever.

In addition, understanding more about exceptional or atypical children gives the reader a more comprehensive account of child development. Some children must cope with special psychological, emotional, and cognitive challenges, such as ADHD or autism, while other children are exposed to environmental insults such as violence and sexualization. These children are often mistreated and misunderstood and have special challenges to overcome.

In this final unit, we provide a wide variety of articles that hopefully will shed light on the new research, implications, and practical interventions that parents, educators and others might utilize to help all children reach their maximum potential in an ever increasingly complex world.

Article   Prepared by: Chris J. Boyatzis, *Bucknell University*

The Touch-Screen Generation

Young children—even toddlers—are spending more and more time with digital technology. What will it mean for their development?

HANNA ROSIN

Learning Outcomes

After reading this article, you will be able to:

- Judge if the article presents compelling evidence of a positive or negative effect on children of using touch-screen technology.

- Describe different kinds of restrictions that parents place on their children's screen time.

- Understand some of the pros and cons in parents' thinking about technology in their children's lives.

On a chilly day last spring, a few dozen developers of children's apps for phones and tablets gathered at an old beach resort in Monterey, California, to show off their games. One developer, a self-described "visionary for puzzles" who looked like a skateboarder-recently-turned-dad, displayed a jacked-up, interactive game called Puzzingo, intended for toddlers and inspired by his own son's desire to build and smash. Two 30-something women were eagerly seeking feedback for an app called Knock Knock Family, aimed at 1- to 4 year-olds. "We want to make sure it's easy enough for babies to understand," one explained.

The gathering was organized by Warren Buckleitner, a long-time reviewer of interactive children's media who likes to bring together developers, researchers, and interest groups—and often plenty of kids, some still in diapers. It went by the Harry Potter–ish name Dust or Magic and was held in a drafty old stone-and-wood hall barely a mile from the sea, the kind of place where Bathilda Bagshot might retire after packing up her wand. Buckleitner spent the breaks testing whether his own

remote-control helicopter could reach the hall's second story, while various children who had come with their parents looked up in awe and delight. But mostly they looked down, at the iPads and other tablets displayed around the hall like so many open boxes of candy. I walked around and talked with developers, and several paraphrased a famous saying of Maria Montessori's, a quote imported to ennoble a touch-screen age when very young kids, who once could be counted on only to chew on a square of aluminum, are now engaging with it in increasingly sophisticated ways: "The hands are the instruments of man's intelligence."

What, really, would Maria Montessori have made of this scene? The 30 or so children here were not down at the shore poking their fingers in the sand or running them along mossy stones or digging for hermit crabs. Instead they were all inside, alone or in groups of two or three, their faces a few inches from a screen, their hands doing things Montessori surely did not imagine. A couple of 3-year-old girls were leaning against a pair of French doors, reading an interactive story called *Ten Giggly Gorillas* and fighting over which ape to tickle next. A boy in a nearby corner had turned his fingertip into a red marker to draw an ugly picture of his older brother. On an old oak table at the front of the room, a giant stuffed Angry Bird beckoned the children to come and test out tablets loaded with dozens of new apps. Some of the chairs had pillows strapped to them, since an 18-month-old might not otherwise be able to reach the table, though she'd know how to swipe once she did.

Not that long ago, there was only the television, which theoretically could be kept in the parents' bedroom or locked behind a cabinet. Now there are smartphones and iPads, which wash up in the domestic clutter alongside keys and gum and stray hair ties. "Mom, everyone has technology but me!" my

4-year-old son sometimes wails. And why shouldn't he feel entitled? In the same span of time it took him to learn how to say that sentence, thousands of kids' apps have been developed—the majority aimed at preschoolers like him. To us (his parents, I mean), American childhood has undergone a somewhat alarming transformation in a very short time. But to him, it has always been possible to do so many things with the swipe of a finger, to have hundreds of games packed into a gadget the same size as *Goodnight Moon.*

In 2011, the American Academy of Pediatrics updated its policy on very young children and media. In 1999, the group had discouraged television viewing for children younger than 2, citing research on brain development that showed this age group's critical need for "direct interactions with parents and other significant care givers." The updated report began by acknowledging that things had changed significantly since then. In 2006, 90 percent of parents said that their children younger than 2 consumed some form of electronic media. Nonetheless, the group took largely the same approach it did in 1999, uniformly discouraging passive media use, on any type of screen, for these kids. (For older children, the academy noted, "high-quality programs" could have "educational benefits.") The 2011 report mentioned "smart cell phone" and "new screen" technologies, but did not address interactive apps. Nor did it broach the possibility that has likely occurred to those 90 percent of American parents, queasy though they might be: that some good might come from those little swiping fingers.

I had come to the developers' conference partly because I hoped that this particular set of parents, enthusiastic as they were about interactive media, might help me out of this conundrum, that they might offer some guiding principle for American parents who are clearly never going to meet the academy's ideals, and at some level do not want to. Perhaps this group would be able to articulate some benefits of the new technology that the more cautious pediatricians weren't ready to address. I nurtured this hope until about lunchtime, when the developers gathering in the dining hall ceased being visionaries and reverted to being ordinary parents, trying to settle their toddlers in high chairs and get them to eat something besides bread.

I fell into conversation with a woman who had helped develop Montessori Letter Sounds, an app that teaches preschoolers the Montessori methods of spelling.

She was a former Montessori teacher and a mother of four. I myself have three children who are all fans of the touch screen. What games did her kids like to play?, I asked, hoping for suggestions I could take home.

"They don't play all that much."

Really? Why not?

"Because I don't allow it. We have a rule of no screen time during the week," unless it's clearly educational.

No screen time? None at all? That seems at the outer edge of restrictive, even by the standards of my overcontrolling parenting set.

"On the weekends, they can play. I give them a limit of half an hour and then stop. Enough. It can be too addictive, too stimulating for the brain."

Her answer so surprised me that I decided to ask some of the other developers who were also parents what their domestic ground rules for screen time were. One said only on airplanes and long car rides. Another said Wednesdays and weekends, for half an hour. The most permissive said half an hour a day, which was about my rule at home. At one point I sat with one of the biggest developers of e-book apps for kids, and his family. The toddler was starting to fuss in her high chair, so the mom did what many of us have done at that moment—stuck an iPad in front of her and played a short movie so everyone else could enjoy their lunch. When she saw me watching, she gave me the universal tense look of mothers who feel they are being judged. "At home," she assured me, "I only let her watch movies in Spanish."

By their pinched reactions, these parents illuminated for me the neurosis of our age: as technology becomes ubiquitous in our lives, American parents are becoming more, not less, wary of what it might be doing to their children. Technological competence and sophistication have not, for parents, translated into comfort and ease. They have merely created yet another sphere that parents feel they have to navigate in exactly the right way. On the one hand, parents want their children to swim expertly in the digital stream that they will have to navigate all their lives; on the other hand, they fear that too much digital media, too early, will sink them. Parents end up treating tablets like precision surgical instruments, gadgets that might perform miracles for their child's IQ and help him win some nifty robotics competition—but only if they are used just so. Otherwise, their child could end up one of those sad, pale creatures who can't make eye contact and has an avatar for a girlfriend.

Norman Rockwell never painted *Boy Swiping Finger on Screen,* and our own vision of a perfect childhood has never adjusted to accommodate that now-common tableau. Add to that our modern fear that every parenting decision may have lasting consequences—that every minute of enrichment lost or mindless entertainment indulged will add up to some permanent handicap in the future—and you have deep guilt and confusion. To date, no body of research has definitively proved that the iPad will make your preschooler smarter or teach her to speak Chinese, or alternatively that it will rust her neural circuitry—the device has been out for only three years, not much more than the time it takes some academics to find funding and gather research subjects. So what's a parent to do?

In 2001, the education and technology writer Marc Prensky popularized the term *digital natives* to describe the first generations of children growing up fluent in the language of computers, video games, and other technologies. (The rest of us are *digital immigrants,* struggling to understand.) This term took on a whole new significance in April 2010, when the iPad was released. iPhones had already been tempting young children, but the screens were a little small for pudgy toddler hands to navigate with ease and accuracy. Plus, parents tended to be more possessive of their phones, hiding them in pockets or purses. The iPad was big and bright, and a case could be made that it belonged to the family. Researchers who study children's media immediately recognized it as a game changer.

Previously, young children had to be shown by their parents how to use a mouse or a remote, and the connection between what they were doing with their hand and what was happening on the screen took some time to grasp. But with the iPad, the connection is obvious, even to toddlers. Touch technology follows the same logic as shaking a rattle or knocking down a pile of blocks: the child swipes, and something immediately happens. A "rattle on steroids," is what Buckleitner calls it. "All of a sudden a finger could move a bus or smush an insect or turn into a big wet gloopy paintbrush." To a toddler, this is less magic than intuition. At a very young age, children become capable of what the psychologist Jerome Bruner called "enactive representation"; they classify objects in the world not by using words or symbols but by making gestures—say, holding an imaginary cup to their lips to signify that they want a drink. Their hands are a natural extension of their thoughts.

Norman Rockwell never painted Boy Swiping Finger on Screen, and our own vision of a perfect childhood has never adjusted to fit that now-common tableau.

I have two older children who fit the early idea of a digital native—they learned how to use a mouse or a keyboard with some help from their parents and were well into school before they felt comfortable with a device in their lap. (Now, of course, at ages 9 and 12, they can create a Web site in the time it takes me to slice an onion.) My youngest child is a whole different story. He was not yet 2 when the iPad was released. As soon as he got his hands on it, he located the Talking Baby Hippo app that one of my older children had downloaded. The little purple hippo repeats whatever you say in his own squeaky voice, and responds to other cues. My son said his name ("Giddy!"); Baby Hippo repeated it back. Gideon poked Baby Hippo; Baby Hippo laughed. Over and over, it was funny every time. Pretty soon he discovered other apps. Old MacDonald, by Duck Duck Moose, was a favorite. At first he would get frustrated trying

to zoom between screens, or not knowing what to do when a message popped up. But after about two weeks, he figured all that out. I must admit, it was eerie to see a child still in diapers so competent and intent, as if he were forecasting his own adulthood. Technically I was the owner of the iPad, but in some ontological way it felt much more his than mine.

Without seeming to think much about it or resolve how they felt, parents began giving their devices over to their children to mollify, pacify, or otherwise entertain them. By 2010, two-thirds of children ages 4 to 7 had used an iPhone, according to the Joan Ganz Cooney Center, which studies children's media. The vast majority of those phones had been lent by a family member; the center's researchers labeled this the "pass-back effect," a name that captures well the reluctant zone between denying and giving.

The market immediately picked up on the pass-back effect, and the opportunities it presented. In 2008, when Apple opened up its App Store, the games started arriving at the rate of dozens a day, thousands a year. For the first 23 years of his career, Buckleitner had tried to be comprehensive and cover every children's game in his publication, *Children's Technology Review.* Now, by Buckleitner's loose count, more than 40,000 kids' games are available on iTunes, plus thousands more on Google Play. In the iTunes "Education" category, the majority of the top-selling apps target preschool or elementary-age children. By age 3, Gideon would go to preschool and tune in to what was cool in toddler world, then come home, locate the iPad, drop it in my lap, and ask for certain games by their approximate description: "Tea? Spill?" (That's Toca Tea Party.)

As these delights and diversions for young children have proliferated, the pass-back has become more uncomfortable, even unsustainable, for many parents:

> He'd gone to this state where you'd call his name and he wouldn't respond to it, or you could snap your fingers in front of his face . . .

> But, you know, we ended up actually taking the iPad away for—from him largely because, you know, this example, this thing we were talking about, about zoning out. Now, he would do that, and my wife and I would stare at him and think, *Oh my God, his brain is going to turn to mush and come oozing out of his ears.* And it concerned us a bit.

This is Ben Worthen, a *Wall Street Journal* reporter, explaining recently to NPR's Diane Rehm why he took the iPad away from his son, even though it was the only thing that could hold the boy's attention for long periods, and it seemed to be sparking an interest in numbers and letters. Most parents can sympathize with the disturbing sight of a toddler, who five minutes earlier had been jumping off the couch, now subdued and staring at a screen, seemingly hypnotized. In the somewhat alarmist *Endangered Minds: Why Children Don't Think—and What We Can Do About It,* author Jane Healy even gives the phenomenon a name, the "'zombie' effect," and raises the possibility that television might "suppress mental activity by putting viewers in a trance."

Ever since viewing screens entered the home, many observers have worried that they put our brains into a stupor. An early strain of research claimed that when we watch television, our brains mostly exhibit slow alpha waves—indicating a low level of arousal, similar to when we are daydreaming. These findings have been largely discarded by the scientific community, but the myth persists that watching television is the mental equivalent of, as one Web site put it, "staring at a blank wall." These common metaphors are misleading, argues Heather Kirkorian, who studies media and attention at the University of Wisconsin at Madison. A more accurate point of comparison for a TV viewer's physiological state would be that of someone deep in a book, says Kirkorian, because during both activities we are still, undistracted, and mentally active.

Because interactive media are so new, most of the existing research looks at children and television. By now, "there is universal agreement that by at least age 2 and a half, children are very cognitively active when they are watching TV," says Dan Anderson, a children's-media expert at the University of Massachusetts at Amherst. In the 1980s, Anderson put the zombie theory to the test, by subjecting roughly 100 children to a form of TV hell. He showed a group of children aged 2 to 5 a scrambled version of *Sesame Street:* he pieced together scenes in random order and had the characters speak backwards or in Greek. Then he spliced the doctored segments with unedited ones and noted how well the kids paid attention. The children looked away much more frequently during the scrambled parts of the show, and some complained that the TV was broken. Anderson later repeated the experiment with babies aged 6 months to 24 months, using *Teletubbies.* Once again he had the characters speak backwards and chopped the action sequences into a nonsensical order—showing, say, one of the Teletubbies catching a ball and then, after that, another one throwing it. The 6- and 12-month-olds seemed unable to tell the difference, but by 18 months, the babies started looking away, and by 24 months, they were turned off by programming that did not make sense.

Anderson's series of experiments provided the first clue that even very young children can be discriminating viewers—that they are not in fact brain-dead, but rather work hard to make sense of what they see and turn it into a coherent narrative that reflects what they already know of the world. Now, 30 years later, we understand that children "can make a lot of inferences and process the information," says Anderson. "And they can learn a lot, both positive and negative." Researchers never abandoned the idea that parental interaction is critical for the development of very young children. But they started to see TV watching in shades of gray. If a child never interacts with adults and always watches TV, well, that is a problem. But if a child is watching TV instead of, say, playing with toys, then that is a tougher comparison, because TV, in the right circumstances, has something to offer.

How do small children actually experience electronic media, and what does that experience do to their development? Since the '80s, researchers have spent more and more time consulting with television programmers to study and shape TV content. By tracking children's reactions, they have identified certain rules that promote engagement: stories have to be linear and easy to follow, cuts and time lapses have to be used very sparingly, and language has to be pared down and repeated. A perfect example of a well-engineered show is Nick Jr.'s *Blue's Clues,* which aired from 1996 to 2006. Each episode features Steve (or Joe, in later seasons) and Blue, a cartoon puppy, solving a mystery. Steve talks slowly and simply; he repeats words and then writes them down in his handy-dandy notebook. There are almost no cuts or unexplained gaps in time. The great innovation of *Blue's Clues* is something called the "pause." Steve asks a question and then pauses for about five seconds to let the viewer shout out an answer. Small children feel much more engaged and invested when they think they have a role to play, when they believe they are actually helping Steve and Blue piece together the clues. A longitudinal study of children older than 2 and a half showed that the ones who watched *Blue's Clues* made measurably larger gains in flexible thinking and problem solving over two years of watching the show.

For toddlers, however, the situation seems slightly different. Children younger than 2 and a half exhibit what researchers call a "video deficit." This means that they have a much easier time processing information delivered by a real person than by a person on videotape. In one series of studies, conducted by Georgene Troseth, a developmental psychologist at Vanderbilt University, children watched on a live video monitor as a person in the next room hid a stuffed dog. Others watched the exact same scene unfold directly, through a window between the rooms. The children were then unleashed into the room to find the toy. Almost all the kids who viewed the hiding through the window found the toy, but the ones who watched on the monitor had a much harder time.

A natural assumption is that toddlers are not yet cognitively equipped to handle symbolic representation. (I remember my older son, when he was 3, asking me if he could go into the TV and pet Blue.) But there is another way to interpret this particular phase of development. Toddlers are skilled at seeking out what researchers call "socially relevant information." They tune in to people and situations that help them make a coherent narrative of the world around them. In the real world, fresh grass smells and popcorn tumbles and grown-ups smile at you or say something back when you ask them a question. On TV, nothing like that happens. A TV is static and lacks one of the most important things to toddlers, which is a "two-way exchange of information," argues Troseth.

A few years after the original puppy-hiding experiment, in 2004, Troseth reran it, only she changed a few things. She turned the puppy into a stuffed Piglet (from the Winnie the Pooh stories). More important, she made the video demonstration explicitly interactive. Toddlers and their parents came into a room where they could see a person—the researcher—on a monitor. The researcher was in the room where Piglet would be hidden and could in turn see the children on a monitor. Before hiding Piglet, the researcher effectively engaged the children in a form of media training. She asked them questions about their siblings, pets, and toys. She played Simon Says with them and invited them to sing popular songs with her. She told them to look for a sticker under a chair in their room. She gave them the distinct impression that she—this person on the screen—could interact with them and that what she had to say was relevant to the world they lived in. Then the researcher told the children she was going to hide the toy and, after she did so, came back on the screen to instruct them where to find it. That exchange was enough to nearly erase the video deficit. The majority of the toddlers who participated in the live video demonstration found the toy.

Blue's Clues was on the right track. The pause could trick children into thinking that Steve was responsive to them. But the holy grail would be creating a scenario in which the guy on the screen did actually respond—in which the toddler did something and the character reliably jumped or laughed or started to dance or talk back.

Like, for example, when Gideon said "Giddy" and Talking Baby Hippo said "Giddy" back, without fail, every time. That kind of contingent interaction (I do something, you respond) is what captivates a toddler and can be a significant source of learning for even very young children—learning that researchers hope the children can carry into the real world. It's not exactly the ideal social partner the American Academy of Pediatrics craves. It's certainly not a parent or caregiver. But it's as good an approximation as we've ever come up with on a screen, and it's why children's-media researchers are so excited about the iPad's potential.

A couple of researchers from the Children's Media Center at Georgetown University show up at my house, carrying an iPad wrapped in a bright-orange case, the better to tempt Gideon with. They are here at the behest of Sandra Calvert, the center's director, to conduct one of several ongoing studies on toddlers and iPads. Gideon is one of their research subjects. This study is designed to test whether a child is more likely to learn when the information he hears comes from a beloved and trusted source. The researchers put the iPad on a kitchen chair; Gideon immediately notices it, turns it on, and looks for his favorite app. They point him to the one they have invented for the experiment, and he dutifully opens it with his finger.

Onto the screen comes a floppy kangaroo-like puppet, introduced as "DoDo." He is a nobody in the child universe, the puppet equivalent of some random guy on late-night public-access TV. Gideon barely acknowledges him. Then the narrator introduces Elmo. "Hi," says Elmo, waving. Gideon says hi and waves back.

An image pops up on the screen, and the narrator asks, "What is this?" (It's a banana.)

"This is a banana," says DoDo.

"This is a grape," says Elmo.

I smile with the inner glow of a mother who knows her child is about to impress a couple strangers. My little darling knows what a banana is. Of course he does! Gideon presses on Elmo. (The narrator says, "No, not Elmo. Try again.") As far as I know, he's never watched *Sesame Street,* never loved an Elmo doll or even coveted one at the toy store. Nonetheless, he is tuned in to the signals of toddler world and, apparently, has somehow figured out that Elmo is a supreme moral authority. His relationship with Elmo is more important to him than what he knows to be the truth. On and on the game goes, and sometimes Gideon picks Elmo even when Elmo says an orange is a pear. Later, when the characters both give made-up names for exotic fruits that few children would know by their real name, Gideon keeps doubling down on Elmo, even though DoDo has been more reliable.

By age 3, Gideon would tune in to what was cool in toddler world, then drop the iPad in my lap and ask for certain games by their approximate description.

As it happens, Gideon was not in the majority. This summer, Calvert and her team will release the results of their study, which show that most of the time, children around age 32 months go with the character who is telling the truth, whether it's Elmo or DoDo—and quickly come to trust the one who's been more accurate when the children don't already know the answer. But Calvert says this merely suggests that toddlers have become even more savvy users of technology than we had imagined. She had been working off attachment theory and thought toddlers might value an emotional bond over the correct answer. But her guess is that something about tapping the screen, about getting feedback and being corrected in real time, is itself instructive and enables the toddlers to absorb information accurately, regardless of its source.

Calvert takes a balanced view of technology: she works in an office surrounded by hardcover books, and she sometimes edits her drafts with pen and paper. But she is very interested in how the iPad can reach children even before they're old enough to access these traditional media.

"People say we are experimenting with our children," she told me. "But from my perspective, it's already happened, and there's no way to turn it back. Children's lives are filled with media at younger and younger ages, and we need to take advantage of what these technologies have to offer. I'm not a Pollyanna. I'm pretty much a realist. I look at what kids are doing and try to figure out how to make the best of it."

Despite the participation of Elmo, Calvert's research is designed to answer a series of very responsible, high-minded questions: Can toddlers learn from iPads? Can they transfer what they learn to the real world? What effect does interactivity have on learning? What role do familiar characters play in children's learning from iPads? All worthy questions, and important, but also all considered entirely from an adult's point of view. The reason many kids' apps are grouped under "Education" in the iTunes store, I suspect, is to assuage parents' guilt (though I also suspect that in the long run, all those "educational" apps merely perpetuate our neurotic relationship with technology, by reinforcing the idea that they must be sorted vigilantly into "good" or "bad"). If small children had more input, many "Education" apps would logically fall under a category called "Kids" or "Kids' Games." And many more of the games would probably look something like the apps designed by a Swedish game studio named Toca Boca.

The founders, Emil Ovemar and Björn Jeffery, work for Bonnier, a Swedish media company. Ovemar, an interactive-design expert, describes himself as someone who never grew up. He is still interested in superheroes, Legos, and animated movies and says he would rather play stuck-on-an-island with his two kids and their cousins than talk to almost any adult. Jeffery is the company's strategist and front man; I first met him at the conference in California, where he was handing out little temporary tattoos of the Toca Boca logo, a mouth open and grinning, showing off rainbow-colored teeth.

In late 2010, Ovemar and Jeffery began working on a new digital project for Bonnier, and they came up with the idea of entering the app market for kids. Ovemar began by looking into the apps available at the time. Most of them were disappointingly "instructive," he found—"drag the butterfly into the net, that sort of thing. They were missing creativity and imagination." Hunting for inspiration, he came upon Frank and Theresa Caplan's 1973 book *The Power of Play*, a quote from which he later e-mailed to me:

What is it that often puts the B student ahead of the A student in adult life, especially in business and creative

professions? Certainly it is more than verbal skill. To create, one must have a sense of adventure and playfulness. One needs toughness to experiment and hazard the risk of failure. One has to be strong enough to start all over again if need be and alert enough to learn from whatever happens. One needs a strong ego to be propelled forward in one's drive toward an untried goal. Above all, one has to possess the ability to play!

Ovemar and Jeffery hunted down toy catalogs from as early as the 1950s, before the age of exploding brand tie-ins. They made a list of the blockbusters over the decades—the first Tonka trucks, the Frisbee, the Hula-Hoop, the Rubik's Cube. Then they made a list of what these toys had in common: None really involved winning or losing against an opponent. None were part of an effort to create a separate child world that adults were excluded from, and probably hostile toward; they were designed more for family fun. Also, they were not really meant to teach you something specific—they existed mostly in the service of having fun.

In 2011, the two developers launched Toca Tea Party. The game is not all that different from a real tea party. The iPad functions almost like a tea table without legs, and the kids have to invent the rest by, for example, seating their own plushies or dolls, one on each side, and then setting the theater in motion. First, choose one of three tablecloths. Then choose plates, cups, and treats. The treats are not what your mom would feed you. They are chocolate cakes, frosted doughnuts, cookies. It's very easy to spill the tea when you pour or take a sip, a feature added based on kids' suggestions during a test play (kids love spills, but spilling is something you can't do all that often at a real tea party, or you'll get yelled at). At the end, a sink filled with soapy suds appears, and you wash the dishes, which is also part of the fun, and then start again. That's it. The game is either very boring or terrifically exciting, depending on what you make of it. Ovemar and Jeffery knew that some parents wouldn't get it, but for kids, the game would be fun every time, because it's dependent entirely on imagination. Maybe today the stuffed bear will be naughty and do the spilling, while naked Barbie will pile her plate high with sweets. The child can take on the voice of a character or a scolding parent, or both. There's no winning, and there's no reward. Like a game of stuck-on-an-island, it can go on for five minutes or forever.

Soon after the release of Toca Tea Party, the pair introduced Toca Hair Salon, which is still to my mind the most fun game out there. The salon is no Fifth Avenue spa. It's a rundown-looking place with cracks in the wall. The aim is not beauty but subversion. Cutting off hair, like spilling, is on the list of things kids are not supposed to do. You choose one of the odd-looking people or creatures and have your way with its hair, trimming it or dyeing it or growing it out. The blow-dryer is genius; it achieves the same effect as Tadao Cern's Blow Job portraits, which depict people's faces getting wildly distorted by high winds. In August 2011, Toca Boca gave away Hair Salon for free for nearly two weeks. It was downloaded more than 1 million times in the first week, and the company took off. Today, many Toca Boca games show up on lists of the most popular education apps.

Are they educational? "That's the perspective of the parents," Jeffery told me at the back of the grand hall in Monterey. "Is running around on the lawn educational? Every part of a child's life can't be held up to that standard." As we talked, two girls were playing Toca Tea Party on the floor nearby. One had her stuffed dragon at a plate, and he was being especially naughty, grabbing all the chocolate cake and spilling everything. Her friend had taken a little Lego construction man and made him the good guy who ate neatly and helped do the dishes. Should they have been outside at the beach? Maybe, but the day would be long, and they could go outside later.

The more I talked with the developers, the more elusive and unhelpful the "Education" category seemed. (Is *Where the Wild Things Are* educational? Would you make your child read a textbook at bedtime? Do you watch only educational television? And why don't children deserve high-quality fun?) Buckleitner calls his conference Dust or Magic to teach app developers a more subtle concept than pedagogy. By *magic,* Buckleitner has in mind an app that makes children's fingers move and their eyes light up. By *dust,* he means something that was obviously (and ploddingly) designed by an adult. Some educational apps, I wouldn't wish on the naughtiest toddler. Take, for example, Counting With the Very Hungry Caterpillar, which turns a perfectly cute book into a tedious app that asks you to "please eat 1 piece of chocolate cake" so you can count to one.

Before the conference, Buckleitner had turned me on to Noodle Words, an app created by the California designer and children's-book writer Mark Schlichting. The app is explicitly educational. It teaches you about active verbs— *spin, sparkle, stretch.* It also happens to be fabulous. You tap a box, and a verb pops up and gets acted out by two insect friends who have the slapstick sensibility of the Three Stooges. If the word is *shake,* they shake until their eyeballs rattle. I tracked down Schlichting at the conference, and he turned out to be a little like Maurice Sendak—like many good children's writers, that is: ruled by id and not quite tamed into adulthood. The app, he told me, was inspired by a dream he'd had in which he saw the word *and* floating in the air and sticking to other words like a magnet. He woke up and thought, *What if words were toys?*

During the course of reporting this story, I downloaded dozens of apps and let my children test them out. They didn't much care whether the apps were marketed as educational or not, as long as they were fun. Without my prompting, Gideon fixated on a game called LetterSchool, which teaches you how to write letters more effectively and with more imagination than any penmanship textbooks I've ever encountered. He loves the Toca Boca games, the Duck Duck Moose games, and random games like Bugs and Buttons. My older kids love The Numberlys, a dark fantasy creation of illustrators who have worked with Pixar that happens to teach the alphabet. And all my kids, including Gideon, play Cut the Rope a lot, which is not exclusively marketed as a kids' game. I could convince myself that the game is teaching them certain principles of physics—it's not easy to know the exact right place to slice the rope. But do I really need that extra convincing? I like playing the game; why shouldn't they?

Every new medium has, within a short time of its introduction, been condemned as a threat to young people. Pulp novels would destroy their morals, TV would wreck their eyesight, video games would make them violent. Each one has been accused of seducing kids into wasting time that would otherwise be spent learning about the presidents, playing with friends, or digging their toes into the sand. In our generation, the worries focus on kids' brainpower, about unused synapses withering as children stare at the screen. People fret about television and ADHD, although that concern is largely based on a single study that has been roundly criticized and doesn't jibe with anything we know about the disorder.

There are legitimate broader questions about how American children spend their time, but all you can do is keep them in mind as you decide what rules to set down for your own child. The statement from the American Academy of Pediatrics assumes a zero-sum game: an hour spent watching TV is an hour not spent with a parent. But parents know this is not how life works. There are enough hours in a day to go to school, play a game, and spend time with a parent, and generally these are different hours. Some people can get so drawn into screens that they want to do nothing else but play games. Experts say excessive video gaming is a real problem, but they debate whether it can be called an addiction and, if so, whether the term can be used for anything but a small portion of the population. If your child shows signs of having an addictive personality, you will probably know it. One of my kids is like that; I set stricter limits for him than for the others, and he seems to understand why.

In her excellent book *Screen Time,* the journalist Lisa Guernsey lays out a useful framework—what she calls the three C's—for thinking about media consumption: content, context, and your child. She poses a series of questions—Do you think the content is appropriate? Is screen time a "relatively small part of your child's interaction with you and the real world"?—and suggests tailoring your rules to the answers, child by child. One of the most interesting points Guernsey makes is about the importance of parents' attitudes toward media. If they treat screen time like junk food, or "like a magazine at the hair salon"—good for passing the time in a frivolous way but nothing more—then the child will fully absorb that attitude, and the neurosis will be passed to the next generation.

"The war is over. The natives won." So says Marc Prensky, the education and technology writer, who has the most extreme parenting philosophy of anyone I encountered in my reporting. Prensky's 7-year-old son has access to books, TV, Legos, Wii—and Prensky treats them all the same. He does not limit access to any of them. Sometimes his son plays with a new app for hours, but then, Prensky told me, he gets tired of it. He lets his son watch TV even when he personally thinks it's a "stupid waste." *SpongeBob SquarePants,* for example, seems like an annoying, pointless show, but Prensky says he used the relationship between SpongeBob and Patrick, his starfish sidekick, to teach his son a lesson about friendship. "We live in a screen age, and to say to a kid, 'I'd love for you to look at a book but I hate it when you look at the screen' is just bizarre. It reflects our own prejudices and comfort zone. It's nothing but fear of change, of being left out."

Prensky's worldview really stuck with me. Are books always, in every situation, inherently better than screens? My daughter, after all, often uses books as a way to avoid social interaction, while my son uses the Wii to bond with friends. I have to admit, I had the exact same experience with *Sponge-Bob*. For a long time I couldn't stand the show, until one day I got past the fact that the show was so loud and frenetic and paid more attention to the story line, and realized I too could use it to talk with my son about friendship. After I first interviewed Prensky, I decided to conduct an experiment. For six months, I would let my toddler live by the Prensky rules. I would put the iPad in the toy basket, along with the remote-control car and the Legos. Whenever he wanted to play with it, I would let him.

Gideon tested me the very first day. He saw the iPad in his space and asked if he could play. It was 8 a.m. and we had to get ready for school. I said yes. For 45 minutes he sat on a chair and played as I got him dressed, got his backpack ready, and failed to feed him breakfast. This was extremely annoying and obviously untenable. The week went on like this—Gideon grabbing the iPad for two-hour stretches, in the morning, after school, at bedtime. Then, after about 10 days, the iPad fell out of his rotation, just like every other toy does. He dropped it under the bed and never looked for it. It was completely forgotten for about six weeks.

Now he picks it up every once in a while, but not all that often. He has just started learning letters in school, so he's back to playing LetterSchool. A few weeks ago his older brother played with him, helping him get all the way through the uppercase and then lowercase letters. It did not seem beyond the range of possibility that if Norman Rockwell were alive, he would paint the two curly-haired boys bent over the screen, one small finger guiding a smaller one across, down, and across again to make, in their triumphant finale, the small *z.*

Critical Thinking

1. Does this article persuade you one way or the other about the value of touch screens in young children's lives? Why or why not?

2. What are some benefits for children from using touch screens? What are possible detrimental effects of too much technology time?

3. If children spend too much time with technology, what is lost from the rest of children's lives and experiences? As a future or current parent, teacher, or adult who may have some role in children's lives, how do your own memories of childhood affect your views of how children "should" spend their time?

Create Central

www.mhhe.com/createcentral

Internet References

American College of Pediatricians
http://www.acpeds.org

Study Finds Touch Screens Don't Help Toddlers Learn
http://www.clickondetroit.com/lifestyle/health/study-finds-touch-screens-dont-help-toddlers-learn/25882550

Touchscreens and Toddlers: The Research is Mostly Good News
http://national.deseretnews.com/article/341/Touchscreens-and-toddlers-The-research-is-mostly-good-news.html#O7DLLYieMMhJS5Cz.

http://national.deseretnews.com/article/341/Touchscreens-and-toddlers-The-research-is-mostly-good-news.html?pg=all

What You Need to Know about Babies, Toddlers, and Screen Time
http://www.npr.org/blogs/alltechconsidered/2013/10/29/228125739/what-to-know-about-babies-and-screen-time-kids-screens-electronics

HANNA ROSIN is a national correspondent for *The Atlantic.*

Rosen, Hanna,"The Touch-Screen Generation," The Atlantic, March 20, 2013. © 2013 The Atlantic Media Co., as first published in The Atlantic Magazine. All rights reserved. Distributed by Tribune Content Agency, LLC

Article   Prepared by: Ellen N. Junn, *California State University, Dominguez Hills*

ADHD among Preschoolers

Identifying and treating attention-deficit hyperactivity disorder in very young children requires a different approach.

BRENDAN L. SMITH

Learning Outcomes

After reading this article, you will be able to:

- Prepare a presentation for parents and teachers on ADHD and controversies surrounding its incidence and treatment.

- Critique the different kinds of therapies for ADHD from medical to behavioral.

Preschoolers can be inattentive or hyperactive even on the best of days, so it can be difficult to accurately diagnose attention-deficit hyperactivity disorder. But a growing body of research has shown that early treatment can help struggling children and frazzled parents.

The diagnosis of young children with ADHD is "very contentious" since there is a blurry line between common developmental changes and symptoms of the mental disorder, says ADHD researcher Stephen Hinshaw, PhD, chair of the psychology department at the University of California at Berkeley. "The symptoms for ADHD are very ubiquitous and very age-relevant," he says. "It's hard to know if you're seeing the signs of a disorder or just the signs of a young kid."

Hinshaw and some other researchers believe ADHD can be reliably diagnosed in children as young as 3 after thorough evaluations. In one study of school-age children, mothers reported that symptoms of ADHD appeared at or before age 4 in two-thirds of the children (*Journal of Developmental & Behavioral Pediatrics*, Vol. 23, No. 1).

Researchers disagree about whether ADHD is overdiagnosed, which may lead to unnecessary medication of healthy children. There is a tendency to overdiagnose young children with ADHD because of a lack of understanding about normative development in toddlerhood and the early preschool years, says Susan Campbell, PhD, a psychology professor at the University of Pittsburgh who has researched ADHD for more than three decades. "The only reason to diagnose a young child is to access appropriate services to help the child and family," she says. "Sometimes the earlier the better."

Overall, more children of all ages are being diagnosed with ADHD since there is greater awareness of the disorder and improvements in treatment, says Russell Barkley, PhD, a psychologist and professor at the Medical University of South Carolina who studies ADHD. Some inaccurate media reports have fueled a public misperception that ADHD is overdiagnosed, Barkley says. But only 20 percent of children with ADHD received any treatment in the 1960s and '70s, compared with roughly 70 percent to 80 percent today, he says.

"The rise in diagnosis is not bad news. It's good news," Barkley says. "Frankly, we were doing an awful job 20 or 30 years ago."

Medication Issues

Often the first line of treatment for ADHD in school-age children is medication with stimulants, which have been found to be generally safe and effective. But drugs have less positive results for preschoolers. "I'm very opposed to the use of medication with young children because we don't really know the implications for brain development," Campbell says.

Approximately 4 million children—or 8 percent of all minors in the United States—have been diagnosed with ADHD, and more than half of them take prescription drugs. Methylphenidate hydrochloride (Ritalin) is the most commonly prescribed medication, but its use in children under 6 years old hasn't been approved by the Food and Drug

Administration, which cites a lack of research for this age group. As a result, doctors are prescribing methylphenidate off label for preschoolers with ADHD.

The most comprehensive study on medication of preschoolers with ADHD showed mixed results for 3- to 5-year-old children. Funded by the National Institute of Mental Health, the multisite Preschool ADHD Treatment Study enrolled 303 preschoolers and their parents in a 10-week behavioral therapy course. Children with severe symptoms who didn't respond to therapy were given low doses of methylphenidate or a placebo. The medicated children showed a marked reduction in symptoms compared with the placebo group, according to the study results published in 2006.

> **"It's crazy to me that we use the same criteria for a 3-year-old as we do for a 35-year-old."**
>
> —George Dupaul, Lehigh University

More troublesome, though, was the fact that almost a third of parents reported that their medicated children experienced moderate to severe side effects, including weight loss, insomnia, loss of appetite, emotional outbursts, and anxiety. Eleven percent of the preschoolers dropped out of the study because of their reactions to methylphenidate. During the study, the medicated children also grew about half an inch less in height and weighed about three pounds less than expected based on average growth rates (*Journal of the American Academy of Child & Adolescent Psychiatry,* Vol. 45, No. 11).

"The bottom line to me is for this age group, I don't believe stimulant medication is a first-line treatment," says George DuPaul, PhD, a professor of school psychology at Lehigh University who studies ADHD.

Embracing Other Methods

Parental training and school-based interventions can be effective in treating preschoolers with ADHD, DuPaul says. His book, "Young Children With ADHD: Early Identification and Intervention" (APA, 2011), co-written with Lehigh University colleague Lee Kern, PhD, describes one of their studies of nondrug interventions with 135 preschoolers with ADHD.

Parents were given 20 training sessions on behavior problems, basic math and language skills, and child safety since children with ADHD often suffer accidental injuries because of their hyperactivity and impulsivity. One group of children also received individual assessments in the home and at preschool

or day care. Both groups of children showed marked improvements in ADHD symptoms, although there was no significant advantage for the children with individual assessments (*School Psychology Review,* Vol. 36, No. 2). One limitation of the study was the lack of a control group because of ethical considerations about providing no treatment.

While older children can sometimes be taught to manage their ADHD symptoms, the training of preschool children has been more difficult, in part because cognitive-behavioral therapy doesn't work, Barkley says. Preschoolers with ADHD are delayed in communication skills, and language hasn't been internalized yet, so they can't use mental instructions or self-monitoring to change their behavior.

"It failed so we abandoned that after multiple studies found it had little or no influence," Barkley says.

But some behavioral management techniques are effective, including a token reward system and praise to provide extra motivation for preschoolers with ADHD, Barkley says. Teachers can seat children with ADHD near the teacher's desk and provide detailed explanations of class rules and disciplinary procedures, such as time-out or loss of tokens. Frequent class breaks and shorter work assignments also can help maintain children's attention and reduce outbursts.

Symptoms of ADHD can be exacerbated in children by impulsive parents who also have ADHD, Campbell says. Parents who are quick to anger and who frequently use physical punishment also can be detrimental. "There is going to be an interaction between the genetic risk and the support or lack of parental support the child has," she says.

Looking Ahead

As the diagnosis of preschoolers with ADHD has increased, so have questions about the lack of age-specific symptoms in the Diagnostic and Statistical Manual of Mental Disorders, Fourth Edition. "It's crazy to me that we use the same criteria for a 3-year-old as we do for a 35-year-old," DuPaul says.

Scheduled for publication in 2013, the fifth DSM edition should require a greater number of symptoms for diagnosing young children with ADHD and more age-specific symptoms instead of generic descriptions such as fidgeting or running around and climbing, DuPaul says. "How do we apply that to a 17-year-old kid in a high school classroom?" he says. "They don't run about and climb on things."

Despite the risks, early identification and treatment of ADHD can provide substantial benefits for children and their families, Campbell says. "It can help so that when the child gets to the first grade, he isn't the only child no one else wants to play with and no teachers want in their class," she says.

Critical Thinking

1. How can you tell if a child has ADHD or is just being a normal preschooler?

2. Do you think ADHD is overdiagnosed? If so, why, and if not, why not?

3. Are there ways to treat ADHD other than medicine? What might be better versus poorer choices?

Create Central

www.mhhe.com/createcentral

Internet References

Children and Adults with ADHD.org
http://www.chadd.org/understanding-adhd.aspx

National Institute of Mental Health.org
http://www.nimh.nih.gov/health/topics/attention-deficit-hyperactivity-disorder-adhd/index.shtml

WebMD.org
http://www.webmd.com/add-adhd

From *Monitor on Psychology* by Brendan L. Smith, July/August 2011, pp. 50–52. Copyright © 2011 by American Psychological Association. Reprinted by permission. No further distribution without permission from the American Psychological Association.

Prepared by: Chris J. Boyatzis, *Bucknell University*
Ellen N. Junn, *California State University, Dominguez Hills*

Article

Is It Really ADHD?

A psychologist and a health economist team up to explore the nation's skyrocketing rates of ADHD diagnoses—and how a global push for performance may be partly to blame.

AMY NOVOTNEY

Learning Outcomes

After reading this article, you will be able to:

- Define and describe ADHD and the most common treatments for this condition for children in the United States today.

- According to this article, it was puzzling to see that states reporting rates of ADHD varied significantly, for example between California and North Carolina. Explain why this significant variance occurs.

- What suggestions might you have for different states to equalize standards for ADHD reporting?

B etween fall 2011 and spring 2012, record numbers of Americans went to their pharmacies to fill prescriptions for Adderall, Ritalin and other stimulants, primarily to treat attention-deficit/hyperactivity disorder (ADHD), only to find the medications were sold out. Several factors contributed to the shortage, but the main reason was that demand had outpaced supply.

The U.S. Drug Enforcement Agency reviewed and subsequently raised the quota for production of stimulants, but this shortage illustrates just how much ADHD diagnoses have ballooned over the past decade. In 2003, 7.8 percent of 4- to 17-year-olds had received a diagnosis of ADHD, according to data from the National Survey of Children's Health, sponsored by the Centers for Disease Control and Prevention.

By 2007, that number had jumped to 9.5 percent, an increase of 22 percent. In 2011, 11 percent of school-age children overall—including nearly one in five high-school-age boys in the United States—had received an ADHD diagnosis (*Journal of the American Academy of Child & Adolescent Psychiatry*, January).

The CDC also found that over two-thirds of children and teens who have been diagnosed with ADHD take medication for it.

What exactly is leading to the growing number of new ADHD diagnoses? Is there a true increase in the disorder—or are we simply expanding our definition of it, or are more aware of it? And why is the chance of receiving an ADHD diagnosis twice as high in Southern states as in Western states?

In their book *The ADHD Explosion: Myths, Medication, Money, and Today's Push for Performance,* (2014, Oxford University Press), University of California, Berkeley, psychologist Stephen Hinshaw, PhD, and health economist Richard Scheffler, PhD, explore how education policies and the nation's increasing push for academic and job performance factor into the rise in diagnoses—and how psychologists can help distinguish ADHD from other mental health conditions.

Is this increase in ADHD diagnoses really warranted?

Hinshaw: The hard part is that ADHD is just like depression, just like autism, just like schizophrenia in that it's a symptom-based mental disorder. We don't have a blood test or a brain scan yet that's definitive. I believe that ADHD is a real condition, but it's on a spectrum, just the way that high blood pressure and autism are. It's always a bit arbitrary as to who is actually above the cut and who is below because we don't know exactly where the cut is.

How did you evaluate the varying state and regional rates of ADHD diagnoses?

Hinshaw: In analyzing the CDC data, it's hard to miss the alarming differences regionally and state by state. The South has much higher rates of diagnosis of ADHD than the West and other regions, and this was a puzzle for us.

So we went on to look at several potential factors and used North Carolina and California as our comparison states. First, we looked at who lives in these states. We thought maybe there was more of a certain racial or ethnic group in one state or the other that might explain it. For example, there are more Hispanics in California than in North Carolina, and traditionally, Hispanics have had the lowest rates of ADHD diagnosis out of any ethnic group. So we equalized the states demographically, and when you do that, it reduces this discrepancy between North Carolina and California a little bit, but not much. There are still twice as many kids diagnosed with ADHD in North Carolina as in California.

Then we thought, well, maybe it's medical practice. We know from other studies that if you have more pediatricians or child psychiatrists in a given region, you might get more diagnoses there. We also thought younger clinicians might be more educated about ADHD and be more likely to diagnose it. So, we looked at all the possible configurations of medical practitioners, but it didn't explain any of the regional differences.

Now we're scratching our heads. We decided to look at the culture of the state. We thought maybe there's a culture of honor in the South or maybe there's rugged individualism out West, or perhaps different standards in the classroom for behavior. But once we started to look at this, we figured out that politics and culture might explain very local variations within a state, but they don't explain the state differences overall.

Scheffler: Finally, we decided to look outside of psychology and outside of the health-care system because inside it, we couldn't explain the discrepancies. [What we are surmising] is that policy had an indirect influence over these diagnoses. We found that during the late 1980s and throughout the 1990s, several states passed consequential accountability laws, which basically changed the philosophy of schools: Instead of funding schools based on the number of students in them, funding became based on their students' standardized math and reading test scores. Schools were rewarded for doing better. At the same time, standardized test scores in the South were the lowest in the nation—and as a result, these states didn't get as much funding.

That's when we knew we were onto something, because if you want to improve test scores, one way of doing that is to have children diagnosed so you can get extra money from the school district to help tutor them or put them in smaller classes. Basically, you diagnose these kids because improving their performance helps the school's performance.

Some states even allowed you to take students diagnosed with ADHD out of the pool that was used to judge your school, with the understanding that these kids probably perform lower, and if you have more of them, that shouldn't be held against you.

What, specifically, did you find out about the effect of these education policies?

Hinshaw: Thirty states, including all of the Southern states, passed these accountability laws before the No Child Left Behind Act—which, like the state consequential accountability laws, sets standards and establishes measurable goals in an effort to improve education outcomes for students—went into effect in 2002, so we were able to compare those 30 states to the other 20 before and after it became federal law to have consequential accountability.

What we found was that standards-based education reform had likely played a large role in the nation's huge increase in ADHD diagnoses. Between 2003 and 2007, in those 20 states that didn't get consequential accountability until No Child Left Behind was implemented, we found a 59 percent increase in ADHD diagnoses among children who were within 200 percent of the federal poverty limit—so among the poorest kids in the state. Among middle- or upper-class kids in those states, there was only a 3 percent increase in ADHD diagnosis. That's a huge and statistically significant difference. But in states that had already passed the accountability laws before No Child Left Behind, rates of ADHD diagnosis only went up 20 percent, which is pretty much the national average, and there was no difference between poor and rich kids. Are we saying that consequential accountability is the cause? No. But there's a really strong association, and it's almost a smoking gun that when test scores really, really count in the public schools, for the poorest kids in a state, ADHD diagnoses go up dramatically shortly thereafter.

What's the sum total of this? School policies really seem to matter, in a way that factors such as ethnicity, medical professionals and culture don't. Can we say they're the absolute and only cause of these state and regional differences? No, but they sure seem to be implicated.

What are some of the dangers of this rise in ADHD diagnoses and the use of medication treatment?

Hinshaw: There's some evidence that if you get diagnosed with ADHD and treated with medication, medicine doesn't just make you sit stiller, it might actually boost test scores. This isn't a bad thing; I'm all for giving it to the kids who really do need it. However, the catch is, how carefully are we making these diagnoses? The average assessment for ADHD is a 10-minute office visit, especially for children on Medicaid.

In addition, while stimulants are usually safe and have relatively manageable side effects if monitored carefully by a knowledgeable professional, they can suppress appetite and interfere with sleep. Other potential side effects are cardiovascular—stimulants have a tendency to raise heart rate and blood pressure slightly. Some evidence also suggests that several years of consistent medication may reduce ultimate adult height by half an inch to an inch. There's also the whole issue of the use of medications for ADHD for people without ADHD. High rates of college students are taking stimulants, without any sign of having ADHD, and the short story is that stimulants are not as beneficial for cognitive performance for the general population as most people think. In those without ADHD, they may help you stay up later, but they don't really increase memory or learning. Importantly, if you don't have ADHD and you're taking these medicines as performance enhancers, there is also a much stronger chance you'll get addicted to the medication, and there are serious consequences of stimulant abuse. So it's another reason to take the diagnosis very seriously and not just dispense the pills if there's any small complaint of poor attention or poor concentration, because it can lead to serious trouble clinically.

What should the standard be, then, for a proper ADHD assessment?

Hinshaw: It has to be at least several hours. You have to get observations from the school or at least ratings from the teacher, normed ratings from parents and a really good developmental history of the child. These are things you can't do in a quick 10-minute office visit. But the national standard is for very quick diagnoses, which will certainly lead to over-diagnoses, because you can mistake all kinds of things for ADHD. But paradoxically, it also leads to under-diagnoses because some doctors will say, "He wasn't tearing up the waiting room," or "She sat very still in the office, so she can't have ADHD." Well, unless you see the child doing homework or when other people are giving directions, you'll miss it.

We also need reimbursement for these thorough assessments so we're not tempted to rule in or rule out ADHD on the basis of very flimsy evidence.

Scheffler: Psychologists also need to understand this academic pressure that happens in the schools, and make their

diagnoses carefully because they may be getting kids sent to them due to these pressures.

Psychologists are the gatekeepers, and they have a lot of responsibility to look into this and make sure they take the time to look into the school, societal and parental pressures while doing a careful diagnosis.

In addition, treating the kid without getting the family and the school involved is not optimal. The problem with an ADHD diagnosis is that it's a catchall for lots of things. It's hyperactivity, it's focus, executive function and the like, but usually the best treatment is to also consider involving the family and teachers in behavioral strategies to help improve focus, and to have everyone lined up to deal with this.

Further Reading

Hinshaw, S. P. & Scheffler, R. M. (2014). *The ADHD explosion: Myths, medications, money, and today's push for performance.* New York: Oxford University Press.

Scheffler, R. M., Brown, T., Fulton, B., Hinshaw, S. P., Levine, P., & Stone, S. I. (2009). Positive association between ADHD medication use and academic achievement during elementary school. *Pediatrics, 123,* 1273–1279.

Visser, S. N., Danielson, M. L., Bitsko, R. H., Holbrook, J. R., Kogan, M. D., Ghandour, R. M. ... Blumberg, S. J. (2014). Trends in the parent-report of health care provider-diagnosed and medicated attention-deficit/hyperactivity disorder: United States, 2003–2011. *Journal of the American Academy of Child and Adolescent Psychiatry, 53,* 34–46.

Critical Thinking

1. Imagine that you have a child you suspect might have ADHD. Based on this article, what factors do you need to take into account when seeking a physician to diagnose your child accurately? What kind of assessment would you want for your child as part of the diagnosing process?

2. Evaluate and assess the various treatment options available for ADHD children. Given this article, which options would you consider? Explain why.

3. Explain why national or federal policies governing K-12 schools might be revised to account for the difference in ADHD reporting by states.

Internet References

Children and Adults with ADHD.org
http://www.chadd.org/Understanding-ADHD/Parents-Caregivers-of-Children-with-ADHD.aspx

KidsHealth.com
http://kidshealth.org/parent/medical/learning/adhd.html

Brain and Behavior Research Foundation

https://bbrfoundation.org/frequently-asked-questions-about-attention-deficit-hyperactivity-disorder-adhd

National Institutes of Mental Health

http://www.nimh.nih.gov/health/topics/attention-deficit-hyperactivity-disorder-adhd/index.shtml

WebMD

http://www.webmd.com/add-adhd/childhood-adhd/frequently-asked-questions-about-attention-deficit-hyperactivity-disorder-adhd

---

AMY NOVOTNEY is a journalist in Chicago.

Novotney, Amy. "Is It Really ADHD? ," *Monitor on Psychology*, April 2014. Copyright © 2014 by American Psychological Association. Reprinted by permission.

Article   Prepared by: Chris J. Boyatzis, *Bucknell University*

1 in 68 Children Now Has a Diagnosis of Autism Spectrum Disorder. Why?

With rates of the disorder yet again rising according to new CDC numbers, a look at how doctors are diagnosing autism spectrum disorder in children, and what might be done better.

ENRICO GNAULATI

Learning Outcomes

After reading this article, you will be able to:

- Understand what it means for a child to receive a false-positive diagnosis and how this diagnosis will influence the child throughout his or her lifetime.

- Create a list of possible reasons for why children are being diagnosed with false-positives. Understand how a slow-to-mature toddler and a would-be-mildly-autistic toddler share many things in common.

- Develop an understanding of what it means to have a "theory of mind" and what it would be like to work with someone who may not have one.

Rates of autism spectrum disorder (ASD) are not creeping up so much as leaping up. New numbers just released by the Centers for Disease Control and Prevention reveal that one in 68 children now has a diagnosis of ASD—a 30 percent increase in just two years. In 2002, about one in 150 children was considered autistic, and in 1991, the figure was one in 500.

The staggering increase in cases of ASD should raise more suspicion in the medical community about its misdiagnosis and overdiagnosis than it does. Promoting early screening for autism is imperative. But, is it possible that the younger in age a child is when professionals screen for ASD—especially its milder cases—the greater the risk that a slow-to-mature child will be misperceived as autistic, thus driving the numbers up?

The science stacks up in favor of catching and treating ASD earlier because it leads to better outcomes. Dr. Laura Schreibman, who directs the Autism Intervention Research Program at the University of California, San Diego, embodies the perspective of most experts when she says, "Psychologists need to advise parents that the 'wait-and-see' approach is not appropriate when ASD is expected. Delaying a diagnosis can mean giving up significant gains of intervention that have been demonstrated before age six."

The younger in age we assess for problems, the greater the potential a slow-to-mature kid will be given a false diagnosis.

There is a universal push to screen for ASD at as young an age as possible and growing confidence that the early signs are clear and convincing. Dr. Jose Cordero, the founding director of the National Center on Birth Defects and Developmental Disabilities conveys this fervor.

"For healthcare providers, we have a message that's pretty direct about ASD. And the message is: The 4-year-old with autism was once a 3-year-old with autism, which was once a 2-year-old with autism."

Many researchers are now on the hunt for atypical behaviors cropping up in infancy that could be telltale signs of ASD. For instance, a team of experts led by Dr. Karen Pierce at the Autism Center of Excellence at the University of California, San Diego, has used eye-tracking technology to determine that infants as young as 14 months who later were diagnosed as autistic showed a preference for looking at movies of geometric shapes over movies of children dancing and doing yoga. This predilection for being engaged by objects rather than "social" images is thought to be a marker for autism.

Even the quality of infants' crying has come under scientific scrutiny as a possible sign of the disorder. Dr. Stephen Sheinkopf and some colleagues at Brown University compared the cries of a group of babies at risk for autism (due to having an autistic sibling) to typically developing babies using cutting-edge acoustic technology. They discovered that the at-risk babies emit higher-pitched cries that are "low in voicing," which is a term for cries that are sharper and reflect tense vocal chords. Dr. Sheinkopf, however, cautioned parents against over-scrutinizing their babies' cries since the distinctions were picked up by sophisticated acoustic technology, not by careful human listening.

"We definitely don't want parents to be anxiously listening to their babies' cries. It's unclear if the human ear is sensitive enough to detect this."

What gets lost in the debate is an awareness of how the younger in age we assess for problems, the greater the potential a slow-to-mature kid will be given a false diagnosis. In fact, as we venture into more tender years to screen for autism, we need to be reminded that the period of greatest diagnostic uncertainty is probably toddlerhood. A 2007 study out of the University of North Carolina at Chapel Hill found that over 30 percent of children diagnosed as autistic at age two no longer fit the diagnosis at age four. Since ASD is still generally considered to be a life-long neuropsychiatric condition that is not shed as childhood unfolds, we have to wonder if a large percentage of toddlers get a diagnosis that is of questionable applicability in the first place.

Expanding autistic phenomena to include picky eating and tantrums can create more befuddlement when applied to small children.

The parallels between a slow-to-mature toddler and a would-be-mildly autistic one are so striking that the prospect of a false diagnosis is great. Let's start with late talkers. Almost one in five 2-year-olds are late talkers. They fall below the expected 50-word expressive vocabulary threshold and appear incapable of stringing together two- and three-word phrases.

Data out of the famed Yale Study Center have demonstrated that toddlers with delayed language development are almost identical to their autistic spectrum disordered counterparts in their use of eye contact to gauge social interactions, the range of sounds and words they produce, and the emotional give-and-take they are capable of. Many tots are in an ASD red-zone who simply don't meet standard benchmarks for how quickly language should be acquired and social interactions mastered.

Expanding autistic phenomena to include picky eating and tantrums can create more befuddlement when applied to small children. Several years ago, a study published in the *Journal of the American Dietetic Association* tracking over 3,000 families found that 50 percent of toddlers are considered picky eaters by their caregivers. The percentage of young children in the U.S. who are picky eaters and have poor appetites is so high that experts writing in the journal *Pediatrics* in 2007 remarked, ". . . it could reasonably be said that eating-behavior problems are a normal feature of toddler life."

Tantrums also are surprisingly frequent and intense during the toddler years. Dr. Gina Mireault, a behavioral scientist at Johnson State College in Vermont, studied kids from three separate local preschools. She discerned that toddlers tantrumed, on average, once every few days. Almost a third of the parents surveyed experienced their offsprings' tantrums as distressing or disturbing.

Too much isolated play, manipulating objects in concrete ways, can also elicit autism concerns. But, relative to young girls, young boys are slower to gravitate toward pretend play that is socially oriented. In a French study of preschoolers' outdoor nursery play published in *PLoS One* in 2011, the lead investigator Stéphanie Barbu concluded, ". . . preschool boys played alone more frequently than preschool girls. This difference was especially marked at 3–4 years."

This is significant, since there is a strong movement to detect autistic spectrum disorder earlier, with the median age of diagnosis now falling between ages 3 and 4. Boys' more solitary style of play during these tender years, without gender-informed observation, can make them appear disordered, rather than different.

Parents and educators shouldn't assume the worst when male toddlers play alone. Many little boys are satisfied engaging in solitary play, or playing quietly alongside someone else, lining up toy trains, stacking blocks, or pursuing any range of sensorimotor activities, more mesmerized by objects than fellow flesh-and-blood kids. According to Dr. Barbu, it's not until about age four or five that boys are involved in associative play to the same extent as girls. That's the kind of play where there's verbal interaction, and give-and-take exchanges of toys and ideas—or, non-autistic-like play.

One in 42 boys is now affected by autism, a ratio that calls into question whether boys' differences get abnormalized.

It is commonly believed that autism spectrum kids lack a "theory of mind." I'll provide a layman's definition of this term first, by a layman. Josh Clark, a senior writer at HowStuffWorks.com, provides a fine, no-frills definition: "It refers to a person's ability to create theories about others' minds—what they may be thinking, how they may be feeling, what they may do next. We are able to make these assumptions easily, without even recognizing that we are doing something fundamentally amazing."

It's this very ability to "mind read," or understand that others have thoughts, feelings, and intentions different from our own, and use this feedback to be socially tuned in, that is considered a hallmark sign of autism. However, between the ages of three and four the average girl is roughly twice as capable as the average boy at reading minds, and the gap doesn't markedly close until they reach about age five or older.

That was the conclusion arrived at by Sue Walker, a professor at Queensland University of Technology, Brisbane, Australia, in her 2005 *Journal of Genetic Psychology* study looking at gender differences in "theory of mind" development in groups of preschoolers. Being mindful of boys' less mindfulness during the early toddler years needs to be considered to prevent an inappropriate diagnosis of mild ASD.

Faulty fine-motor skills are often seen as part of an autistic profile. Yet, preschool aged boys have been shown to lag behind their female classmates in this domain. A classic study of preschoolers by Drs. Allen Burton and Michael Dancisak out of the University of Minnesota discovered that females in the 3- to 5-year-old range significantly outperform boys at this age in their acquisition of the "tripod" pencil grip. The so-called "tripod" pencil grip, where the thumb is used to stabilize a pencil pressed firmly against the third and forth digits, with the wrist slightly extended, is generally considered by teachers and occupational therapists as the most effective display of fine-motor dexterity when it comes to writing and drawing.

Finger pointing is one of the fundamental ways that young children express and share their interests, as well as manifest curiosity in the outside world. It's scant use is seen as a warning sign of autism. However, researchers at the University of Sussex in England conducted tests at monthly intervals on 8-month-old infants as they emerged into toddlerhood and found that girls learn to point earlier than boys.

Which is all to say that young boys' social-communication approaches, play styles, and pace of fine-motor development leave them living closer to the autistic spectrum than girls. This confound may explain why boys are five times more likely than girls to be ascribed the diagnosis. One in 42 boys are now affected by autism, a ratio that calls into question whether boys' different pace at acquiring social, emotional, and fine-motor skills gets abnormalized.

It's important to not overstate the case. The possibility that a slow-to-mature toddler will be confused as a moderately or severely autistic is slim. On the extreme end, autism is, more often than not, a conspicuous, lifelong, disabling neurological condition.

Roy Richard Grinker, in his acclaimed book *Unstrange Minds,* masterfully documents the challenges he faced raising Isabel, his daughter with pronounced autism. At age two, she only made passing eye contact, rarely initiated interactions, and had trouble responding to her name in a consistent fashion.

Her play often took the form of rote activities such as drawing the same picture repeatedly or rewinding a DVD to watch identical film clips over and over. Unless awakened each morning with the same greeting, "Get up! Get up!," Isabel became quite agitated. She also tended to be very literal and concrete in her language comprehension: expressions like "I'm so tired I could die" left her apprehensive about actual death. By age five, Isabel remained almost completely nonverbal.

When the signs of autism spectrum disorder are indisputable, as in Isabel's case, early detection and intervention are crucial to bolster verbal communication and social skills. The brain is simply more malleable when children are young. Isabel's story in *Unstrange Minds* is a heroic testament to the strides a child can make when afforded the right interventions at the right time.

Diagnostic conundrums enter the picture when we frame autism as a spectrum disorder (as it is now officially designated in the newly minted *Diagnostic and Statistical Manual 5th Edition,* the psychiatric handbook used to diagnose it) and try to draw a bold line between a slow-to-mature toddler and one on the mild end of the spectrum. What is a doctor to make of a chatty, intellectually advanced, three-year-old patient presenting with a hodgepodge of issues, such as poor eye contact, clumsiness, difficulties transitioning, overactivity or under-activity, tantruming, picky eating, quirky interests, and social awkwardness? Does this presentation indicate mild ASD? Or, does it speak to a combination of off-beat developmental events that result in a toddler experiencing transitory stress, who is otherwise normal, in the broad sense?

We entrust our children to professionals like psychiatrists and psychologists to tease apart the delicate distinctions between mild ASD and a slower pace of development. The trained professionals are supposed to know best. But, do they? A pediatrician is the professional who is most likely to be consulted when a child is suspected of having ASD. While most pediatricians are adequately educated and trained to assess for ASD, a good many of them aren't. How many pediatricians who actually call themselves pediatricians have specialized training in pediatric medicine and/or pediatric mental health?

Several years ago, Gary L. Freed, MD, chief of the Division of General Pediatrics at the University of Michigan, initiated a survey of physicians listed as pediatricians on state licensure files in eight states across the United States: Ohio, Wisconsin, Texas, Mississippi, Massachusetts, Maryland, Oregon, and Arizona. According to the survey, 39 percent of state-identified pediatricians hadn't completed a residency in pediatrics. And even for those who had, their training in pediatric mental health was minimal.

Currently, the American Academy of Pediatrics estimates that less than a quarter of pediatricians around the country have specialized training in child mental health beyond what they receive in a general pediatric residency. The latest data examining pediatricians who have launched themselves into practice reveals that 62 percent of them feel that mental health issues were not adequately covered in medical school. These figures hardly inspire widespread confidence as regards relying on pediatricians to accurately diagnose ASD.

In a 2010 study, 45 percent of graduate students in child psychology had little exposure to coursework in child/adolescent lifespan development.

This brings me to my own cherished profession: child psychology. What does survey data tell us about the current training of child psychologists that speaks directly to their ability to separate out abnormalcy from normalcy?

Poring over the numbers of a 2010 study out of the University of Hartford in Connecticut, I discovered that 45 percent of graduate students in child psychology had either no exposure to or had just an introductory-level exposure to coursework in child/adolescent lifespan development. It is in these classes that emerging child psychologists learn about what is developmentally normal to expect in children.

It would appear that the education and training of a sizable percentage of pediatricians and child psychologists leaves them ill-equipped to tease apart the fine distinction between mild ASD and behaviors that fall within the broad swath of normal childhood development.

When the uptick in ASD numbers was made public by the Centers for Disease Control and Prevention the week before last, Dr. Marshalyn Yeargin-Allsopp, chief of their Developmental Disabilities Branch, said in a press release, "The most important thing for parents to do is to act early when there is a concern about a child's development. If you have a concern about how your child plays, learns, speaks, acts, or moves, take action. Don't wait."

On the one hand, a clarion call of this nature is the push the parents of a child with an unmistakable case of moderate-to-severe ASD (like Isabel above) absolutely need. On the other hand, Dr. Yeagin-Alsopp's remark seems to stoke the very anxiety that haunts the average parent of a slow-to-mature, but otherwise normal kid, edging that parent to transport the kid to a doctor, where there's a good chance that doctor will lack a solid knowledge-template as to what constitutes normal.

Early screening and treatment for ASD must remain a top public health priority, but the numbers make it clear that professionals would benefit from familiarizing and re-familiarizing themselves with the broad range of what is considered normal early childhood development, and with how young boys and girls differ in behaviors that resemble autistic phenomena. Otherwise, the ASD numbers will rise, yet again, with a pool of slow-to-mature children being falsely diagnosed.

Critical Thinking

1. What are some of the serious benefits and drawbacks of early screening for autism in children? Do you think that one of the options outweighs the other?

2. What do you think should be done with the information that "over 30 percent of children diagnosed as autistic at age two no longer fit the diagnosis at age four"? What do you believe is happening to these children?

3. How does gender play a role in the diagnosing of autism? Do you believe that gender differences should be accounted for when conducting early screenings?

Create Central

www.mhhe.com/createcentral

Internet References

American Speech-Language-Hearing Association
   http://www.asha.org/public/speech/disorders/autism
AutismSpeaks.org
   http://www.autismspeaks.org/family-services/tool-kits/100-day-kit/ten-things-every-child-autism-wishes-you-knew
HelpGuide.org
   http://www.helpguide.org/mental/autism_help.htm
KidsHealth.org
   http://kidshealth.org/kid/health_problems/brain/autism.html
National Autistic Society.uk
   http://www.autism.org.uk/about-autism/all-about-diagnosis/diagnosis-the-process-for-children.aspx

Gnaulati, Enrico, "1 in 68 Children Now Has a Diagnosis of Autism Spectrum Disorder. Why?", April 2014. © 2014 The Atlantic Media Co., as first published in The Atlantic Magazine. All rights reserved. Distributed by Tribune Content Agency, LLC

Prepared by: Chris J. Boyatzis, *Bucknell University*
Ellen N. Junn, *California State University, Dominguez Hills*

Article

Unlocking Emily's World

Cracking the code of silence in children with autism who barely speak

CHRIS BERDIK

Learning Outcomes

After reading this article, you will be able to:

- Describe and define what autism is and how the diagnosis is made.
- Understand some of the prevailing theories about the causes of autism.
- Be aware of what treatments exist for autism and describe the research supporting the various treatments.

E mily Browne is laughing, and nobody really knows why. The 14-year-old with a broad face and a mop of curly brown hair has autism. She drifts through her backyard in Boston's Dorchester neighborhood, either staring into the distance or eyeballing a visitor chatting with her dad, Brendan, and her 15-year-old sister, Jennifer, on the nearby patio. That's where the laughter started—a conversational chuckle from somebody on the patio that Emily answered with a rollicking, high-pitched guffaw. Then another, and another, and another.

Emily is growing up, her father says. She is learning new words in her classroom at Joseph Lee School in Dorchester.

Emily can't join the conversation. She is among the 30 percent of children with autism who never learn to speak more than a few words—those considered "nonverbal" or "minimally verbal." Emily was diagnosed with autism at two, but Brendan and his wife, Jeannie, knew something was wrong well before then.

"There was no babbling. She didn't play with anything. You could be standing beside her and call her name, and she wouldn't look at you," says her dad. "Emily was in her own little world."

"We were worried about Emily from pretty much her 12-month checkup … and we had talked with the doctor about the fact that she didn't make any sounds. She didn't really pay attention to anybody, which seemed a little unusual."

But why? What is it about the brains of "minimally verbal" kids like Emily that short circuits the connections between them and everyone else? And can it be overcome? That's the research mission of Boston University's new Center for Autism Research Excellence, where Emily is a study subject.

Partly because of the expanding parameters of what is considered autism, the number of American children diagnosed with autism spectrum disorder has shot up in recent years, from one in 155 children in 1992 to one in 68 in 2014, according to the Centers for Disease Control and Prevention. And Helen Tager-Flusberg, a BU College of Arts & Sciences professor of psychology who has studied language acquisition and autism for three decades and heads the Autism Center, says minimally verbal children are among the most "seriously understudied" of that growing population.

Backed by a five-year, $10 million grant from the National Institutes of Health awarded in late 2012, her team includes researchers and clinicians from Massachusetts General Hospital, Harvard Medical School, Beth Israel Deaconess Medical Center, Northeastern University, and Albert Einstein College of Medicine in New York City. The researchers are focusing on the areas of the brain used for understanding speech, the motor areas activated to produce speech, and the connections between the two. They'll combine functional magnetic resonance imaging (fMRI), electroencephalography (EEG), and neural models of how brains understand and make speech. The models were developed at BU by Barbara Shinn-Cunningham, a professor of biomedical engineering in the College of Engineering, and Frank Guenther, a professor of speech, language, and hearing sciences at BU's Sargent College of Health & Rehabilitation Sciences. They'll also run the first clinical trials of a novel therapy using music and drumming to help minimally verbal children acquire spoken language.

Ultimately, Tager-Flusberg and her colleagues hope to crack the code of silence in the brains of minimally verbal children and give them back their own voices. Getting these kids to utter complete sentences and fully participate in conversation is years away. For now, the goal is to teach words and phrases in a way that can rewire the brain for speech and allow more traditional speech therapy to take hold.

"Imagine if you were stuck in a place where you could not express anything and people were not understanding you," says Tager-Flusberg, who is also a professor of anatomy and neurobiology and of pediatrics on Boston University's Medical Campus. "Can you imagine how distressing and frustrating that would be?"

On a hot, muggy morning in late August, Emily's dad escorts her into the Autism Center on Cummington Mall for a couple hours of tests. It's part of a sound-processing study comparing minimally verbal adolescents with high-functioning autistic adolescents who can speak, as well as normal adolescents and adults.

The investigation is painstaking, because every study must be adapted for subjects who not only don't speak but may also be prone to easy distraction, extreme anxiety, aggressive outbursts, and even running away. "[Minimally verbal children] do tend to understand more than they can speak," says Tager-Flusberg. "But they won't necessarily demonstrate in any situation that they are following what you are saying."

"The study at BU especially was interesting to us because it focused on the kind of autism that Emily has … I know autistic children can behave a certain way—they can be antisocial and so forth—but no one seemed to be addressing the fact that some of these kids can't communicate."

That's obvious in Emily's first task, a vocabulary test. Seated before a computer, she watches as pictures of everyday items pop up on the screen, such as a toothbrush, a shirt, a car, and a shoe. When a computer-generated voice names one of these objects, Emily's job is to tap the correct picture. Emily's earlier pilot testing of this study showed that she understands more than 100 words. But today, she's just not interested. Between short flurries of correct answers, Emily weaves her head, slumps in her chair, or flaps her elbows as the computer voice drones on—car … car … car and then umbrella … umbrella …

umbrella. When one of the researchers tries to get Emily back on task, she simply taps the same spot on the screen over and over. Finally, she gives the screen a hard smack.

The next session is smoother. Emily is given a kind of IQ test in which she quickly and (mostly) correctly matches shapes and colors, identifies patterns, and points out single items within increasingly complicated pictures of animals playing in the park, kids at a picnic, or cluttered yard sales.

Emily's First Words

Emily is minimally verbal, not nonverbal. "Words do come out of her," her dad explains. She'll say "car" when she wants to go for a ride or "home" when she's out somewhere and has had enough. Sometimes she communicates with a combination of sounds and signs or gestures, because she has trouble saying words with multiple syllables. For instance, when she needs a "bathroom," her version sounds like, "ba ba um," but she combines it with a closed hand tilting 90 degrees—pantomiming a toilet flush.

"That's a handy one," her dad says. "She uses it to get out of things. When she's someplace she doesn't want to be, she'll ask to go to the bathroom five or six times."

The first word Emily ever said was "apple" when she was four years old. "We were going through the supermarket, and she grabbed an apple. Said it, and ate it. It was amazing to me," her dad recalls.

The final item on the morning agenda is an EEG study, in which Emily must wear a net of moist electrodes fitted over her head while she listens to a series of beeps in a small, soundproof booth. The researchers have tried EEG with Emily twice before in pilot testing. The first time, she tolerated the electrode net. The second time, she refused. This time, with her dad to comfort her and a rewarding snack of gummi bears, Emily dons the neural net without protest.

The point of this study is to see how well Emily's brain distinguishes differences in sound—a key to understanding speech. For instance, normally developing children learn very early, well before they can speak, to separate out somebody talking from the birds chirping outside the window or an airplane overhead. They also learn to pay attention to deviations in speech that matter—the word "cat" versus "cap"—and to ignore those that don't—cat is cat whether mommy or daddy says it.

"The brain filters out what's important based on what it learns," says Shinn-Cunningham. Some of this sound filtering is automatic, what brain researchers call "subcortical." The rest is more complicated, a top-down process of organizing sounds and focusing the brain's limited attention and processing power on what's important.

EEG measures electrical fields generated by neuron activity in different parts of the brain. "Novel sounds should elicit a larger-than-normal brain response, and that should register on the EEG signal," Shinn-Cunningham explains. There are 128 tiny EEG sensors surrounding Emily's head and upper neck. Each sensor is represented as a line jogging along on the computer monitor outside the darkened booth where Emily sits with her dad holding her hand, watching a silent version of her favorite movie, *Shrek*.

Today's experiment is focused on the automatic end of sound-processing. A constant stream of beeps in one pitch is occasionally interrupted by a higher-pitched beep. How will Emily's brain respond? Most of the time, the 128 EEG lines are tightly packed as they move across the screen. However, muscle movements generate large, visible peaks and troughs in the signals when Emily blinks or lolls her head from side to side. Once, just after a gummi bear break, several large, concentrated spikes show her chewing.

Shifts in attention are much more subtle, and the raw data will have to be processed before anything definitive can be said about Emily's brain. The readout is time-coded with every beep, and the researchers will be particularly interested in the signals from the auditory areas in the brain's temporal cortex, located behind the temples.

The beep test has six five-minute trials. But, after about twenty minutes, Emily is getting restless. It's been a long morning. She starts scratching at the net of sensors in her hair. She's frustrated that *Shrek* is silent. The EEG signals start to swing wildly. From inside the booth, stomping and moans of protest can be heard. When the booth's door is opened at the end of the fourth trial, Emily's eyes are red. She's crying. Her father and the researchers try to cajole her into continuing.

"Just two more, Emmy," her dad says. "Can you do two more for daddy?" And Emily answers with a word she can speak, quite loudly. "Noooo!" They call it a day. Emily will return to the center as the experiments move from beeps to words, and they can finish the last two trials then. All in all, it's been a successful morning. "She did great," says Tager-Flusberg.

In one room at the Autism Center, the researchers have rigged up a mock MRI, using a padded roller board that can slide into a cloth tunnel supported by those foam "noodles" kids use in swimming pools. It's for helping the children in these studies learn what to expect in the real brain scanners operated by Massachusetts General Hospital.

"We've been finishing up our pilot projects for the scanning protocols and trimming them down to a time the kids will tolerate," says Tager-Flusberg. "At first, the imaging folks at MGH

said we need 40 to 50 minutes in the scanner for each subject. I said, 'well that's not happening. These kids won't last that long.'"

The brain scans will be done with the adolescents as well as a group of younger minimally verbal kids, aged six to ten. The younger kids will also participate in an intervention study of a new therapy called Auditory-Motor Mapping Training (AMMT). The therapy was developed by Gottfried Schlaug, a neurologist who runs the Music and Neuroimaging Lab at Beth Israel Deaconess Medical Center. In AMMT, a therapist guides a child through a series of words and phrases, sung in two pitches, while tapping on electronic, tonal drum pads.

"The idea, from a neuroscience perspective," says Schlaug, is that, "maybe in autistic children's brains one of the problems is that the regions that have to do with hearing don't communicate with the regions that control oral motor activity."

"The first time she ever actually said a word to me that I understood, we were in Stop & Shop ... She reached into the bin and she picked up an apple and said 'apple.'"

Many of the same brain areas activated when we move our hands and gesture are also activated when we speak. So, combining the word practice with drumming could help reconnect what Schlaug calls the "hearing and doing" regions of the brain. The initial results, from pilot work on a handful of children in 2009 and 2010, were promising. After five weeks of AMMT, kids who had never spoken before were able to say things like, "more please" and "coat on." That's when Schlaug sought out Tager-Flusberg.

Being Involved in Research

"I was aware of her importance in the field of autism research, and we wanted to discuss these findings with somebody who was an expert to ask if what we were seeing was believable," says Schlaug, who is one of the principal investigators for the Autism Center. For the intervention study, the researchers aim to recruit about 80 minimally verbal children who will be randomized to either 25 sessions of AMMT or a similar therapy that differs in a few vital respects. (The control group subjects will have the option of getting AMMT after the study is complete.)

All the children will get brain scans before and after the therapy to see if improvements in vocal ability correspond with

standard of care and improve access to services for traumatized children, their families, and communities. The network offers training and education on childhood trauma, a wealth of resources and ways to get immediate help for children online or by calling the National Child Abuse Hotline at (800) 4-A-Child.

Future Directions

With the large influx of unaccompanied minor children dropping from summertime peaks, media and public attention have moved on. But the humanitarian crisis is far from over, says Kennedy. Migrant rates could soar again next year, while children and adolescents who are already here—but not receiving needed psychological and other services—are at risk for dropping out of school, being unemployed and possibly winding up in prison.

So what's needed? Funding, for one, both for schools and school-based services as well as for direct immigrant services through the U.S. Department of Health and Human Services, say experts. Early last year, President Obama requested an additional $1.8 billion to help care for unaccompanied minors, but Congress did not pass the request.

More counselors trained in these children's special needs and cultures are also needed. The NLPA, under the leadership of Consoli, Chavez-Dueñas and Torres Fernandez, has developed guidelines for detention center workers and mental health professionals to better help unaccompanied minors, which will be published on the NLPA site. Some keys: making sure unaccompanied minors receive mental health screenings once in U.S. custody and having culturally responsive assessments. The guidelines include a variety of interventions and therapeutic approaches to use with these children, such as narrative therapy or allowing children to process their grief and loss through a memorial wall.

Consoli hopes that as the spotlight on the border kids has shifted, attention won't similarly pass without necessary measures being taken.

"Even though right now it's a really hot issue, it is a longstanding issue," he says. "We're hoping that it won't peak and pass—that it will get the actions that are needed."

Critical Thinking

1. What should the US government do to support and protect the immigrant children fleeing their countries?

2. How would you counsel parents in Mexico and elsewhere who are encouraging or permitting their children to try and cross the US boarder alone and unaccompanied?

3. Critique the United States' legal and immigration response to this new surge of children into the United States.

Internet References

Administration for Children and Families, Health Human Services .gov
  http://www.acf.hhs.gov/unaccompanied-children-frequently-asked-questions

ImmigrationPolicyCenter.org
  http://www.immigrationpolicy.org/just-facts/unaccompanied-children-resource-page

National Journal.com
  http://www.nationaljournal.com/domesticpolicy/why-90-000-children-flooding-our-border-is-not-an-immigration-story-20140616

National Network for Immigrant and Refugee Rights.com
  http://www.nnirr.org/drupal/migrant-children

New York Times.com
  http://www.nytimes.com/2014/07/10/world/americas/fleeing-gangs-children-head-to-us-border.html

Collier, Lorna. "Helping Immigrant Children Heal," *Monitor on Psychology,* March 2015. Copyright © 2015 by American Psychological Association. Reprinted by permission.

Article

Prepared by: Chris J. Boyatzis, *Bucknell University*
Ellen N. Junn, *California State University, Dominguez Hills*

The Sexualization of Girls: Is the Popular Culture Harming Our Kids?

GWEN DEWAR

Learning Outcomes

After reading this article, you will be able to:

- Discuss and explain the increasing trends in the media and elsewhere to sexualize young girls.

- What are the negative consequences of heightened sexuality for girls at a young age and into adulthood?

- Visit your local department store and examine the young girls' clothing sections. Do your observations support the findings in this article? Why do manufacturers produce this more sexualized clothing if parents do not favor this practice?

W hat do psychologists mean by the "sexualization of girls"?

According to the American Psychological Association, sexualization occurs when "individuals are regarded as sex objects and evaluated in terms of their physical characteristics and sexiness."

This doesn't sound like something that the parents of young children should have to worry about. Yet the popular culture seems increasingly accepting of the sexualization of children.

Examples come from many quarters:

- A photo editorial in Paris Vogue that portrays pre-adolescent girls as heavily made-up, sophisticated *femme fatales*

- Clothing—including thong underwear—marketed for preschoolers and elementary school kids that feature printed slogans like "Eye Candy" or "Wink Wink"

- Fashion dolls marketed at 6-year-old girls that feature sexualized clothing, like fishnet stockings

- Beauty pageants for little girls, complete with heavy mascara, high heels, and bathing suits

- Pornography and sexually explicit pop music videos that feature young women dressed to resemble little girls

The examples are creepy. But what exactly is *bad* about them?

The most common worries are that girls will learn to view themselves as sex objects, or that girls will develop anxieties when they fail to meet popular standards of beauty.

But I'm also concerned about the effects on the population at large. Do media images of sexualized girls change the way we view children? Are people liable to judge children as more sophisticated than they really are? Are we more likely to believe that young girls are willing participants in sexual activity?

There is surprisingly little research on the subject. Still, the worries don't seem far-fetched.

For example, there is evidence that being self-conscious about one's sexual attractiveness interferes with intellectual performance. People do more poorly on math tests when they are forced to think about their looks.

It also seems that certain kinds of sexual imagery can make ordinary people form unconscious links between children and sex. Here are the details.

How Concern with Body Image Makes People Less Smart

Barbara Frederickson wondered if being concerned with one's physical appearance might impair one's ability to think clearly. So she and her colleagues devised an experiment in which they asked 82 college students to change their clothes (Frederickson et al 1998).

Each student was randomly assigned to try on EITHER a crewneck sweater OR a one-piece bathing suit. Next, the student was asked to evaluate the garment and the way it made him or her look. Afterward, the student was given a math test.

How did the clothing experience relate to the students' subsequent performance on the math test?

For male students, there was no difference between conditions. But for female students, the swimming suit experience had a more negative effect: Women performed significantly worse on the math test after changing into the bathing suit.

A subsequent study found that both sexes were adversely affected by the swimming suit experience (Hebl et al. 2004). Does something akin to the "stupid swimming suit" effect apply to our kids? Nobody yet has done the research. But it seems rather likely.

Evidence that Sexual Images of Minors Influence the Way We View Children

Does the sexualization of young girls affect the way ordinary people regard kids? This isn't easy to test. As you might imagine, ethical considerations make experiments very difficult.

The most relevant study to date tested the effects of "barely legal" pornography, in which an 18-year-old model is made to look younger. Researchers Bryant Paul and Daniel Linz presented 154 undergraduates—the majority of whom were women—with sexually explicit images.

Some images depicted adult women who appeared to be at least 21 years old. Other images depicted females who appeared to be minors.

After presenting these images, the researchers administered a classic test of unconscious association. They presented the study participants with a series of images and words on a computer screen. The test worked like this:

First an image was flashed on the screen—e.g., a non-sexual image of a girl who appeared to be about 12 years old.

Next, a series of letters appeared. Sometimes, these letters spelled out a word (e.g., "beauty"). In other cases, the letters spelled out a nonsense word (e.g., "bartey").

Participants were instructed to press the "W" key as soon as they could tell whether or not the letters spelled out a genuine word. If the letters spelled out a nonsense word, participants were to press the "N" key.

Study participants evaluated an array of words, including neutral words ("window," basket," cloudy") and words with sexual connotations ("sexy," "erotic," and "arousing").

The researchers measured reaction times, and compared them with the reaction times of people who had been shown pornographic images of apparently adult women. How long did it take people to accurately classify the words and nonsense words?

It depended on the words and the images.

The people who'd seen the "barely legal porn" were quicker to recognize words with sexual connotations when those words were presented immediately after an *nonsexual,* image of a girl who appeared to be around 12 years old.

Implications

Did the viewers of barely legal porn become more tolerant of child sexual abuse? Researchers found no evidence of this.

But the most accepted interpretation of word association effects is that people have an easier time recognizing words when these words are already "on our minds."

It's called spreading activation—the idea that viewing an image makes your mind activate memories and associations that are linked with the image. So if you see a table, some part of your mind is ready to think about chairs, too.

The "barely legal" study suggests that ordinary—people who aren't pedophiles—have no trouble learning to associate 12-year-old girls with sexuality. And that was after only a brief exposure to simulated images of *teen* sexuality in the laboratory.

What happens when people are repeatedly exposed? What happens when the imagery features 7-year-old girls, rather than adolescents? And what happens when pedophiles see the popular culture endorsing the sexualization of children?

These questions haven't been addressed by current research. But the stakes seem high. Perhaps in the next few years, new studies will help us understand the true costs of sexualizing children.

References

Fortenberry JD. 2009. An article and commentaries on the sexualization of girls. *J Sex Res.* 46(4):249.

Fredrickson BL, Roberts TA, Noll SM, Quinn DM, and Twenge JM. 1998. That swimsuit becomes you: sex differences in self-objectification, restrained eating, and math performance. *J Pers Soc Psychol.* 75(1):269–84.

Hebl MR, King EB, and Lin J. 2004. The swimsuit becomes us all: ethnicity, gender, and vulnerability to self-objectification. *Pers Soc Psychol Bull.* 30(10):1322–31.

Paul B and Linz D. 2008. The effects of exposure to virtual child pornography on viewer cognitions and attitudes toward deviant sexual behavior. *Communication Research* 35(1): 3–38.

Sherman AM and Zurbriggen. 2014. "Boys Can Be Anything": Effect of Barbie Play on Girls' Career Cognitions. *Sex Roles* 70(5): 195–208.

Wonderlich AL, Ackard DM, and Henderson JB. 2005. Childhood beauty pageant contestants: associations with adult disordered eating and mental health. *Eat Disord.* 13(3):291–301.

See more at: http://www.parentingscience.com/sexualization-of-girls. html#sthash.3K4i9jxU.dpuf

Critical Thinking

1. Imagine you are a parent of a young girl, how might you help to counteract this early sexualization of girls for your own daughter? What specific steps would you take to reduce these negative consequences?

2. Based on the research, how does this early sexualization contribute to lower self-esteem in girls and potentially increase violence against women by males?

3. Compare and contrast this early sexualization of girls in other countries. What accounts for these cultural and international differences and what long-term impact might it have on society?

Internet References

American Psychological Association

http://www.apa.org/pi/women/programs/girls/report.aspx

http://www.apa.org/pi/women/programs/girls/report-full.pdf

http://www.apa.org/pi/women/programs/girls/

CNN

http://www.cnn.com/2011/09/12/opinion/henson-toddlers-tiaras/

Huffington Post

http://www.huffingtonpost.com/dr-jim-taylor/the-disturbing-sexualization_b_1948451.html

PBS.org

http://www.pbs.org/newshour/updates/social_issues-july-dec13-sexualization_12-21/

Psychology Today.com

https://www.psychologytoday.com/blog/overcoming-child-abuse/201203/the-sexualization-women-and-girls

Dewar, Gwen. "The Sexualization of Girls: Is the Popular Culture Harming Our Kids?," *Parenting Science*, 2012. Copyright © 2012 by Gwen Dewar, Ph.D. Reprinted by permission.

Prepared by: Chris J. Boyatzis, *Bucknell University*
Ellen N. Junn, *California State University, Dominguez Hills*

Article

Selling a New Generation on Guns

MIKE MCINTIRE

Learning Outcomes

After reading this article, you will be able to:

- Describe organizations interested in selling guns to a new generation of future gun owners by marketing to parents of children. What is your opinion of the gun industry's interest in recruiting more youth to become gun users?

- Discuss and defend both a pro-gun and an anti-gun view of exposing children to toy guns or actual gun use as a child or young adult. What are the benefits or dangers for each position?

Threatened by long-term declining participation in shooting sports, the firearms industry has poured millions of dollars into a broad campaign to ensure its future by getting guns into the hands of more, and younger, children.

The industry's strategies include giving firearms, ammunition and cash to youth groups; weakening state restrictions on hunting by young children; marketing an affordable military-style rifle for "junior shooters" and sponsoring semi-automatic-handgun competitions for youths; and developing a target-shooting video game that promotes brand-name weapons, with links to the websites of their makers.

The pages of Junior Shooters, an industry-supported magazine that seeks to get children involved in the recreational use of firearms, once featured a smiling 15-year-old girl clutching a semiautomatic rifle. At the end of an accompanying article that extolled target shooting with a Bushmaster AR-15—an advertisement elsewhere in the magazine directed readers to a coupon for buying one—the author encouraged youngsters to share the article with a parent.

"Who knows?" it said. "Maybe you'll find a Bushmaster AR-15 under *your* tree some frosty Christmas morning!"

The industry's youth-marketing effort is backed by extensive social research and is carried out by an array of nonprofit groups financed by the gun industry, an examination by *The New York Times* found. The campaign picked up steam about five years ago with the completion of a major study that urged a stronger emphasis on the "recruitment and retention" of new hunters and target shooters.

The overall objective was summed up in another study, commissioned last year by the shooting sports industry, that suggested encouraging children experienced in firearms to recruit other young people. The report, which focused on children ages 8 to 17, said these "peer ambassadors" should help introduce wary youngsters to guns slowly, perhaps through paintball, archery or some other less intimidating activity.

"The point should be to get newcomers started shooting something, with the natural next step being a move toward actual firearms," said the report, which was prepared for the National Shooting Sports Foundation and the Hunting Heritage Trust.

Firearms manufacturers and their two primary surrogates, the National Rifle Association of America and the National Shooting Sports Foundation, have long been associated with high-profile battles to fend off efforts at gun control and to widen access to firearms. The public debate over the mass shootings in Newtown, Conn., and elsewhere has focused largely on the availability of guns, along with mental illness and the influence of violent video games.

Little attention has been paid, though, to the industry's youth-marketing initiatives. They stir passionate views, with proponents arguing that introducing children to guns can provide a safe and healthy pastime, and critics countering that it fosters a corrosive gun culture and is potentially dangerous.

The N.R.A. has for decades given grants for youth shooting programs, mostly to Boy Scout councils and 4-H groups, which traditionally involved single-shot rimfire rifles, BB guns, and archery. Its $21 million in total grants in 2010 was nearly double what it gave out five years earlier.

Newer initiatives by other organizations go further, seeking to introduce children to high-powered rifles and handguns while invoking the same rationale of those older, more traditional programs: that firearms can teach "life skills" like responsibility, ethics, and citizenship. And the gun industry points to injury statistics that it says show a greater likelihood of getting hurt cheerleading or playing softball than using firearms for fun and sport.

Still, some experts in child psychiatry say that encouraging youthful exposure to guns, even in a structured setting with an emphasis on safety, is asking for trouble. Dr. Jess P. Shatkin, the director of undergraduate studies in child and adolescent mental health at New York University, said that young people are naturally impulsive and that their brains "are engineered to take risks," making them ill suited for handling guns.

"There are lots of ways to teach responsibility to a kid," Dr. Shatkin said. "You don't need a gun to do it."

Steve Sanetti, the president of the National Shooting Sports Foundation, said it was better to instruct children in the safe use of a firearm through hunting and target shooting, and engage them in positive ways with the heritage of guns in America. His industry is well positioned for the task, he said, but faces an unusual challenge: introducing minors to activities that involve products they cannot legally buy and that require a high level of maturity.

Ultimately, Mr. Sanetti said, it should be left to parents, not the government, to decide if and when to introduce their children to shooting and what sort of firearms to use.

"It's a very significant decision," he said, "and it involves the personal responsibility of the parent and personal responsibility of the child."

Trying to Reverse a Trend

The shooting sports foundation, the tax-exempt trade association for the gun industry, is a driving force behind many of the newest youth initiatives. Its national headquarters is in Newtown, just a few miles from Sandy Hook Elementary School, where Adam Lanza, 20, used his mother's Bushmaster AR-15 to kill 20 children and 6 adults last month.

The foundation's $26 million budget is financed mostly by gun companies, associated businesses and the foundation's SHOT Show, the industry's annual trade show, according to its latest tax return.

Although shooting sports and gun sales have enjoyed a rebound recently, the long-term demographics are not favorable, as urbanization, the growth of indoor pursuits like video games and changing cultural mores erode consumer interest. Licensed hunters fell from 7 percent of the population in 1975 to fewer than 5 percent in 2005, according to federal data.

Galvanized by the declining share, the industry redoubled its efforts to reverse the trend about five years ago.

The focus on young people has been accompanied by foundation-sponsored research examining popular attitudes toward hunting and shooting. Some of the studies used focus groups and telephone surveys of teenagers to explore their feelings about guns and people who use them, and offered strategies for generating a greater acceptance of firearms.

The *Times* reviewed more than a thousand pages of these studies, obtained from gun industry websites and online archives, some of them produced as recently as last year. Most were prepared by consultants retained by the foundation, and at least one was financed with a grant from the United States Fish and Wildlife Service.

In an interview, Mr. Sanetti said the youth-centered research was driven by the inevitable "tension" the industry faces, given that no one under 18 can buy a rifle or a shotgun from a licensed dealer or even possess a handgun under most circumstances. That means looking for creative and appropriate ways to introduce children to shooting sports.

"There's nothing alarmist or sinister about it," Mr. Sanetti said. "It's realistic."

Pointing to the need to "start them young," one study concluded that "stakeholders such as managers and manufacturers should target programs toward youth 12 years old and younger."

"This is the time that youth are being targeted with competing activities," it said. "It is important to consider more hunting and target-shooting recruitment programs aimed at middle school level, or earlier."

Aware that introducing firearms to young children could meet with resistance, several studies suggested methods for smoothing the way for target-shooting programs in schools. One cautioned, "When approaching school systems, it is important to frame the shooting sports only as a mechanism to teach other life skills, rather than an end to itself."

In another report, the authors warned against using human silhouettes for targets when trying to recruit new shooters and encouraged using words and phrases like "sharing the experience," "family," and "fun." They also said children should be enlisted to prod parents to let them join shooting activities: "Such a program could be called 'Take Me Hunting' or 'Take Me Shooting.'"

The industry recognized that state laws limiting hunting by children could pose a problem, according to a "Youth Hunting Report" prepared by the shooting sports foundation and two other groups. Declaring that "the need for aggressive recruitment is urgent," the report said a primary objective should be to "eliminate or reduce age minimums." Still another study recommended allowing children to get a provisional license to hunt with an adult, "perhaps even before requiring them to take hunter safety courses."

The effort has succeeded in a number of states, including Wisconsin, which in 2009 lowered the minimum hunting age to 10 from 12, and Michigan, where in 2011 the age minimum for hunting small game was eliminated for children accompanied by an adult mentor. The foundation cited statistics suggesting that youth involvement in hunting, as well as target shooting, had picked up in recent years amid the renewed focus on recruitment.

Gun companies have spent millions of dollars to put their recruitment strategies into action, either directly or through the shooting sports foundation and other organizations. The support takes many forms.

The Scholastic Steel Challenge, started in 2009, introduces children as young as 12 to competitive handgun shooting using steel targets. Its "platinum" sponsors include the shooting sports foundation, Smith & Wesson and Glock, which donated 60, 9-millimeter semiautomatic pistols, according to the group's website.

The site features a quote from a gun company executive praising the youth initiative and saying that "anyone in the firearms industry that overlooks its potential is missing the boat."

Larry Potterfield, the founder of MidwayUSA, one of the nation's largest sellers of shooting supplies and a major sponsor of the Scholastic Steel Challenge, said he did not fire a handgun until he was 21, adding that they "are the most difficult guns to learn to shoot well." But, he said, he sees nothing wrong with children using them.

"Kids need arm strength and good patience to learn to shoot a handgun well," he said in an e-mail, "and I would think that would come in the 12 to 14 age group for most kids."

Another organization, the nonprofit Youth Shooting Sports Alliance, which was created in 2007, has received close to $1 million in cash, guns and equipment from the shooting sports foundation and firearms-related companies, including ATK, Winchester and Sturm, Ruger & Company, its tax returns show. In 2011, the alliance awarded 58 grants. A typical grant: 23 rifles, 4 shotguns, 16 cases of ammunition and other materials, which went to a Michigan youth camp.

The foundation and gun companies also support *Junior Shooters* magazine, which is based in Idaho and was started in 2007. The publication is filled with catchy advertisements and articles about things like zombie targets, pink guns and, under the heading "Kids Gear," tactical rifle components with military-style features like pistol grips and collapsible stocks.

Gun companies often send new models to the magazine for children to try out with adult supervision. Shortly after Sturm, Ruger announced in 2009 a new, lightweight semiautomatic rifle that had the "look and feel" of an AR-15 but used less expensive .22-caliber cartridges, *Junior Shooters* received one for review. The magazine had three boys aged 14 to 17 fire it and wrote that they "had an absolute ball!"

Junior Shooters' editor, Andy Fink, acknowledged in an editorial that some of his magazine's content stirred controversy.

"I have heard people say, even shooters that participate in some of the shotgun shooting sports, such things as, 'Why do you need a semiautomatic gun for hunting?' " he wrote. But if the industry is to survive, he said, gun enthusiasts must embrace all youth shooting activities, including ones "using semiautomatic firearms with magazines holding 30 to 100 rounds."

In an interview, Mr. Fink elaborated. Semiautomatic firearms are actually not weapons, he said, unless someone chooses to hurt another person with them, and their image has been unfairly tainted by the news media. There is no legitimate reason children should not learn to safely use an AR-15 for recreation, he said.

"They're a tool, not any different than a car or a baseball bat," Mr. Fink said. "It's no different than a junior shooting a .22 or a shotgun. The difference is in the perception of the viewer."

The Weapon of Choice

The AR-15, the civilian version of the military's M-16 and M-4, has been aggressively marketed as a cool and powerful step up from more traditional target and hunting rifles. But its appearance in mass shootings—in addition to Newtown, the gun was also used last year in the movie theater massacre in Aurora, Colo., and the attack on firefighters in Webster, N.Y.—has prompted calls for tighter restrictions. The AR-15 is among the guns included in a proposed ban on a range of semiautomatic weapons that was introduced in the Senate last week.

Given the gun's commercial popularity, it is perhaps unsurprising that AR-15-style firearms have worked their way into youth shooting programs. At a "Guns 'n Grillin" weekend last fall, teenagers at a Boy Scout council in Virginia got to shoot AR-15s. They are used in youth competitions held each year at a National Guard camp in Ohio, and in "junior clinics" taught by Army or Marine marksmanship instructors, some of them sponsored by gun companies or organizations they support.

ArmaLite, a successor company to the one that developed the AR-15, is offering a similar rifle, the AR-10, for the grand prize in a raffle benefiting the Illinois State Rifle Association's "junior high-power" team, which uses AR-15s in its competitions. Bushmaster has offered on its website a coupon worth $350 off the price of an AR-15 "to support and encourage junior shooters."

Military-style firearms are prevalent in a target-shooting video game and mobile app called Point of Impact, which was sponsored by the shooting sports foundation and *Guns & Ammo* magazine. The game—rated for ages 9 and up in the iTunes store—allows players to shoot brand-name AR-15 rifles and semiautomatic handguns at inanimate targets, and it provides links to gun makers' websites as well as to the foundation's "First Shots" program, intended to recruit new shooters.

Upon the game's release in January 2011, foundation executives said in a news release that it was one of the industry's "most unique marketing tools directed at a younger audience." Mr. Sanetti of the shooting sports foundation said sponsorship of the game was an experiment intended to deliver safety tips to players, while potentially generating interest in real-life sports.

The confluence of high-powered weaponry and youth shooting programs does not sit well even with some proponents of those programs. Stephan Carlson, a University of Minnesota environmental science professor whose research on the positive effects of learning hunting and outdoor skills in 4-H classes has been cited by the gun industry, said he "wouldn't necessarily go along" with introducing children to more powerful firearms that added nothing useful to their experience.

"I see why the industry would be pushing it, but I don't see the value in it," Mr. Carlson said. "I guess it goes back to the skill base we're trying to instill in the kids. What are we preparing them for?"

For Mr. Potterfield of MidwayUSA, who said his own children started shooting "boys' rifles" at age 4, getting young people engaged with firearms—provided they have the maturity and the physical ability to handle them—strengthens an endangered American tradition.

Mr. Potterfield and his wife, Brenda, have donated more than $5 million for youth shooting programs in recent years, a campaign that he said was motivated by philanthropy, not "return on investment."

"Our gifting is pure benevolence," he said. "We grew up and live in rural America and have owned guns, hunted and fished all of our lives. This is our community, and we hope to preserve it for future generations."

Critical Thinking

1. Think back to when you were a child. Did you engage in playing with toy guns and did your parents encourage pretend gun play? Reflect on and discuss how those childhood experiences may have influenced your attitudes toward guns and gun control today as an adult.

2. Do you think that American beliefs about gun ownership and usage is different from other countries? Explain why or why not. Why might prominent gun play by children in other countries (e.g., Japan where there gun ownership is extremely restricted) may not have serious societal consequences?

3. Given this article, if you are not already a gun owner, do you envision yourself becoming a future owner and/or encouraging your own children to become familiar with guns? Why or why not?

Internet References

ColoraBaby.com
    http://www.calorababy.co.za/kids/toy-guns-real-dangers.html
National Center for Biotechnology Information, NIH.gov
    http://www.ncbi.nlm.nih.gov/pubmed/3969326
ParentMap.com
    https://www.parentmap.com/article/weapons-ban-just-how-bad-are-toy-guns-for-kids
PoliceOne.com
    http://www.policeone.com/Officer-Safety/articles/7959040-How-police-can-educate-the-public-about-dangers-of-toy-guns/
Youth Shooting Sports Alliance
    http://www.youthshootingsa.com/

McIntire, Mike. "Selling a New Generation on Guns," *The New York Times,* January 2013. Copyright © 2013 by New York Times. Reprinted by permission.

Article

Prepared by: Chris J. Boyatzis, *Bucknell University*
Ellen N. Junn, *California State University, Dominguez Hills*

Biology Doesn't Justify Gender Divide for Toys

There is concern at the increasing segregation of toys and books for boys and girls. Is there any scientific justification, asks the author of Delusions of Gender.

CORDELIA FINE

Learning Outcomes

After reading this article, you will be able to:

- Summarize the recent trends in marketing toys by gender. Explain why stores and manufacturers continue this practice and why parents appear to accept this practice?

- Discuss the research showing the negative effects of stereotyping toy preferences for girls and boys. Should manufacturers and society stop portraying toys as gendered?

- When you buy toys for a new baby or a niece or nephew, explain why you choose the toys you do. Given this article, explain whether your choices of gifts might change in the future. Why or why not?

C aught on camera in the "pink aisle" of a US toy store, 5-year-old Riley posed a multibillion dollar question: "Why does all the girls have to buy pink stuff, and all the boys have to buy different coloured stuff?"

Her impassioned critique of profit-boosting gendered toy marketing has been viewed over 4 million times on YouTube. She isn't a lone voice. Campaigns such as Let Toys Be Toys in the UK have also expressed frustration at the way manufacturers and shops have increasingly restricted the interests of girls to the narrow domain between the twin pink pillars of femininity—being caring and being pretty—while the broader, "different coloured" terrain is for boys.

The group has recently expanded its focus to include books, after the publication of titles such as *The Brilliant Boys' Colouring Book* and *The Beautiful Girls' Colouring Book*. It argues that, if the purpose of books is "opening minds and hearts … broadening horizons," such titles do the opposite.

In a recent UK parliamentary debate, politicians Jenny Willott, Elizabeth Truss and Chi Onwurah also expressed concern that the "pinkification" of toys for girls was adding to gender inequality in careers in science, technology, engineering and mathematics. Willott, for instance, drawing on a basic tenet of early education, observed that "children learn through play; it's how they develop skills and interests."

But the detrimental effects of this kind of marketing, though clearly only one factor in a mix of many influences on the young, may run broader and deeper. It polarises children into stereotypes. It's not just that vehicles, weapons and construction sets are presented as "for boys," while toys of domesticity and beautification are "for girls." Toys for boys facilitate competition, control, agency and dominance; those for girls promote cooperation and nurturance. These gender stereotypes, acquired in childhood, underlie a host of well-documented biases against women in traditionally masculine domains and roles, and hinder men from sharing more in the responsibilities and rewards of domestic life.

Relentless Stereotyping

True, there is no research linking gendered marketing of toys and books and later occupational discrimination or sharing of household chores. But the smart money would say the effects won't be trivial, given that children are enveloped in some of the most relentless stereotyping to be found in the 21st century.

A common rebuttal to movements towards more gender-neutral marketing, of the sort recently promised by store chain Marks & Spencer, for example, is that what we see on the shelves reflects "innate" sex differences. Even monkeys, we are told, have gendered toy preferences, and there are no sexist toy ads in monkey society.

Newborn boys and girls, untouched by the forces of gender socialisation, supposedly show stereotypical preferences for looking at hanging mobiles versus faces, respectively. And, we are told, girls with congenital adrenal hyperplasia (CAH), who are exposed to unusually high levels of testosterone in the womb, prefer "boy toys."

But these findings are far less compelling than they appear. For instance, if the preference of female rhesus monkeys for stuffed animals shows that love of dolls is "innate" in girls, what do we make of the fact that the favourite toy of male vervet monkeys was a stuffed dog, which they played with more than a third longer than a toy car?

Recent experiments, more methodologically rigorous than the much-cited mobiles versus faces newborn study, found no sex differences in the preferences of babies for looking at objects versus faces. Both preferred the latter to an equal extent. And girls with CAH—born with atypical or masculinised genitalia, who undergo intensive medical and psychiatric intervention and have physical characteristics inconsistent with cultural ideals of feminine attractiveness—may be more willing to play with "boy toys" because of unconsidered effects of the condition on their psychosexual development, rather than because their brains have been "wired for wheels."

Self-socialisation

Existing science simply doesn't support the view that gender-neutral toys or books are, at best, a pointless railing against nature or, at worse, politically correct meddling with children's "true" natures. Social experience isn't something that interferes with the emergence of a child's "real," underlying design. It is an integral part of the construction, step by step, of the developmental pathway—destination uncertain.

Moreover, developmental psychologists have found that children are very aware of the importance placed on the social category of gender, and highly motivated to discover what is "for boys" and what is "for girls." Socialisation isn't just imposed by others; a child actively self-socialises. Once a child realises (at about 2 to 3 years of age) on which side of the great gender divide they belong, the well-known dynamics of norms, in-group preference and out-group prejudice kick-in.

When Riley's adult companion makes the common mollifying observation that, "If boys want to buy pink they can buy pink, right?," he is only right in the way that it's technically correct to say that men can wear dresses to work, if they want.

Gendered toy and book marketing doesn't create gender stereotypes, roles and norms, but it does reinforce them. It may be profitable to corporations, but there is a social cost—and science offers no moral comfort that there is a biological justification.

Why do all the girls have to buy pink stuff? Let's keep asking.

Critical Thinking

1. Design a new toy campaign for a major toy store that would not rely on gender typing of toys.

2. Imagine that you are a parent. Based on this article, what concrete steps will you take in selecting toys for your child and how will you respond if your child shows strong preferences for traditionally opposite toys?

3. Think back to when you were growing up. What kind of toys did your parents buy for you? What kinds of toys did you want? Reflect on your past experiences and integrate the research to explain your feelings now.

Internet References

Atlantic
    http://www.theatlantic.com/business/archive/2014/12/toys-are-more-divided-by-gender-now-than-they-were-50-years-ago/383556/
Change.org
    https://www.change.org/p/toys-r-us-stop-marketing-gender-stereotypes-to-children
Huffington Post
    http://www.huffingtonpost.com/rob-watson/hey-toys-r-us-stop-thrusting-gender-roles-on-my-kids_b_4025214.html
National Association for the Education of Young Children
    http://www.naeyc.org/content/what-research-says-gender-typed-toys

Fine, Cordelia. "Biology Doesn't Justify Gender Divide for Toys," *New Scientist Magazine,* March 2014. Copyright © 2014 by Tribune Content Agency (TMS). Reprinted by permission.

A Court Put a 9-Year-Old in Shackles for Stealing Chewing Gum — an Outrage That Happens Every Single Day by Bryan Schatz

153

Article

Prepared by: Chris J. Boyatzis, *Bucknell University*
Ellen N. Junn, *California State University, Dominguez Hills*

A Court Put a 9-Year-Old in Shackles for Stealing Chewing Gum—an Outrage That Happens Every Single Day

Research shows that shackling is bad for kids and unnecessary for courtroom safety. So why do judges keep doing it?

BRYAN SCHATZ

Learning Outcomes

After reading this article, you will be able to:

- Define juvenile shackling and understand the legal implications.

- Cite the pros and cons for the use of juvenile shackling.

- Be familiar with whether juvenile shackling is used extensively throughout the United States and whether the trend is increasing or decreasing in recent years.

The nine-year-old stole [1] a 14-stick pack of Trident "Layers" chewing gum, Orchard Peach and Ripe Mango flavor, worth $1.48. He'd lingered by the beverage isle of the Super 1 Foods in Post Falls, Idaho, for a while before bailing out the front door. The theft led to a missed court appearance, which led to an arrest and a night spent in a juvenile jail. The next day, the third-grader appeared in court, chained and shackled.

At least 100,000 children are shackled in the US every year, according to estimates by David Shapiro, a campaign manager at the Campaign Against Indiscriminate Juvenile Shackling. (Formal data on numbers of shackled kids does not exist.) As juvenile justice practices have grown more punitive over the past several decades, shackling has become far more common. This month, the American Bar Association (ABA) passed a resolution calling for an end to this practice because it is harmful to juveniles, largely unnecessary for courtroom safety—and contradicts existing law. "We're not just talking handcuffs here. These kids are virtually hog-tied," says John D. Elliott, a South Carolina defense attorney who worked on the resolution. "The only difference is their hands are in front."

The restraints—which include handcuffs, belly chains, and leg irons—are used on kids of all ages and often don't fit the severity of their crime: The majority of kids are in court for non-violent offenses, like shoplifting or truancy.

The ABA says that this practice is contrary to law because it undermines the accused's right to be presumed innocent. In adult criminal court, if the defendant is seen by the jury in any sort of restraint, that's almost always considered a mistrial, explains Judge Jay Blitzman from Massachusetts, who worked on the ABA's resolution and helped pass anti-shackling policy for juveniles in his state. "You're sending a message, and it's not subliminal. It's: 'This guy is dangerous.'" The ABA argues that these anti-shackling principles observed in adult court should apply with equal, if not greater, force for children.

"We're not just talking handcuffs here. These kids are virtually hog-tied."

There's plenty of behavioral science establishing that harsh treatment of young offenders is counterproductive. Even one day of unnecessary detention can have profoundly negative impacts on children's mental and physical health. And shackling, the ABA argues, goes against the therapeutic goals of the juvenile justice system because it humiliates kids: Child psychologists have testified that publicly shackling children can be so damaging to their developing personal identity that it can lead to further criminal behavior in the future.

Indeed, the mother of the nine-year-old alluded to this in an interview with Idaho's *Coeur d'Alene Press:* "He feels already like he's the outcast of the family, like he's not as good as everybody else," she said, adding that he fears becoming like his father, who has served time in jail.

The rise in juvenile shackling began in the 1980s, when states started passing tough-on-crime laws in response to a perceived rise in youth crime. Influential criminologists predicted a coming wave of "superpredator" juvenile criminals, including "elementary school youngsters who pack guns instead of lunches." The prediction didn't come true, but it spurred a rush toward harsher punishment for kids, including life without parole, mandatory minimums, and automatic transfer to adult court for certain offenses. This hardened approach extended to courthouse security after multiple fatal shootings in courts across the country, most notably a 2005 incident in an Atlanta courthouse that left two people dead. As Elliott puts it, the courts became "virtually unyielding" after that.

Massachusetts implemented an anti-shackling rule in 2010 and since then "there really have never been issues with its implementation."

To this day, many judges, prosecutors, and law enforcement officers argue that juvenile shackling preserves courtroom safety and order. But there's little evidence to support that claim, argues the ABA, especially given that several states have curtailed the practice with little to no ill effects. Since Florida's Miami-Dade County outlawed shackling kids in 2006, not one of the more than 20,000 children who have appeared in court unbound has escaped or harmed anyone, according to 2011 data. Florida eliminated indiscriminate shackling statewide in 2009, and in the two years following the ruling, officials reported only one disruptive incident. Massachusetts implemented an anti-shackling rule in 2010 and since then "there really have never been issues with its implementation," says Blitzman.

Several states are currently considering legislation or court orders to limit the use of shackling, including Nebraska, Indiana, Connecticut, Minnesota, Utah, and Tennessee.

Colorado is also debating an anti-shackling bill. Ann Roan, the state training director for the Colorado Office of the State Public Defender, says she is optimistic that it will pass during this year's legislative session. She explains why: "It's just hard to come up with any research at all that says shackling doesn't harm children."

Critical Thinking

1. What is your opinion about whether juveniles should be shackled or not? What evidence would you cite for your views?

2. Do you think shackling of alleged juvenile defendants serves a deterrent purpose? Given the cognitive development of juveniles, why or why not?

3. How would you feel if you were shackled as a juvenile? What might be the future psychological consequences of being shackled? How can you balance the needs of the juvenile versus the victim?

Internet References

American Bar Association, ABAjournal.com
http://www.abajournal.com/news/article/should_juveniles_be_shackled_in_court_or_sentenced_to_life_without_parole_a

Juvenile Justice Information Exchange, JJIE.org
http://jjie.org/aclu-wants-supreme-court-to-review-shackling-of-juveniles/

National Conference of State Legislators, NCSL.org
http://www.ncsl.org/research/civil-and-criminal-justice/states-that-limit-or-prohibit-juvenile-shackling-and-solitary-confinement635572628.aspx

National Association for Public Defense.us
http://www.publicdefenders.us/?q=node/450

National Juvenile Defender Center, njdc.info
http://njdc.info/campaign-against-indiscriminate-juvenile-shackling/
http://njdc.info/wp-content/uploads/2014/01/Shackling-Inno-Brief-2013.pdf

Schatz, Bryan. "A Court Put a 9-Year-Old in Shackles for Stealing Chewing Gum—an Outrage That Happens Every Single Day," *Mother Jones,* February 2015. Copyright © 2015 by Mother Jones. Reprinted by permission.

Prepared by: Chris J. Boyatzis, *Bucknell University*
Ellen N. Junn, *California State University, Dominguez Hills*

Article

85 Million Children Work in Dangerous Conditions: Are Governments Fulfilling Their Promise to Prevent This?

JODY HEYMANN, ALETA SPRAGUE, AND NICOLAS DE GUZMAN CHORNY

Learning Outcomes

After reading this article, you will be able to:

- Describe the use of child labor around the world and its immediate and long-term impact on children.
- Describe the Convention on the Rights of the Child and how nations have respected, or not, its protections for children.
- Understand different types of labor that children conduct in different parts of the world.

Mining is a notoriously dangerous job. Tunnels can collapse, explosions and falling rocks are common, and the air is often filled with dust or even toxic gases. While the world breathed a collective sigh of relief when the 33 Chilean miners were rescued in 2010, around 12,000 people die in similar accidents each year.

So why do we let so many children do it—in 2014?

Mining falls squarely within the definition of "hazardous work," as defined by the International Labour Organization (ILO). According to the ILO, there are 168 million child laborers worldwide, including 85 million in jobs that directly endanger their health and safety. In countries around the world, kids work in gold mines, salt mines, and stone quarries—while millions more toil in fields, factories, or construction sites.

As noted in the first post in our series last week, November 20th marks the 25th anniversary of the Convention on the Rights of the Child (CRC), a landmark U.N. agreement that laid the foundation for strengthening children's rights around

the world. Among other fundamental rights, the CRC recognizes "the right of the child to be protected … from performing any work that is likely to be hazardous" and explicitly calls on ratifying countries to take legislative measures to ensure implementation of these rights. Yet a quarter century later, how much progress has the world really made toward ending child labor and shielding children from dangerous work conditions?

As it turns out, while a majority of CRC States parties have passed legislation to prevent hazardous child labor, only 53 percent legally protect children from hazardous work in all circumstances. In nearly a quarter of States parties, the minimum age for hazardous work is under 18, while 2 percent haven't established a minimum age whatsoever. In an additional 21 percent of States parties, although the minimum age is 18, legal exceptions allow younger children to do hazardous work in certain circumstances.

And while the problem is particularly severe in lower-income countries, child labor remains a global phenomenon—especially in the agricultural sector. In the U.S. (one of only three countries that are not parties to the CRC), federal regulations include exceptions that allow children to perform agricultural work at *any* age, subject to some limitations on work during school hours. Even when not technically classified as "hazardous," agricultural work often involves direct contact with poisonous pesticides, strenuous work, and long hours under the sun.

Earlier this year, in a survey of child workers in U.S. tobacco fields aged seven to 17, Human Rights Watch found that most children worked 50–60 hours per week, while 66 percent reported symptoms consistent with acute nicotine poisoning. According to the Bureau of Labor Statistics, the rate of fatalities for children aged 15–17 engaged in agricultural work is

4.4 times higher compared to children working in other jobs. Yet despite these risks, legal loopholes mean millions of children labor in fields around the world.

The consequences of child labor last a lifetime. Whether the work is hazardous or not, evidence shows that child laborers tend to have poorer health and complete less education than children who do not work. A study conducted in Guatemala, for example, showed that having worked between the ages of six and 14 increased the probability of health problems as an adult by over 40 percent. Another study conducted in Vietnam showed that the highest grade attained by working children was three grades lower than for children who did not work, even after controlling for family and regional characteristics.

Enacting laws that protect all children from performing hazardous work is a first step toward improving children's health and access to education. Yet full accountability for ending child labor and upholding children's other fundamental rights will also require participation from citizens to ensure adequate protections are both legislated and implemented. Citizens all over the world should have access to simple tools to monitor their countries' progress and pitfalls.

That's why in commemoration of the CRC's 25th anniversary, the WORLD Policy Analysis Center is releasing a series of maps, factsheets, and infographics that show where countries currently stand and what they could achieve. With this information, we hope to empower citizens all over the world to make change happen. Only when policymakers can identify viable solutions to eliminating child labor while supporting adequate family income, and citizens can access tools to hold their leaders accountable for commitments made, will child labor truly become a relic of the past.

Critical Thinking

1. Why is child labor still used in many countries? What are some political and economic reasons child labor still exists in some places?

2. What is your personal or moral position on child labor? Do you feel there are important distinctions in the acceptability between different types of labor and in different circumstances? Is running a lemonade stand in one's neighborhood "child labor"? Why or why not? In what ways does a 10-year-old mowing the family's lawn differ from a 10-year-old working for many hours a day collecting tobacco leaves on a tobacco farm?

3. If human-rights organizations learn that some nations are making children engage in exploitive and dangerous child labor, what can the rest of the world do? Should other countries intervene?

Internet References

The Atlantic
http://www.theatlantic.com/business/archive/2014/12/how-common-is-chid-labor-in-the-us/383687/

Bureau of Labor Statistics
http://www.bls.gov/opub/rylf/pdf/chapter2.pdf

Child Labor Public Education Project (University of Iowa)
https://www.continuetolearn.uiowa.edu/laborctr/child_labor/about/us_laws.html

https://www.continuetolearn.uiowa.edu/laborctr/child_labor/about/us_history.html

U.S. Department of Labor
http://www.dol.gov/dol/topic/youthlabor/

http://www.dol.gov/whd/childlabor.htm

Heymann, Jody; Sprague, Aleta;de Guzman Chorny, Nicolas. "85 Million Children Work in Dangerous Conditions: Are Governments Fulfilling Their Promise to Prevent This?," *Huffington Post*, November 2014. Copyright © 2014 by Dr. Jody Heymann. Reprinted by permission.